Canadian Living

THE SPECIAL OCCASIONS
COOKBOOK

Bibliothèque et Archives nationales du Québec
and Library and Archives Canada cataloguing in
publication

Main entry under title :
    The complete special occasions menu book
Includes index.

    1. Holiday cooking. 2. Cookbooks. I. Canadian
Living Test Kitchen.

TX739.C65 2016   641.5'68   C2016-941337-3

10-16

© 2016, Juniper Publishing, a division of
Sogides Group Inc., a subsidiary of
Quebecor Media Inc. (Montreal, Quebec)

All rights reserved.

Legal deposit: 2016
Bibliothèque et Archives nationales du Québec
Library and Archives Canada

ISBN 978-1-988002-34-7

Printed in Canada

EXCLUSIVE DISTRIBUTOR
FOR CANADA & USA
Simon & Schuster Canada
166 King Street East, Suite 300
Toronto ON M5A 1J3

Tel: 647-427-8882
Toll Free: 800-387-0446
Fax: 647-430-9446

simonandschuster.ca

canadianliving.com/books

Government of Quebec – Tax credit for book publishing –
Administered by SODEC. **sodec.gouv.qc.ca**

This publisher gratefully acknowledges the support of the Société
de développement des enterprises culturelles du Québec.

Canada Council   Conseil des arts
for the Arts   du Canada

We gratefully acknowledge the support of the Canada Council
for the Arts for its publishing program.

We acknowledge the financial support of our publishing activity
by the Government of Canada through the Canada Book Fund.

ART DIRECTOR
Colin Elliott

PROJECT EDITOR
Martin Zibauer

COPY EDITOR
Ruth Hanley

INDEXER
Beth Zabloski

Canadian Living

THE SPECIAL OCCASIONS
COOKBOOK

250+ RECIPES FOR MEMORABLE GATHERINGS

BY THE CANADIAN LIVING TEST KITCHEN

JUNIPER
PUBLISHING
A Quebecor Media Corporation

MEMORABLE
FOOD MAKES
UNFORGETTABLE
GATHERINGS

CONTENTS

TESTED TILL PERFECT **p.293**   INDEX **p.294**   NUTRITIONAL INFORMATION **p.303**

SPRING

ST. PATRICK'S DAY FEAST **p.8**

MAKE-AHEAD EASTER DINNER **p.16**

PASSOVER DINNER **p.24**

CABANE À SUCRE **p.34**

MOTHER'S DAY BRUNCH **p.42**

AFTERNOON TEA **p.48**

BABY SHOWER **p.56**

SEASONAL SUNDAY SUPPER **p.64**

SUMMER

FATHER'S DAY COOKOUT **p.74**

IT'S A PARADE **p.82**

CANADA DAY MAKE-AHEAD MENU **p.90**

CANADA DAY BARBECUE **p.100**

GARDEN PARTY GRILL **p.108**

A DAY AT THE COTTAGE **p.116**

BLOCK PARTY **p.124**

FAMILY REUNION PICNIC **p.132**

MARKET DAY **p.140**

SEASONAL SUNDAY SUPPER **p.148**

AUTUMN

SEAFOOD SUPPER **p.156**

MAKE-AHEAD THANKSGIVING **p.164**

THANKSGIVING FEAST **p.176**

GAME NIGHT **p.186**

HARVEST TABLE **p.192**

SEASONAL SUNDAY SUPPER **p.200**

WINTER

TREE TRIMMING PARTY **p.208**

HANUKKAH GET–TOGETHER **p.216**

MAKE-AHEAD CHRISTMAS DINNER **p.224**

CHRISTMAS BUFFET **p.234**

HOLIDAY BRUNCH **p.244**

NEW YEAR'S EVE DROP-IN **p.250**

APRÈS-SKI FONDUE **p.260**

GONG HEI FAT CHOI **p.264**

VALENTINE'S DAY DINNER **p.272**

RED CARPET EXTRAVAGANZA **p.278**

SEASONAL SUNDAY SUPPER **p.284**

SPRING

ST. PATRICK'S DAY FEAST p.8

MAKE-AHEAD EASTER DINNER p.16

PASSOVER DINNER p.24

CABANE À SUCRE p.34

MOTHER'S DAY BRUNCH p.42

AFTERNOON TEA p.48

BABY SHOWER p.56

SEASONAL SUNDAY SUPPER p.64

ST. PATRICK'S DAY FEAST

About 1 in 7 Canadians have some roots in Ireland, and vibrant Celtic influences can be felt across the country. Celebrate St. Patrick's Day with a meal of authentic, honest Irish cooking, which relies on abundant seafood, farm-fresh produce and the versatile potato— but not a drop of green food colouring.

MENU FOR 8

IRISH BROWN BREAD **p.10**

SMOKED MACKEREL PÂTÉ **p.10**

IRISH ROOT SOUP
WITH CASHEL BLUE CHEESE **p.12**

FRESH SHUCKED OYSTERS **p.12**

ROAST PORK WITH CIDER CREAM SAUCE **p.13**

BOXTY POTATO CAKES **p.14**

LEMON BRUSSELS SPROUTS **p.14**

STICKY DATE PUDDING
WITH IRISH WHISKEY TOFFEE SAUCE **p.15**

HAZELNUT IRISH COFFEE **p.15**

IRISH BROWN BREAD

opposite

HANDS-ON TIME	TOTAL TIME	MAKES
15 MINUTES	1 HOUR	1 LOAF, ABOUT 12 SLICES

1 cup	all-purpose flour (approx)
1 cup	whole wheat flour
½ cup	quick-cooking rolled oats (not instant)
¼ cup	wheat germ
1½ tsp	each baking soda and caraway seeds
½ tsp	salt
½ cup	cold butter, cubed
1 cup	buttermilk
2 tbsp	cooking or fancy molasses

In large bowl, whisk together 1 cup all-purpose flour, the whole wheat flour, oats, wheat germ, baking soda, caraway seeds and salt. Using pastry blender or 2 knives, cut in butter until mixture resembles fine crumbs. Whisk buttermilk with molasses; stir into flour mixture to make soft dough.

Turn out onto lightly floured work surface; knead lightly about 10 times. Shape into 8-inch (20 cm) long oval; dust top with flour. Using serrated knife, cut shallow slash lengthwise down centre; transfer to greased 9- × 5-inch (2 L) loaf pan.

Bake in 375°F (190°C) oven until loaf sounds hollow when tapped, about 45 minutes. Let cool in pan on rack for 5 minutes. Turn out onto rack; let cool completely before slicing. *(Make-ahead: Store in airtight container for up to 4 days or freeze for up to 2 weeks.)*

NUTRITIONAL INFORMATION, PER SLICE: about 183 cal, 4 g pro, 9 g total fat (5 g sat. fat), 23 g carb (2 g dietary fibre), 21 mg chol, 332 mg sodium. % RDI: 4% calcium, 10% iron, 7% vit A, 14% folate.

SMOKED MACKEREL PÂTÉ

opposite

HANDS-ON TIME	TOTAL TIME	MAKES
15 MINUTES	15 MINUTES	2 CUPS

340 g	smoked mackerel (about 3 fillets)
½ cup	fresh bread crumbs
⅓ cup	whipping cream (35%)
¼ cup	butter, softened
1 tbsp	lemon juice
pinch	cayenne pepper
2 tbsp	each finely chopped fresh parsley and green onion

Remove skin and bones from fish; discard. In food processor, pulse together fish, bread crumbs, cream, butter, lemon juice and cayenne just until smooth. Stir in parsley and green onion. *(Make-ahead: Refrigerate in airtight container for up to 5 days. Let come to room temperature before serving.)*

NUTRITIONAL INFORMATION, PER 1 TBSP: about 46 cal, 3 g pro, 4 g total fat (2 g sat. fat), 1 g carb (0 g dietary fibre), 17 mg chol, 95 mg sodium. % RDI: 1% calcium, 1% iron, 2% vit A, 2% vit C, 1% folate.

FROM TOP: FRESH SHUCKED OYSTERS; IRISH BROWN BREAD; AND SMOKED MACKEREL PÂTÉ

IRISH ROOT SOUP
WITH CASHEL BLUE CHEESE

HANDS-ON TIME	**TOTAL TIME**	**MAKES**
35 MINUTES	1¼ HOURS	8 SERVINGS

3 tbsp	butter
2	leeks (white and light green parts only), thinly sliced
1	onion, thinly sliced
4 cups	diced peeled rutabaga
1	each carrot and russet potato, peeled and diced
¾ tsp	salt
¼ tsp	each pepper and nutmeg
4 cups	sodium-reduced chicken broth
1 cup	10% cream or milk
1 tsp	cider vinegar or white wine vinegar
⅓ cup	crumbled Cashel blue cheese
2 tbsp	finely chopped fresh chives or parsley

In Dutch oven or large heavy-bottomed saucepan, melt butter over medium heat; cook leeks and onion, stirring often, until translucent, about 12 minutes.

Add rutabaga, carrot, potato, salt, pepper and nutmeg; cook, stirring, for 5 minutes.

Stir in broth and 2 cups water; bring to boil. Reduce heat, cover and simmer until vegetables are tender, about 30 minutes.

Working in batches, purée soup in blender until smooth. *(Make-ahead: Refrigerate in airtight container for up to 3 days; add water to thin out as needed.)*

Return to Dutch oven. Stir in cream and vinegar; bring just to boil over medium heat. Ladle into bowls. Garnish with blue cheese and chives.

NUTRITIONAL INFORMATION, PER SERVING: about 164 cal, 5 g pro, 9 g total fat (6 g sat. fat), 16 g carb (2 g dietary fibre), 26 mg chol, 662 mg sodium. % RDI: 11% calcium, 6% iron, 27% vit A, 28% vit C, 12% folate.

12

FRESH SHUCKED OYSTERS

In Ireland (as in Canada), oysters are a national treasure. They are especially tasty with a pint of smooth Irish stout. Serve them freshly shucked on a platter with lemon wedges, freshly grated horseradish and hot pepper sauce, alongside Irish Brown Bread and Smoked Mackerel Pâté (recipes, page 10).

ROAST PORK
WITH CIDER CREAM SAUCE

p.8

HANDS-ON TIME
25 MINUTES

TOTAL TIME
4 HOURS

MAKES
8 SERVINGS

PORK Stir together oil, garlic, sage, thyme, salt and pepper; rub all over pork. Cover and refrigerate for 2 hours. *(Make-ahead: Refrigerate for up to 24 hours.)*

Place pork on lightly greased rack in roasting pan. Roast in 375°F (190°C) oven until instant-read thermometer inserted into centre reads 160°F (71°C), about 90 minutes. Transfer to cutting board; cover loosely with foil and let stand for 15 minutes before slicing.

CIDER CREAM SAUCE While pork is resting, skim fat from pan juices. Add butter to pan and cook over medium heat until melted. Add apples and onion; cook, stirring often, for 5 minutes. Stir in cider and bring to boil, scraping up any browned bits. Stir in broth, cream and mustard; cook until reduced by half, about 8 minutes.

Mix cornstarch with 1 tbsp water; whisk into apple mixture. Cook, stirring, until thickened, about 1 minute. Serve with pork.

NUTRITIONAL INFORMATION, PER SERVING: about 397 cal, 34 g pro, 23 g total fat (10 g sat. fat), 11 g carb (1 g dietary fibre), 128 mg chol, 493 mg sodium. % RDI: 6% calcium, 11% iron, 10% vit A, 5% vit C, 4% folate.

13

PORK

2 tbsp	vegetable oil
3	cloves garlic, minced
1 tbsp	each minced fresh sage and thyme (or ½ tsp each crumbled dried sage and dried thyme)
1 tsp	salt
½ tsp	pepper
1.35 kg	boneless pork loin centre roast, rolled and tied

CIDER CREAM SAUCE

2 tbsp	butter
2	Granny Smith apples, peeled, quartered, cored and thinly sliced crosswise
1	onion, diced
1 cup	alcoholic or nonalcoholic apple cider
1 cup	sodium-reduced chicken broth
¾ cup	whipping cream (35%)
1 tbsp	grainy or Dijon mustard
1 tsp	cornstarch

TIP FROM THE TEST KITCHEN

An instant-read digital thermometer is the best tool to ensure meat is cooked perfectly. Insert the probe into the thickest part of a roast to check its internal temperature. If you're cooking a bone-in roast, be sure the probe isn't touching a bone (which can skew the reading).

BOXTY POTATO CAKES

p.8

HANDS-ON TIME	**TOTAL TIME**	**MAKES**
45 MINUTES	45 MINUTES	8 SERVINGS

1.5 kg	russet potatoes
3	green onions, thinly sliced
½ cup	all-purpose flour
1 tsp	baking powder
½ tsp	salt
¾ cup	buttermilk
3 tbsp	each butter and vegetable oil

Peel half of the potatoes; cut into large chunks. In saucepan of boiling salted water, cook potato chunks until tender, about 15 minutes. Drain well; transfer to large bowl and mash.

Meanwhile, peel and grate remaining potatoes. Wrap potatoes in kitchen towel; squeeze out liquid. Add grated potatoes, green onions, flour, baking powder and salt to mashed potatoes; mix well. Stir in buttermilk.

In large skillet, heat 1 tbsp each of the butter and oil over medium-high heat; working in batches and adding remaining butter and oil as needed, scoop potato mixture by heaping ¼ cup into skillet, leaving 1 inch (2.5 cm) between each. Using spatula, flatten to ½-inch (1 cm) thickness. Cook, turning once, until crisp and golden, about 8 minutes. *(Make-ahead: Let cool. Refrigerate in airtight container for up to 24 hours; add about 8 minutes to heating time.)* Reheat in 375°F (190°C) oven until hot, about 5 minutes.

NUTRITIONAL INFORMATION, PER SERVING: about 237 cal, 4 g pro, 10 g total fat (3 g sat. fat), 34 g carb (2 g dietary fibre), 12 mg chol, 405 mg sodium. % RDI: 6% calcium, 9% iron, 4% vit A, 27% vit C, 15% folate.

LEMON BRUSSELS SPROUTS

p.8

HANDS-ON TIME	**TOTAL TIME**	**MAKES**
15 MINUTES	15 MINUTES	8 SERVINGS

8 cups	brussels sprouts (about 1 kg total), trimmed and halved
¼ cup	butter, softened
2 tsp	grated lemon zest
4 tsp	lemon juice
pinch	each salt and pepper

In large saucepan of boiling salted water, cook brussels sprouts until tender-crisp, about 6 minutes. Drain and return to pan. *(Make-ahead: Chill in ice water; drain. Wrap in towels. Refrigerate in airtight container for up to 24 hours. Reheat in boiling water for 2 minutes; drain and return to pan.)*

Add butter, lemon zest, lemon juice, salt and pepper; cook over medium heat, stirring, until butter is melted.

NUTRITIONAL INFORMATION, PER SERVING: about 89 cal, 3 g pro, 6 g total fat (4 g sat. fat), 9 g carb (4 g dietary fibre), 15 mg chol, 287 mg sodium. % RDI: 3% calcium, 9% iron, 12% vit A, 102% vit C, 26% folate.

STICKY DATE PUDDING
WITH IRISH WHISKEY TOFFEE SAUCE

HANDS-ON TIME
30 MINUTES

TOTAL TIME
2 HOURS

MAKES
12 SERVINGS

Grease 10-cup (2.5 L) Bundt or tube pan; dust with flour. Set aside.

In saucepan, bring dates, baking soda and 1½ cups water to boil; let cool.

In large bowl, beat 1 cup of the butter with the granulated sugar until fluffy; beat in eggs, 1 at a time. Stir in vanilla. In separate bowl, whisk flour with baking powder; stir into butter mixture, alternating with date mixture, making 2 additions of flour mixture and 1 of date mixture. Scrape into prepared pan. Bake in 350°F (180°C) oven for 45 minutes.

While pudding is baking, in saucepan, melt remaining butter over medium heat; stir in brown sugar until dissolved. Add cream; bring to simmer. Cook, stirring occasionally, until slightly thickened, about 5 minutes. Stir in whiskey; keep warm.

While pudding is still in pan, use skewer or toothpick to poke holes all over cake; pour ⅓ cup of the whiskey mixture evenly over top. Continue baking until cake tester inserted in centre comes out clean, about 15 minutes. Let cool in pan on rack for 10 minutes.

Invert cake onto platter. Poke holes all over; pour ⅓ cup whiskey mixture over cake. *(Make-ahead: Let cool completely. Wrap in plastic wrap; store in airtight container at room temperature for up to 2 days. Cover remaining sauce and refrigerate for up to 2 days. Reheat before serving.)*

Before serving, cut into slices; drizzle with remaining whiskey mixture.

NUTRITIONAL INFORMATION, PER SERVING: about 585 cal, 6 g pro, 34 g total fat (21 g sat. fat), 66 g carb (3 g dietary fibre), 152 mg chol, 488 mg sodium. % RDI: 7% calcium, 15% iron, 30% vit A, 29% folate.

1⅓ cups	chopped pitted dates
2 tsp	baking soda
1¾ cups	butter, softened
½ cup	granulated sugar
4	eggs
1 tsp	vanilla
2½ cups	all-purpose flour
2 tsp	baking powder
1¼ cups	packed dark brown sugar
¾ cup	whipping cream (35%)
¼ cup	Irish whiskey (such as Bushmills or Jameson)

HAZELNUT IRISH COFFEE
In mug, stir together ⅓ cup freshly brewed hot coffee; 1 oz each hazelnut liqueur (such as Frangelico) and Irish cream liqueur and 2 tbsp 10% cream. Top with whipped cream (optional).

MAKE-AHEAD EASTER DINNER

So much is wrapped up in this holiday: the deep significance for many of the religious observance, the celebration of the seasonal abundance of spring and the excitement of the egg hunts and parades. Ham is often at the centre of the Easter meal; traditionally, the first hams of the year were ready in early spring.

MENU FOR 16

PINEAPPLE-GLAZED HAM p.18

ROASTED ASPARAGUS SALAD WITH PARMESAN CROUTONS p.19

TWIN PEAS WITH ROASTED GARLIC BUTTER p.20

SLOW COOKER SCALLOPED POTATOES p.20

HONEY-LIME CARROTS WITH CIPOLLINI ONIONS p.22

LEMON AMARETTO TIRAMISU p.23

PINEAPPLE-GLAZED HAM

p.16

HANDS-ON TIME
40 MINUTES

TOTAL TIME
5 HOURS

MAKES
24 TO 46 SERVINGS

3½ cups   pineapple juice
1½ cups   packed brown sugar
1   piece (3 inches/8 cm) fresh ginger, peeled and sliced
6.5 kg   fully cooked smoked bone-in ham

In saucepan, stir together 2 cups of the pineapple juice, the brown sugar and two-thirds of the ginger; bring to boil over medium-high heat. Cook, stirring, until sugar is dissolved, about 5 minutes. Reduce heat to medium-low; simmer, stirring occasionally, until glaze is reduced by half and thick enough to coat back of spoon, about 35 minutes. Let cool slightly, about 20 minutes.

While pineapple glaze is simmering, pour remaining pineapple juice and 1 cup water into roasting pan; add remaining ginger. Place ham, fat side up, on greased rack in roasting pan. Cover tightly with foil; roast on bottom rack in 325°F (160°C) oven until instant-read thermometer inserted in centre reads 130°F (55°C), about 4 hours.

Uncover ham; peel off and discard outer skin. Trim fat layer to ¼-inch (5 mm) thickness. Using paring knife, diagonally score remaining fat to make diamond pattern on ham. Brush half of the pineapple glaze over ham.

Roast, uncovered, in 375°F (190°C) oven, brushing with remaining glaze several times throughout (reheat glaze to loosen, if necessary), until glaze is caramelized and golden and instant-read thermometer inserted in centre reads 140°F (60°C), about 30 minutes.

Remove ham to cutting board; cover loosely with foil. Let stand for 15 minutes before carving.

NUTRITIONAL INFORMATION, PER EACH OF 46 SERVINGS (100 G): about 248 cal, 19 g pro, 15 g total fat (5 g sat. fat), 8 g carb (trace dietary fibre, 9 g sugar), 55 mg chol, 1,059 mg sodium, 279 mg potassium. % RDI: 1% calcium, 6% iron, 3% vit C, 2% folate.

ROASTED ASPARAGUS SALAD
WITH PARMESAN CROUTONS

p.21

HANDS-ON TIME	TOTAL TIME	MAKES
25 MINUTES	1 HOUR	16 SERVINGS

LEMON-TARRAGON DRESSING In small bowl, whisk together lemon juice, mustard, honey, garlic, salt and pepper. Gradually whisk in oil. *(Make-ahead: Refrigerate in airtight container for up to 3 days. Let stand at room temperature for 20 minutes and whisk just before serving.)* Stir in tarragon.

PARMESAN CROUTONS On parchment paper–lined rimmed baking sheet, toss baguette with oil. Gather closely together in single layer; sprinkle with Parmesan. Bake in 400°F (200°C) oven until golden, about 12 minutes. Let cool to room temperature; break apart. *(Make-ahead: Store in airtight container for up to 24 hours.)*

SALAD While croutons are cooling, in large bowl, toss together asparagus, oil, salt and pepper. Spread on 2 rimmed baking sheets. Roast in top and bottom thirds of 425°F (220°C) oven, switching and rotating sheets halfway through, until tender, about 15 minutes. Let cool to room temperature. *(Make-ahead: Refrigerate in airtight container for up to 24 hours. Let stand at room temperature for 20 minutes before continuing with recipe.)*

ASSEMBLY In large bowl, combine asparagus, tomatoes, arugula, spinach and croutons; add dressing and toss to coat. Serve immediately.

NUTRITIONAL INFORMATION, PER SERVING: about 116 cal, 4 g pro, 8 g total fat (1 g sat. fat), 10 g carb (2 g dietary fibre, 4 g sugar), 3 mg chol, 194 mg sodium, 309 mg potassium. % RDI: 7% calcium, 10% iron, 19% vit A, 22% vit C, 58% folate.

LEMON-TARRAGON DRESSING

¼ cup	lemon juice
4 tsp	each Dijon mustard and liquid honey
1	small clove garlic, minced
¼ tsp	each salt and pepper
⅓ cup	extra-virgin olive oil
3 tbsp	chopped fresh tarragon

PARMESAN CROUTONS

half	baguette (8 inches/20 cm), cut in ½-inch (1 cm) cubes
1 tbsp	extra-virgin olive oil
½ cup	finely grated Parmesan cheese

SALAD

2 kg	asparagus (about 4 bunches), trimmed and cut in 1½-inch (4 cm) lengths
1 tbsp	extra-virgin olive oil
¼ tsp	each salt and pepper
3 cups	grape tomatoes, halved
1	pkg (142 g) baby arugula
1	pkg (142 g) baby spinach

TWIN PEAS
WITH ROASTED GARLIC BUTTER

opposite

HANDS-ON TIME	TOTAL TIME	MAKES
15 MINUTES	1 HOUR	16 SERVINGS

ROASTED GARLIC BUTTER

1	head garlic
1 tsp	olive oil
¼ cup	butter, softened

PEAS

8 cups	whole sugar snap peas (about 750 g total), trimmed
4 cups	frozen green peas
1 tsp	salt
¼ tsp	pepper
2 tbsp	chopped fresh tarragon (optional)

ROASTED GARLIC BUTTER Slice off top third of garlic head to expose cloves. Place garlic head on small square of foil; drizzle cut side with oil and fold foil over to seal. Roast in 375°F (190°C) oven until tender, about 45 minutes. Let cool slightly. Squeeze out cloves into small bowl; stir in butter until well combined. *(Make-ahead: Cover with plastic wrap; refrigerate for up to 2 days. Soften at room temperature for 20 minutes before continuing with recipe.)*

PEAS In large saucepan of boiling salted water, cook snap peas for 1 minute; add frozen peas and cook until heated through, about 30 seconds. Drain well.

In large bowl, toss together peas, garlic butter, salt and pepper until butter is melted. Sprinkle with tarragon (if using).

NUTRITIONAL INFORMATION, PER SERVING: about 74 cal, 3 g pro, 3 g total fat (2 g sat. fat), 8 g carb (3 g dietary fibre, 3 g sugar), 8 mg chol, 361 mg sodium, 146 mg potassium. % RDI: 3% calcium, 10% iron, 13% vit A, 38% vit C, 14% folate.

SLOW COOKER SCALLOPED POTATOES

opposite

HANDS-ON TIME	TOTAL TIME	MAKES
30 MINUTES	5½ HOURS	16 SERVINGS

2.25 kg	yellow-fleshed potatoes, peeled and cut in scant ¼-inch (5 mm) thick rounds
1	bulb fennel, trimmed, cored and thinly sliced
1 tbsp	chopped fresh thyme
3	cloves garlic, minced
2 tsp	salt
½ tsp	pepper
1 cup	whipping cream (35%)
2 tbsp	potato starch
1 cup	shredded Gruyère cheese
3	strips bacon, chopped

In large bowl, gently toss together potatoes, fennel, thyme, garlic, salt and pepper until well combined. In small bowl, whisk cream with potato starch until smooth.

In lightly greased slow cooker, layer half of the potato mixture. Sprinkle with one-quarter of the Gruyère and half of the bacon. Pour in half of the cream mixture. Top with remaining potato mixture, another quarter of the Gruyère and remaining bacon and cream mixture.

Cover and cook on high until potatoes are tender, about 4½ hours. Turn off slow cooker; sprinkle with remaining Gruyère. Cover and let stand until Gruyère is melted and some of the liquid has absorbed, about 15 minutes.

NUTRITIONAL INFORMATION, PER SERVING: about 206 cal, 6 g pro, 9 g total fat (6 g sat. fat), 26 g carb (3 g dietary fibre, 2 g sugar), 29 mg chol, 367 mg sodium, 828 mg potassium. % RDI: 10% calcium, 9% iron, 7% vit A, 37% vit C, 9% folate.

CLOCKWISE, FROM TOP LEFT: TWIN PEAS WITH ROASTED GARLIC BUTTER AND HONEY-LIME CARROTS WITH CIPOLLINI ONIONS; ROASTED ASPARAGUS SALAD; LEMON AMARETTO TIRAMISU; AND SLOW COOKER SCALLOPED POTATOES

HONEY-LIME CARROTS
WITH CIPOLLINI ONIONS

p.21

HANDS-ON TIME	TOTAL TIME	MAKES
1 HOUR	1 HOUR	16 SERVINGS

4	bags (each 175 g) cipollini onions
¼ cup	butter
1.5 kg	carrots
2 tbsp	liquid honey
1 tsp	salt
¼ tsp	pepper
1 tsp	grated lime zest
2 tbsp	lime juice

In saucepan of boiling water, cook onions until skins begin to loosen, about 1 minute. Drain and rinse under cold water. Peel onions, trimming root ends if necessary. Cut onions through root end into quarters.

In large skillet, melt one-quarter of the butter over medium heat; cook onions, stirring occasionally and adding 1 to 2 tbsp water, as needed (about every 4 minutes) if onions begin to stick to skillet, until softened and golden, about 40 minutes. *(Make-ahead: Refrigerate in airtight container for up to 2 days.)*

While onions are cooking, peel carrots and cut crosswise on the diagonal into 2-inch (5 cm) lengths. Cut lengthwise into ½-inch (1 cm) thick pieces. In large saucepan of boiling salted water, cook carrots until tender-crisp, about 8 minutes. Drain and transfer to bowl of ice water to chill. Drain and pat dry with clean towel. *(Make-ahead: Refrigerate in airtight container for up to 24 hours.)*

In large skillet, melt remaining butter over medium-high heat; cook carrots, stirring often, until light golden, about 4 minutes. Stir in onions, honey, salt and pepper; cook, stirring often, just until carrots are tender, about 2 minutes. Remove from heat; stir in lime zest and lime juice.

NUTRITIONAL INFORMATION, PER SERVING: about 76 cal, 1 g pro, 3 g total fat (2 g sat. fat), 12 g carb (3 g dietary fibre, 6 g sugar), 8 mg chol, 361 mg sodium, 229 mg potassium. % RDI: 3% calcium, 3% iron, 116% vit A, 8% vit C, 7% folate.

LEMON AMARETTO TIRAMISU

p.21

HANDS-ON TIME
1 HOUR

TOTAL TIME
13½ HOURS

MAKES
16 TO 20 SERVINGS

Toss almonds with egg white to coat; stir in ¼ cup of the granulated sugar until well combined. Spread on parchment paper–lined rimmed baking sheet. Bake in 350°F (180°C) oven, stirring once, until light golden, about 12 minutes. Let cool on sheet. *(Make-ahead: Store in airtight container for up to 2 days.)*

While almonds are baking, in large heatproof bowl, whisk together egg yolks, 1½ cups of the granulated sugar, the lemon zest and lemon juice. Set bowl over saucepan of simmering water; cook, stirring, until thick enough to coat back of spoon, about 12 minutes. Remove from heat; stir in butter, 1 tbsp at a time. Strain through fine-mesh sieve into clean bowl. Place plastic wrap directly on surface. Refrigerate until curd is thick enough to mound firmly on spoon, about 1 hour. *(Make-ahead: Refrigerate for up to 2 days.)*

While curd is chilling, in saucepan, cook remaining granulated sugar with ¼ cup water over medium heat, stirring, until sugar is dissolved; let cool completely. Stir in amaretto. Quickly dip both sides of ladyfingers in amaretto mixture; arrange in single layer in 13- × 9-inch (3 L) baking dish.

In large bowl, beat together mascarpone, icing sugar and vanilla until smooth. In separate bowl, beat 1½ cups of the cream until stiff peaks form; fold into mascarpone mixture. Spoon mixture over ladyfingers, spreading to edges. Spread lemon curd evenly over top. Cover and refrigerate for 12 hours. *(Make-ahead: Refrigerate for up to 24 hours. Let stand at room temperature for 10 minutes before continuing with recipe.)*

In bowl, beat remaining cream until stiff peaks form. Spoon over lemon curd, leaving border of curd. Sprinkle with almonds.

NUTRITIONAL INFORMATION, PER EACH OF 20 SERVINGS: about 535 cal, 8 g pro, 37 g total fat (20 g sat. fat), 44 g carb (1 g dietary fibre, 36 g sugar), 222 mg chol, 121 mg sodium, 143 mg potassium. % RDI: 11% calcium, 9% iron, 32% vit A, 10% vit C, 14% folate.

1½ cups	sliced natural (skin-on) almonds
1	egg white
2 cups	granulated sugar
12	egg yolks
4 tsp	grated lemon zest
1 cup	lemon juice
1 cup	cold butter, cubed
⅓ cup	amaretto liqueur
18	ladyfingers (about 4 inches/10 cm long)
1	tub (475 g) mascarpone cheese
2 cups	icing sugar
1 tsp	vanilla
2½ cups	whipping cream (35%)

23

PASSOVER DINNER

Passover brings families to the table to share traditions and teach children the significance of those traditions in modern society. Even after the Seder, family dinners are important gatherings during this festival. Flavourful kosher dishes with traditional ingredients such as lamb, apples and walnuts will make for memorable meals.

MENU FOR 12

CHOPPED LIVER PÂTÉ **p.26**

APPLE WALNUT CHUTNEY **p.27**

ROASTED EGGPLANT DIP **p.29**

ROAST LEG OF LAMB
WITH CARAMELIZED ONION GRAVY **p.30**

LAYERED "KNISH" BAKE **p.31**

SAUTÉED SPRING ASPARAGUS AND MUSHROOMS **p.32**

HONEY-GLAZED CARROTS **p.32**

DAIRY-FREE GLUTEN-FREE
MOLTEN CHOCOLATE LAVA CAKES **p.33**

CHOPPED LIVER PÂTÉ

p.28

HANDS-ON TIME	TOTAL TIME	MAKES
30 MINUTES	6½ HOURS	2⅔ CUPS

450 g	chicken livers
2 tbsp	kosher pareve margarine or kosher olive oil
2	small onions, thinly sliced
3 tbsp	lemon juice
2 tbsp	kosher-for-Passover red wine
¼ cup	chopped fresh parsley
½ tsp	each salt and pepper
2	hard-cooked eggs, diced

Rinse livers; trim and pat dry. Set aside.

In large skillet, melt half of the margarine over medium heat; cook onions, stirring occasionally, until softened and golden, 5 to 8 minutes. Transfer to food processor.

Add remaining margarine to skillet; sauté livers over medium-high heat until browned but still slightly pink in centre, 5 to 8 minutes. Add lemon juice and wine; cook for 1 minute. Add to food processor.

Add parsley, salt and pepper to food processor; purée, scraping down side occasionally, until smooth. Scrape into bowl; fold in eggs. Scrape into plastic wrap–lined mini loaf pan or dish; smooth surface. Place plastic wrap directly on surface; refrigerate for 6 hours. *(Make-ahead: Refrigerate for up to 24 hours.)* Before serving, unwrap and invert onto serving platter.

NUTRITIONAL INFORMATION, PER 1 TBSP: about 20 cal, 2 g pro, 1 g total fat (trace sat. fat), 1 g carb (trace dietary fibre, trace sugar), 55 mg chol, 44 mg sodium, 36 mg potassium. % RDI: 7% iron, 54% vit A, 7% vit C, 26% folate.

26

APPLE WALNUT CHUTNEY

p.28

HANDS-ON TIME
25 MINUTES

TOTAL TIME
1¼ HOURS

MAKES
ABOUT 2 CUPS

In saucepan, heat oil over medium heat; cook onion, stirring occasionally, until softened, about 5 minutes.

Stir in apples, apricot, pear, brown sugar, lemon zest, lemon juice, cinnamon and ⅓ cup water; cook, stirring occasionally, until apples are tender, about 15 minutes. Stir in walnuts. Let cool, about 45 minutes. *(Make-ahead: Refrigerate in airtight container for up to 2 days.)*

NUTRITIONAL INFORMATION, PER 1 TBSP: about 43 cal, 1 g pro, 3 g total fat (trace sat. fat), 5 g carb (1 g dietary fibre, 4 g sugar), 0 mg chol, 1 mg sodium, 53 mg potassium. % RDI: 1% calcium, 1% iron, 2% vit C, 2% folate.

2 tsp	kosher olive oil
1	small onion, finely diced
2	Empire or Granny Smith apples, peeled, cored and chopped
¼ cup	chopped dried apricot
¼ cup	chopped dried pear
3 tbsp	packed brown sugar
1 tsp	grated lemon zest
3 tbsp	lemon juice
pinch	cinnamon
1 cup	chopped walnuts

27

FROM TOP: CHOPPED LIVER PÂTÉ, APPLE WALNUT CHUTNEY AND ROASTED EGGPLANT DIP

ROASTED EGGPLANT DIP

opposite

HANDS-ON TIME
20 MINUTES

TOTAL TIME
2¾ HOURS

MAKES
ABOUT 4 CUPS

Using fork, prick eggplants all over; place on lightly greased rimmed baking sheet. Set aside.

Remove 2 cloves garlic from garlic head; peel, mince and set aside. Slice off top third of remaining garlic head to expose cloves. Place garlic head on small square of foil; drizzle cut side with 1 tsp oil, fold foil over to seal. Add to baking sheet. Bake in 375°F (190°C) oven, turning eggplants once, until softened, 35 to 40 minutes. Let stand until eggplants are cool enough to handle.

While eggplants are cooling, in large skillet, heat remaining oil over medium heat; cook onion and coriander, stirring occasionally, until onion is golden, about 15 minutes. Scrape into food processor.

Cut eggplants in half. Using spoon, scoop flesh into food processor; discard skin. Squeeze out cloves of roasted garlic into food processor.

Add minced garlic, the tahini, lemon juice, salt and pepper in food processor; purée until smooth. Stir in parsley. Cover and refrigerate for 2 hours. *(Make-ahead: Refrigerate in airtight container for up to 2 days.)*

NUTRITIONAL INFORMATION, PER 1 TBSP: about 16 cal, trace pro, 1 g total fat (trace sat. fat), 2 g carb (1 g dietary fibre, 1 g sugar), 0 mg chol, 33 mg sodium, 33 mg potassium. % RDI: 1% iron, 2% vit C, 2% folate.

2	large eggplants
1	head garlic
4 tsp	kosher olive oil
1	sweet onion, thinly sliced
1½ tsp	ground coriander
½ cup	kosher tahini
¼ cup	lemon juice
¾ tsp	each salt and pepper
¼ cup	chopped fresh parsley

29

ROAST LEG OF LAMB
WITH CARAMELIZED ONION GRAVY

p.24

HANDS-ON TIME	**TOTAL TIME**	**MAKES**
30 MINUTES	3¼ HOURS	12 SERVINGS

ROAST LAMB

2.7 kg	kosher bone-in leg of lamb
2	cloves garlic, thinly sliced lengthwise
2	sprigs fresh rosemary
¼ tsp	each salt and pepper

CARAMELIZED ONION GRAVY

2 tsp	kosher-for-Passover beef consommé instant soup mix (such as Lieber's) or 2 cups homemade kosher beef broth
2 tsp	kosher olive oil
2	cloves garlic, minced
1	onion, thinly sliced
¼ cup	kosher-for-Passover red wine
¼ tsp	pepper
1 tsp	kosher potato starch

ROAST LAMB Trim all but thin layer of fat from lamb. Using thin sharp knife, poke about twelve 1½-inch (4 cm) deep slits into top. Stuff each slit with 1 slice garlic. Remove leaves from rosemary sprigs; stuff 4 or 5 leaves into each slit. Cover and refrigerate for 1 hour. *(Make-ahead: Refrigerate for up to 24 hours.)* Sprinkle with salt and pepper.

Place lamb on greased rack in roasting pan; roast in 350°F (180°C) oven until instant-read thermometer inserted in thickest part of lamb reads 145°F (63°C) for medium-rare, about 2 hours. Transfer to cutting board and cover loosely with foil; let stand for 15 minutes before carving.

CARAMELIZED ONION GRAVY Meanwhile, in glass measure, whisk soup mix with 2 cups water (omit water if using homemade broth); set aside.

In saucepan, heat oil over medium heat; cook garlic, stirring, for 1 minute. Add onion; cook, stirring occasionally, until golden, about 8 minutes. Stir in wine; cook, stirring, for 1 minute. Add soup mix and pepper; bring to boil. Remove from heat.

Drain fat from roasting pan; heat pan over medium-high heat. Add onion mixture and bring to boil, scraping up any browned bits. Mix potato starch with ¼ cup water; whisk into roasting pan and cook, stirring, until slightly thickened, about 3 minutes. Serve with lamb.

NUTRITIONAL INFORMATION, PER SERVING: about 275 cal, 38 g pro, 12 g total fat (5 g sat. fat), 2 g carb (trace dietary fibre, 1 g sugar), 129 mg chol, 292 mg sodium, 653 mg potassium. % RDI: 2% calcium, 18% iron, 1% vit A, 10% folate.

VARIATION
NONKOSHER ROAST LEG OF LAMB
WITH CARAMELIZED ONION GRAVY

For gravy, use red wine of your choice, replace soup mix and water with 2 cups sodium-reduced beef broth and replace potato starch with cornstarch.

LAYERED "KNISH" BAKE

HANDS-ON TIME
40 MINUTES

TOTAL TIME
1 HOUR

MAKES
16 SERVINGS

In large skillet, heat oil over medium heat; cook onions, ¼ tsp of the salt and pinch of the pepper, stirring occasionally, until deep golden, about 30 minutes.

Meanwhile, in large saucepan of boiling water, cook potatoes and garlic until potatoes are tender, about 10 minutes. Drain and return to pan. Mash until smooth; stir in nutmeg and remaining salt and pepper. Let cool for 5 minutes. Stir in eggs and chives.

In greased 13- × 9-inch (3 L) baking dish, spread half of the potato mixture. Top with onion mixture. Spread remaining potato mixture over top. *(Make-ahead: Cover and refrigerate for up to 24 hours. Dot with margarine. Bake, covered, in 350°F/180°C oven until warmed through, about 1 hour. Uncover and bake until golden, about 30 minutes.)*

Dot with margarine; bake, uncovered, in 350°F (180°C) oven until golden, about 20 minutes.

NUTRITIONAL INFORMATION, PER SERVING: about 123 cal, 3 g pro, 3 g total fat (1 g sat. fat), 22 g carb (2 g dietary fibre, 5 g sugar), 23 mg chol, 242 mg sodium, 499 mg potassium. % RDI: 3% calcium, 8% iron, 2% vit A, 22% vit C, 12% folate.

2 tbsp	kosher olive oil
4	sweet onions, thinly sliced
1½ tsp	salt
½ tsp	pepper
8	large russet potatoes, peeled and cut in 1-inch (2.5 cm) chunks
1	head garlic, cloves separated and peeled
¼ tsp	nutmeg
2	eggs, lightly beaten
¼ cup	chopped fresh chives
1 tbsp	kosher pareve margarine

31

VARIATION
SPINACH, ONION AND POTATO BAKE
Reduce onions to 2. When onions are cooked, add 12 cups chopped fresh spinach; cook, stirring, until wilted.

SAUTÉED SPRING ASPARAGUS AND MUSHROOMS

HANDS-ON TIME
20 MINUTES

TOTAL TIME
20 MINUTES

MAKES
12 SERVINGS

2 tbsp	kosher olive oil
5	cloves garlic, minced
675 g	mixed fresh mushrooms (such as oyster, shiitake and cremini), sliced
900 g	asparagus (about 2 bunches), trimmed, peeled and halved
3 tbsp	chopped fresh chives
2 tsp	grated lemon zest
2 tbsp	lemon juice
¼ tsp	each salt and pepper
3 tbsp	sliced almonds, toasted

In large skillet, heat oil over medium-high heat; cook garlic, stirring, until fragrant, about 1 minute.

Add mushrooms; cook, stirring often, until light golden and almost no liquid remains, about 8 minutes.

Add asparagus; cook, stirring often, until asparagus is tender-crisp and mushrooms are golden, about 8 minutes.

Add chives, lemon zest, lemon juice, salt and pepper; toss to combine. Serve sprinkled with almonds.

NUTRITIONAL INFORMATION, PER SERVING: about 60 cal, 3 g pro, 3 g total fat (trace sat. fat), 7 g carb (2 g dietary fibre, 2 g sugar), 0 mg chol, 62 mg sodium, 361 mg potassium. % RDI: 2% calcium, 7% iron, 6% vit A, 10% vit C, 40% folate.

HONEY-GLAZED CARROTS

HANDS-ON TIME
25 MINUTES

TOTAL TIME
25 MINUTES

MAKES
12 SERVINGS

2.25 kg	carrots (about 4 bunches), trimmed and peeled
1 tbsp	chicken schmaltz or beef schmaltz
2	shallots, finely diced
2 tbsp	kosher liquid honey
1 tbsp	chopped fresh thyme
½ tsp	each salt and pepper

Cut carrots in half lengthwise; cut crosswise into 1½-inch (4 cm) pieces.

In large skillet, heat schmaltz over medium-high heat; cook shallots, stirring frequently, until softened, about 3 minutes.

Add carrots, tossing to coat; cook until slightly softened, about 5 minutes.

Add ¾ cup water, the honey and thyme; cook until no liquid remains, about 5 minutes.

Stir in additional ½ cup water; cook, stirring, until carrots are tender and no liquid remains, 3 to 5 minutes. Sprinkle with salt and pepper; toss to combine.

NUTRITIONAL INFORMATION, PER SERVING: about 74 cal, 1 g pro, 1 g total fat (trace sat. fat), 15 g carb (4 g dietary fibre, 8 g sugar), 1 mg chol, 182 mg sodium, 356 mg potassium. % RDI: 4% calcium, 4% iron, 253% vit A, 10% vit C, 10% folate.

DAIRY-FREE GLUTEN-FREE
MOLTEN CHOCOLATE LAVA CAKES

HANDS-ON TIME
30 MINUTES

TOTAL TIME
50 MINUTES

MAKES
12 SERVINGS

In heatproof bowl set over saucepan of hot (not boiling) water, melt chocolate with margarine, stirring until smooth. Slice vanilla pod in half lengthwise. Scrape seeds into chocolate mixture; stir. Remove from heat.

Whisk in sugar. Whisk in eggs and egg yolks, 1 at a time. Sift cocoa; whisk into chocolate mixture with salt. Divide batter among 12 greased ramekins; place on rimmed baking sheet. *(Make-ahead: Cover and refrigerate for up to 24 hours; add 5 minutes to baking time.)*

Bake in 425°F (220°C) oven until edges are set and centres are slightly jiggly when tapped, about 15 minutes. Let cool for 3 minutes. Run knife around edges and turn out onto plates. Garnish with strawberries and whipped topping (if using).

NUTRITIONAL INFORMATION, PER SERVING: about 387 cal, 7 g pro, 18 g total fat (8 g sat. fat), 51 g carb (4 g dietary fibre, 45 g sugar), 195 mg chol, 108 mg sodium, 132 mg potassium. % RDI: 3% calcium, 16% iron, 16% vit A, 28% vit C, 15% folate.

VARIATION
FLOURLESS CHOCOLATE LAVA CAKES
Substitute butter for margarine, and whipping cream (35%) for whipped topping.

340 g	kosher pareve bittersweet chocolate (12 oz) or semisweet chocolate (such as Lieber's), chopped
½ cup	kosher pareve margarine, cubed
1	vanilla pod
2 cups	granulated sugar
6	eggs
6	egg yolks
¼ cup	kosher pareve cocoa powder (such as Ghirardelli)
pinch	salt
340 g	strawberries, hulled and diced
	kosher nondairy whipped topping (optional)

33

CABANE À SUCRE
SUGAR SHACK

When the sun is bright and the snow is melting, it's time for a trip to the sugar bush. As the sweet sap is boiled off to make syrup, let's sit down for a meal of springtime favourites from Quebec, featuring the unique flavour of the maple tree.

35

MENU FOR 8

PINEAPPLE AND MAPLE HAM p.36

**CHARD AND APPLE SALAD
WITH MAPLE BACON VINAIGRETTE** p.37

CHEESE AND MAPLE SOUFFLÉS p.38

MAPLE FRENCH TOAST STICKS p.38

SWEET POTATO CAKES p.39

MAPLE MAYO p.39

MAPLE TAFFY ON VANILLA ICE CREAM p.41

MAPLE FUDGE p.41

PINEAPPLE AND MAPLE HAM

p.34

HANDS-ON TIME	**TOTAL TIME**	**MAKES**
25 MINUTES	4 HOURS	16-20 SERVINGS

4 cups	pineapple juice
1 cup	maple syrup
	grated zest and juice of half orange
¼ cup	each brown sugar and Dijon mustard
pinch	pepper
4 kg	fully cooked bone-in ham
4	pineapple slices (optional)
¼ cup	each unsalted butter and flour

In saucepan, stir together 1½ cups of the pineapple juice, ¾ cup of the maple syrup, orange zest, orange juice, brown sugar, mustard and pepper; bring to boil over medium-high heat. Cook, stirring, until brown sugar is dissolved, about 5 minutes. Reduce heat to medium-low; simmer, stirring occasionally, until glaze is reduced by half and thick enough to coat back of spoon, about 25 minutes. Let cool slightly, about 15 minutes.

Meanwhile, pour remaining pineapple juice and remaining maple syrup into roasting pan. Place ham, fat side up, on rack in roasting pan. Arrange pineapple slices (if using) around ham; cover pan with foil. Roast on bottom rack in 325°F oven until instant-read thermometer inserted into centre reads 130°F (55°C), about 3 hours.

Uncover ham; peel off and discard outer skin. Trim fat layer to ¼-inch (5 mm) thickness. Using paring knife, score remaining fat to make diamond pattern on ham. Brush half of the pineapple glaze over ham.

Roast, uncovered, in 375°F (190°C) oven, brushing with remaining glaze several times throughout, until glaze is caramelized and instant-read thermometer inserted into centre reads 140°F (60°C), about 30 minutes.

Remove ham to cutting board; let stand for 15 minutes before slicing or shredding.

While ham is resting, tilt roasting pan so juices collect at end. Skim fat from surface; discard. In large saucepan, melt butter over medium-high heat. Add flour; cook, stirring, until golden, about 1 minute. Whisk in juices from roasting pan and enough water to make 4 cups. Bring to boil. Reduce heat; cook, stirring, until thickened, about 5 minutes. Chop pineapple slices (if using); stir into sauce.

NUTRITIONAL INFORMATION, PER EACH OF 20 SERVINGS: about 426 cal, 50 g pro, 14 g total fat (6 g sat. fat), 23 g carb (trace dietary fibre), 117 mg chol, 1,800 mg sodium.

CHARD AND APPLE SALAD
WITH MAPLE BACON VINAIGRETTE

HANDS-ON TIME
35 MINUTES

TOTAL TIME
35 MINUTES

MAKES
6 SERVINGS

In nonstick skillet, cook bacon with oil over medium-high heat until bacon begins to sizzle; reduce heat to medium and cook until golden and beginning to crisp, about 8 minutes.

Remove bacon to paper towel–lined plate, reserving fat. Wipe out skillet. Return bacon fat to skillet; cook shallots over medium heat until beginning to soften, about 1 minute. Remove to large bowl; stir in maple syrup, vinegar, mustard and salt. Add Swiss chard, radicchio, apples, Camembert and bacon to bowl; toss to coat.

NUTRITIONAL INFORMATION, PER SERVING: about 260 cal, 11 g pro, 16 g total fat (7 g sat. fat), 19 g carb (2 g dietary fibre, 12 g sugar), 33 mg chol, 545 mg sodium, 540 mg potassium. % RDI: 15% calcium, 10% iron, 17% vit A, 27% vit C, 35% folate.

6	strips thick-cut bacon, sliced crosswise in ½-inch (1 cm) pieces
2 tbsp	vegetable oil
2	shallots, minced
3 tbsp	maple syrup
3 tbsp	cider vinegar
1 tsp	Dijon mustard
pinch	salt
10 cups	torn stemmed Swiss chard (1 large bunch)
8 cups	thickly sliced cored halved radicchio (3 small heads)
2	tart apples, cored and thinly sliced
2 cups	cubed (½ inch/1 cm) Camembert cheese (about 195 g)

CHEESE AND MAPLE SOUFFLÉS

p.40

HANDS-ON TIME	**TOTAL TIME**	**MAKES**
15 MINUTES	35 MINUTES	8 SERVINGS

8	eggs, separated
½ cup	milk
¼ cup	maple syrup
3 tbsp	flour
2 tbsp	finely chopped fresh chives
½ tsp	salt
pinch	each nutmeg and pepper
1 cup	grated aged Cheddar cheese

In large bowl, whisk together egg yolks, milk, syrup, flour, chives, salt, nutmeg and pepper. Stir in Cheddar. Set aside.

In separate bowl, beat egg whites until stiff peaks form. Fold one-quarter of egg whites into yolk mixture. Fold in remaining whites. Pour into 8 buttered and floured 1-cup (250 mL) ramekins. Run tip of thumb around inside edge of ramekins to wipe clean.

Bake in 400°F oven until soufflés are puffed, golden and firm when pressed gently, 20 to 25 minutes. Serve immediately.

NUTRITIONAL INFORMATION, PER SERVING: about 178 cal, 11 g pro, 10 g total fat (5 g sat. fat), 10 g carb (trace dietary fibre, 7 g sugar), 209 mg chol, 305 mg sodium, 122 mg potassium. % RDI: 14% calcium, 8% iron, 15% vit A, 17% folate.

MAPLE FRENCH TOAST STICKS

p.40

HANDS-ON TIME	**TOTAL TIME**	**MAKES**
15 MINUTES	30 MINUTES	8 SERVINGS

1½ cups	panko bread crumbs
⅓ cup	grated unsweetened coconut
8	eggs
½ cup	each milk and maple syrup
1 tsp	vanilla
¼ tsp	cinnamon
8	1-inch (2.5 cm) thick white bread slices, crusts removed, cut into 1-inch (2.5-cm) strips
¼ cup	each butter and vegetable oil (approx)

In shallow dish, combine bread crumbs and coconut. Set aside.

In bowl, whisk together eggs, milk, maple syrup, vanilla and cinnamon. Pour into separate shallow dish.

Dip bread strips in egg mixture, turning to coat and shaking off any excess. Cover in bread crumb mixture, turning to coat all over and pressing lightly to adhere.

In large skillet, melt 1 tbsp butter with 1 tbsp oil over medium heat. Working in batches, cook bread strips, pressing down lightly with a spatula, turning halfway through and adding more butter and oil as needed, until golden and crisp, about 4 minutes. Transfer to rimmed baking sheet; keep warm in 250°F (120°C) oven.

NUTRITIONAL INFORMATION, PER SERVING: about 415 cal, 10 g pro, 19 g total fat (7 g sat. fat), 50 g carb (1 g dietary fibre), 146 mg chol, 275 mg sodium.

SWEET POTATO CAKES

p.40

HANDS-ON
25 MINUTES

TOTAL TIME
25 MINUTES

MAKES
12 PIECES

Pat sweet potatoes and onion in paper towel to dry. In large bowl, combine potatoes, onion, eggs, flour, baking powder, salt and pepper.

In large skillet, heat 1 tbsp oil over medium heat. Working in batches, pour in scant ¼ cup batter per cake; spread slightly. Cook, turning occasionally and adding more oil as needed, until golden and crisp, about 8 minutes. Transfer to rimmed baking sheet; cover and keep warm in 250°F (120°C) oven. *(Make-ahead: Cover and refrigerate overnight. Reheat in 350°F oven until crisp, about 15 minutes.)* Serve with Maple Mayo (see recipe, below).

NUTRITIONAL INFORMATION, PER PIECE: about 91 cal, 2 g pro, 6 g total fat (1 g sat. fat), 9 g carb (1 g dietary fibre, 2 g sugar), 32 mg chol, 81 mg sodium, 102 mg potassium. % RDI: 2% calcium, 4% iron, 54% vit A, 8% vit C, 5% folate.

2	sweet potatoes (about 500 g total), peeled and grated
1	small onion, grated
2	eggs, lightly beaten
¼ cup	flour
½ tsp	baking powder
¼ tsp	salt
pinch	pepper
¼ cup	peanut oil or vegetable oil (approx)

39

MAPLE MAYO

p.40

In bowl, whisk together ½ cup mayonnaise, 1 tbsp maple syrup and ¼ tsp fleur de sel. *(Make-ahead: Cover and refrigerate for up to 2 days.)*
MAKES ABOUT ½ CUP

NUTRITIONAL INFORMATION, PER 1 TBSP: about 105 cal, trace pro, 11 g total fat (2 g sat. fat), 2 g carb (0 g dietary fibre, 2 g sugar), 5 mg chol, 111 mg sodium, 7 mg potassium. % RDI: 1% iron, 1% vit A.

CLOCKWISE FROM TOP LEFT: SWEET POTATO CAKES WITH MAPLE MAYONNAISE; MAPLE FRENCH TOAST STICKS; AND CHEESE AND MAPLE SOUFFLÉS

MAPLE TAFFY ON VANILLA ICE CREAM

HANDS-ON
15 MINUTES

TOTAL TIME
4¼ HOURS

MAKES
16 TO 20 SERVINGS

Spread ice cream into 13- × 9-inch dish. Cover and freeze until firm, about 4 hours.

In small saucepan over medium heat, boil syrup, without stirring, until candy thermometer reads 235°F (115°C) or a few drops of syrup dropped into very cold water form firm taffy-like threads, about 10 minutes.

Drizzle ¼ of maple syrup over ice cream. Let stand until just beginning to set, about 30 seconds. Repeat with remaining maple syrup.

NUTRITIONAL INFORMATION, PER EACH OF 20 SERVINGS: about 150 cal, 2 g pro, 6 g total fat (4 g sat. fat), 77 g carb (trace dietary fibre), 2 mg chol, 45 mg sodium.

| 8 cups | vanilla ice cream, softened |
| 1 cup | maple syrup |

MAPLE FUDGE

HANDS-ON TIME
30 MINUTES

TOTAL TIME
3½ HOURS

MAKES
36 SQUARES

Grease side of heavy saucepan. Add brown sugar, cream, maple syrup, butter and pinch of the baking soda; cook over medium heat, stirring constantly with wooden spoon, until boiling. If mixture does not foam up high when boiling, stir in remaining baking soda. Boil, without stirring, until candy thermometer reads 238°F (114°C) or ½ tsp of mixture dropped into very cold water forms soft ball that flattens when removed from water, about 8 minutes. Immediately pour into greased wide bowl, without scraping pan clean. Let cool on rack until candy thermometer reads 100°F (38°C), 1 to 2 hours.

Using wooden spoon, beat in vanilla until mixture is very thick and most of the gloss disappears, about 7 minutes. (Or use heavy-duty mixer with paddle attachment and beat at medium-low speed for about 8 minutes.) Immediately scrape into parchment paper–lined 8-inch (2 L) square baking dish; smooth top. Let cool on rack. Lift out onto cutting board; cut into 36 squares.

NUTRITIONAL INFORMATION, PER SQUARE: about 85 cal, trace g pro, 3 g total fat (2 g sat. fat), 15 g carb (0 g dietary fibre, 14 g sugar), 10 mg chol, 47 mg sodium, 57 mg potassium. % RDI: 2% calcium, 2% iron, 3% vit A.

2 cups	packed brown sugar
1 cup	whipping cream (35%)
½ cup	pure maple syrup
2 tbsp	butter, cut in small pieces
1 tsp	baking soda (approx)
1 tsp	vanilla

MOTHER'S DAY BRUNCH

Perhaps she would be satisfied with only a card,
but a brunch in her honour, made by the people she loves
is one of the best ways to thank your mom (or the other
special women in your life) for everything she does.

43

MENU FOR 8

BOSTON LETTUCE SALAD
WITH GREEN GODDESS DRESSING **p.44**

PINEAPPLE MIMOSAS **p.44**

HAM HOCK HASH AND POACHED EGGS **p.45**

SAUTÉED GARLIC SWISS CHARD **p.46**

APPLE CHEDDAR DROP BISCUITS **p.46**

CREAMY LEMON MERINGUE PIE **p.47**

BOSTON LETTUCE SALAD
WITH GREEN GODDESS DRESSING

HANDS-ON TIME	TOTAL TIME	MAKES
10 MINUTES	10 MINUTES	8 SERVINGS

GREEN GODDESS DRESSING

1	anchovy fillet or 1 tsp anchovy paste (optional)
1 cup	chopped fresh parsley
½ cup	each sour cream and mayonnaise
2 tbsp	thinly sliced fresh chives or green onions
2 tbsp	white wine vinegar
1 tbsp	dried tarragon
¼ tsp	each salt and pepper

SALAD

6 cups	torn Boston lettuce
2 cups	baby arugula or baby spinach
4	radishes, thinly sliced

GREEN GODDESS DRESSING Soak anchovy fillet (if using) in cold water for 5 minutes; drain, pat dry and finely chop.

In food processor, pulse together parsley, sour cream, mayonnaise, chives, vinegar, tarragon, salt, pepper and anchovy (if using) until smooth. *(Make ahead: Refrigerate in airtight container for up to 24 hours.)*

SALAD In large bowl, toss together lettuce, arugula and radishes. Divide among salad bowls; spoon dressing over top.

NUTRITIONAL INFORMATION, PER SERVING: about 135 cal, 2 g pro, 13 g total fat (3 g sat. fat), 3 g carb (1 g dietary fibre), 11 mg chol, 168 mg sodium. % RDI: 6% calcium, 7% iron, 17% vit A, 28% vit C, 27% folate.

PINEAPPLE MIMOSAS

Pour 2 oz pineapple juice (about ¼ cup) into champagne flute; top with 3 oz sparkling dry white wine or Champagne (about 6 tbsp). Garnish rim with fresh pineapple spear.

MAKES 1 SERVING

NUTRITIONAL INFORMATION, PER SERVING: about 91 cal, trace pro, 0 g total fat (0 g sat. fat), 9 g carb (trace dietary fibre), 0 mg chol, 5 mg sodium. % RDI: 2% calcium, 3% iron, 23% vit C, 6% folate.

HAM HOCK HASH AND POACHED EGGS

p.42

HANDS-ON TIME
45 MINUTES

TOTAL TIME
3¼ HOURS

MAKES
8 SERVINGS

HAM HOCK In large saucepan, add ham hock, onion, carrot, parsley, thyme, cloves, bay leaves, garlic, peppercorns. Pour enough cold water to cover; bring to boil. Reduce heat to low; cover and cook for 2 hours, skimming off foam as necessary.

Transfer ham hock to bowl; let cool enough to handle. Remove skin and slice into strips; discard fat and bone. Using 2 forks, shred ham. Set aside.

Strain ham cooking liquid through fine-mesh sieve into large saucepan; skim off fat. Remove ¼ cup of the liquid to small bowl; bring remaining liquid to boil.

HASH Add potatoes to ham cooking liquid; cook over medium-high heat just until tender, 5 to 7 minutes. Drain. *(Make-ahead: Refrigerate ham and potatoes in separate airtight containers for up to 24 hours.)*

In large heavy skillet, heat oil over medium heat; cook onions, stirring occasionally, until softened, about 5 minutes. Add mushrooms, garlic, thyme, salt and pepper; cook, stirring, until mushrooms are browned, about 8 minutes. Stir in paprika. Add vinegar and reserved ham cooking liquid, scraping up any browned bits. Reduce heat to simmer; cook until no liquid remains. Add potatoes, ham skin, ham hock and parsley; cook, stirring, until heated through, about 6 minutes. Serve with eggs.

NUTRITIONAL INFORMATION, PER SERVING: about 335 cal, 28 g pro, 14 g total fat (4 g sat. fat), 23 g carb (2 g dietary fibre), 231 mg chol, 191 mg sodium. % RDI: 5% calcium, 15% iron, 10% vit A, 17% vit C, 20% folate.

PERFECT POACHED EGGS

In large, shallow saucepan or Dutch oven, pour enough water to come 3 inches (8 cm) up side; bring to boil. Add 1 tsp vinegar; reduce heat to simmer.

Break egg into small dish; gently slip into simmering water and cook until desired doneness, about 5 minutes for soft yolks and firm whites. Remove with slotted spoon, patting bottom of spoon with towel to dry egg.

HAM HOCK

900 g	smoked ham hock
1	onion, quartered
1	carrot, quartered
3 sprigs	each fresh parsley and thyme
4	whole cloves
2	bay leaves
2	cloves garlic
½ tsp	black peppercorns

HASH

900 g	russet or yellow-fleshed potatoes (6 to 8), peeled and cut in ½-inch (1 cm) cubes
2 tbsp	vegetable oil
2	onions, chopped
1	pkg (227 g) cremini mushrooms, sliced
3	cloves garlic, minced
1 tsp	finely chopped fresh thyme (or ½ tsp dried thyme)
¼ tsp	each salt and pepper
¾ tsp	smoked or sweet paprika
2 tbsp	white wine vinegar
¼ cup	chopped fresh parsley
8	poached eggs (see recipe, left)

SAUTÉED GARLIC SWISS CHARD

p.42

HANDS-ON TIME 10 MINUTES	**TOTAL TIME** 10 MINUTES	**MAKES** 8 SERVINGS

1 kg	Swiss chard (about 2 bunches), trimmed and coarsely chopped
3 tbsp	olive oil
3	cloves garlic, minced
¼ tsp	salt
¼ tsp	hot pepper flakes

In large saucepan of salted boiling water, cover and cook Swiss chard, until tender-crisp, 2 to 4 minutes. Drain, squeezing out excess liquid. Pat dry. *(Make-ahead: Refrigerate in airtight container for up to 24 hours.)*

In skillet, heat oil over medium-high heat; cook garlic, salt and hot pepper flakes, stirring, until garlic is golden, about 30 seconds. Add Swiss chard; cook, tossing, until heated through, 3 to 5 minutes.

NUTRITIONAL INFORMATION, PER SERVING: about 82 cal, 2 g pro, 5 g total fat (1 g sat. fat), 8 g carb (3 g dietary fibre), 0 mg chol, 93 mg sodium. % RDI: 14% calcium, 2% iron, 36% vit A, 27% vit C, 4% folate.

46

APPLE CHEDDAR DROP BISCUITS

p.42

HANDS-ON TIME 15 MINUTES	**TOTAL TIME** 30 MINUTES	**MAKES** 12 BISCUITS

1¾ cups	all-purpose flour
4 tsp	baking powder
1 tbsp	granulated sugar
½ tsp	salt
¼ cup	cold butter, cubed
1 cup	shredded extra-old Cheddar cheese
1 cup	grated cored peeled Cortland or Spartan apple, about 1
2	green onions, finely chopped
¾ cup	milk

In large bowl, whisk together flour, baking powder, sugar and salt. Using pastry blender or 2 knives, cut in butter until mixture resembles coarse crumbs with a few larger pieces. Stir in Cheddar, apple and green onions. Using fork, stir in milk to form ragged dough.

Drop by ¼ cup, 1½ inches (4 cm) apart, onto parchment paper–lined rimless baking sheet. Bake in 425°F (220°C) oven until lightly browned, 13 to 15 minutes.

NUTRITIONAL INFORMATION, PER BISCUIT: about 157 cal, 5 g pro, 8 g total fat (5 g sat. fat), 17 g carb (1 g dietary fibre, 3 g sugar), 21 mg chol, 290 mg sodium, 69 g potassium. % RDI: 12% calcium, 8% iron, 7% vit A, 2% vit C, 14% folate.

CREAMY LEMON MERINGUE PIE

HANDS-ON TIME
35 MINUTES

TOTAL TIME
5 HOURS

MAKES
8 SERVINGS

SOUR CREAM PASTRY In bowl, whisk flour with salt. Using pastry blender or 2 knives, cut in butter and lard until mixture resembles fine crumbs with a few larger pieces.

Whisk ice water with sour cream; drizzle over flour mixture, tossing with fork to form ragged dough. Shape into disc; wrap in plastic wrap. Refrigerate until chilled, about 30 minutes. *(Make-ahead: Refrigerate for up to 24 hours.)*

On lightly floured work surface, roll out dough to ⅛-inch (3 mm) thickness. Fit into 9-inch (23 cm) pie plate. Trim to fit, leaving 1-inch (2.5 cm) overhang; fold under and flute edge.

Line crust with foil; fill with pie weights or dried beans. Bake on bottom rack of 400°F (200°C) oven for 15 minutes. Remove weights and foil. Using fork, prick shell all over. Bake until crust is golden, about 10 minutes. Let cool on rack. *(Make-ahead: Cover for up to 24 hours.)*

LEMON FILLING In bowl, beat egg yolks with lemon zest until light, about 2 minutes. Beat in condensed milk and lemon juice; pour into cooled crust, smoothing top. Bake in 325°F (160°C) oven for 7 minutes.

MERINGUE While filling is baking, in small microwaveable bowl, whisk cornstarch with ⅓ cup water. Microwave on high, stirring twice, until thickened, about 40 seconds. Cover with plastic wrap; keep warm.

In bowl, beat egg whites with cream of tartar until soft peaks form. Beat in sugar, 1 tbsp at a time, until stiff peaks form. Beat in cornstarch mixture, 1 tbsp at a time.

Starting at edge and using spatula, spread meringue around edge of hot filling, sealing to crust. Spread meringue over remaining filling, making peaks with back of spoon. Bake in 325°F (160°C) oven until peaks are golden, about 20 minutes. Let cool on rack until set, about 3 hours.

NUTRITIONAL INFORMATION, PER SERVING: about 419 cal, 9 g pro, 20 g total fat (10 g sat. fat), 52 g carb (1 g dietary fibre), 141 mg chol, 207 mg sodium. % RDI: 15% calcium, 9% iron, 14% vit A, 15% vit C, 28% folate.

SOUR CREAM PASTRY

1¼ cups	all-purpose flour
¼ tsp	salt
¼ cup	cold butter, cubed
¼ cup	cold lard, cubed
2 tbsp	ice water
4 tsp	sour cream

LEMON FILLING

4	egg yolks
1 tbsp	grated lemon zest
1	can (300 mL) condensed milk
½ cup	lemon juice

MERINGUE

1 tbsp	cornstarch
4	egg whites (room temperature)
¼ tsp	cream of tartar
⅓ cup	fruit/berry (instant dissolving) sugar

AFTERNOON TEA

You don't need a holiday on the calendar to create a special occasion. Just invite your friends around for afternoon tea. Keep it simple: a few sandwiches, scones, a perfect cup of tea and good conversation. For you, afternoon tea is easy to put together; for your guests, it's a brilliant and unexpected change of pace.

49

MENU FOR 8

CURRIED EGG SALAD SANDWICHES **p.50**

TUNA OLIVE SALAD SANDWICHES **p.50**

HAM PICKLE SPREAD SANDWICHES **p.51**

PIMIENTO CHEESE SPREAD SANDWICHES **p.51**

CRUDITÉS WITH HERB DIP **p.51**

OAT DEMERARA SHORTBREAD **p.52**

ROSEHIP CREAM SANDWICH COOKIES **p.53**

MINI LEMON SCONES
WITH STRAWBERRIES AND CREAM **p.54**

THE PERFECT CUP OF TEA **p.54**

TEA SANDWICHES

p.48

A simple filling between 2 slices of bread is just a sandwich. Take a little extra care in assembling, cutting and presenting the same sandwich, and it becomes a treat. Here are some of our favourite sandwich-making techniques (use any of the filling recipes at right in the sandwiches below).

Triangle Sandwiches

Spread 16 thin slices white or whole wheat sandwich bread with ⅓ cup butter, softened. Spread desired filling evenly over 8 of the slices; top with remaining slices, buttered side down, pressing lightly. Place on rimmed baking sheet and cover with damp tea towel; cover tightly with plastic wrap and refrigerate until firm, about 1 hour. Trim off crusts. Cut each sandwich into 4 triangles.

MAKES 32 PIECES

Square Sandwiches

Make sandwiches as in Triangle Sandwiches above except use 8 thin slices white and 8 thin slices whole wheat sandwich bread. Cut each sandwich into quarters.

MAKES 32 PIECES

Finger Sandwiches

Make sandwiches as in Triangle Sandwiches above. Cut each sandwich lengthwise into 4 fingers.

MAKES 32 PIECES

Pinwheel Sandwiches

Ask your bakery to slice a white or whole wheat sandwich loaf horizontally. Trim off crusts from 5 slices. Using rolling pin, flatten slices slightly. Spread with ⅓ cup butter, softened; top with desired filling.

Place 1 spear asparagus (or 2 baby gherkins) along 1 short end of each slice. Starting at asparagus, roll up tightly without squeezing. Wrap each roll tightly in plastic wrap. Refrigerate for 1 hour. Using serrated knife, trim ends; cut each roll into 6 slices.

MAKES 30 PIECES

CURRIED EGG SALAD

MAKES 1⅔ CUPS

8	hard-cooked eggs, peeled and finely chopped
⅓ cup	light mayonnaise
1 tsp	Dijon mustard
½ tsp	mild curry paste
¼ tsp	pepper
pinch	salt

Stir together eggs, mayonnaise, mustard, curry paste, pepper and salt.

TUNA OLIVE SALAD

MAKES 1⅔ CUPS

2	cans (each 170 g) chunk white tuna, drained
⅓ cup	light mayonnaise
¼ cup	finely chopped celery
2 tbsp	finely chopped black olives
1	green onion, finely chopped
pinch	pepper

In bowl, finely flake tuna with fork. Stir in mayonnaise, celery, olives, green onion and pepper.

HAM PICKLE SPREAD

MAKES 1⅔ CUPS

340 g	Black Forest ham, cubed
⅓ cup	drained sweet pickle relish
⅓ cup	light mayonnaise
2 tsp	Dijon mustard

In food processor, pulse ham until consistency of coarse bread crumbs. Scrape into bowl. Sir in relish, mayonnaise and mustard.

PIMIENTO CHEESE SPREAD

MAKES 1⅔ CUPS

1	jar (128 mL) pimientos, drained and rinsed
1 cup	cream cheese, softened
⅓ cup	light mayonnaise
1 cup	shredded extra-old Cheddar cheese
¼ tsp	pepper

Pat pimientos dry; dice and set aside. In bowl, beat cream cheese with mayonnaise until smooth. Stir in Cheddar, pimientos and pepper.

CRUDITÉS
WITH HERB DIP

MAKES 8 SERVINGS

½ cup	each light mayonnaise and light sour cream
1	green onion, finely chopped
4 tsp	lemon juice
1 tbsp	finely chopped fresh parsley
¼ tsp	dried dill
pinch	each salt and pepper
4 cups	assorted cut vegetables (carrots, celery, cucumber, radishes and/or asparagus)

In small bowl, whisk together mayonnaise, sour cream, green onion, lemon juice, parsley, dill, salt and pepper. Cover and refrigerate for 1 hour. *(Make-ahead: Refrigerate for up to 24 hours.)* Serve with vegetables.

NUTRITIONAL INFORMATION, PER SERVING: about 82 cal, 2 g pro, 6 g total fat (1 g sat. fat), 7 g carb (1 g dietary fibre), 7 mg chol, 145 mg sodium. % RDI: 5% calcium, 2% iron, 19% vit A, 28% vit C, 10% folate.

51

TIP FROM THE TEST KITCHEN

A platter of crunchy raw vegetables and dip is a reliable favourite at any party. Plan to serve ½–1 cup cut vegetables per person, depending on how much other food is on the table. To keep your crudité selection interesting, freshen up the familiar options—celery, carrots, cauliflower and peppers—with a few surprises. Try sliced fennel, celery root or zucchini cut in sticks, wedges of turnip or jicama, or Belgian endive spears. Mix in colourful heirloom tomatoes and carrots with the usual varieties. You can also serve some vegetables, such as green beans and asparagus, lightly blanched instead of raw.

OAT DEMERARA SHORTBREAD

HANDS-ON TIME	**TOTAL TIME**	**MAKES**
10 MINUTES	1 HOUR	12 TO 16 WEDGES

SHORTBREAD

½ cup	large-flake rolled oats
1 cup	unsalted butter, softened
½ cup	packed Demerara sugar or dark brown sugar
½ tsp	salt
1½ cups	all-purpose flour
¼ cup	cornstarch

TOPPING

| 2 tbsp | large-flake rolled oats |

SHORTBREAD On baking sheet, bake oats in 325°F (160°C) oven until lightly toasted, 7 to 10 minutes. Let cool.

In large bowl, beat butter, Demerara sugar and salt until fluffy. In separate bowl, whisk flour, cornstarch and oats; stir into butter mixture just until combined.

Press into parchment paper–lined 9-inch (2.5 L) springform pan. Score into 12 to 16 wedges.

TOPPING Prick wedges with fork; sprinkle with oats and press lightly into dough.

Bake in 325°F (160°C) oven until browned, about 50 minutes. Let cool in pan on rack for 5 minutes. Cut through score lines. Let cool completely.

NUTRITIONAL INFORMATION, PER EACH OF 16 WEDGES: about 192 cal, 2 g pro, 12 g total fat (7 g sat. fat), 20 g carb (1 g dietary fibre, 0 g sugar), 30 mg chol, 77 mg sodium, 53 mg potassium. % RDI: 1% calcium, 6% iron, 10% vit A, 11% folate.

ROSEHIP CREAM SANDWICH COOKIES

HANDS-ON TIME
40 MINUTES

TOTAL TIME
1¼ HOURS

MAKES
36 COOKIES

COOKIES In large bowl, beat butter with sugar until fluffy; beat in egg and vanilla. In seaparate bowl, whisk together flour, baking powder and salt; stir into butter mixture to form smooth dough.

On lightly floured work surface, roll out dough to scant ¼-inch (5 mm) thickness. Using 1½-inch (4 cm) round cookie cutter, cut out shapes, rerolling scraps. Arrange, about 1 inch (2.5 cm) apart, on parchment paper–lined rimless baking sheets.

Bake, 1 sheet at a time, in 350°F (180°C) oven until edges are golden, about 10 minutes per sheet. Transfer to racks; let cool.

ROSEHIP CREAM FILLING Meanwhile, in small saucepan, bring cream and rosehips to boil; reduce heat and simmer for 30 seconds. Remove from heat; cover and let stand for 15 minutes.

Strain through fine-mesh sieve into bowl, pressing with back of spoon to release liquid and some of the pulp; set aside and let cool completely.

In separate bowl, beat butter with icing sugar and salt until mixture resembles fine crumbs; beat in rosehip cream. Spoon or pipe about 1 tsp icing onto centre of half of the cookies; sandwich with remaining cookies, pressing gently to push icing to edge. *(Make-ahead: Store in single layer in airtight container for up to 2 days.)*

NUTRITIONAL INFORMATION, PER COOKIE: about 97 cal, 1 g pro, 5 g total fat (3 g sat. fat), 13 g carb (0 g dietary fibre, 8 g sugar), 17 mg chol, 27 mg sodium, 12 mg potassium. % RDI: 1% calcium, 2% iron, 4% vit A, 2% vit C, 7% folate.

COOKIES

½ cup	unsalted butter, softened
½ cup	granulated sugar
1	egg
1 tsp	vanilla
2 cups	all-purpose flour
1 tsp	baking powder
¼ tsp	salt

ROSEHIP CREAM FILLING

⅓ cup	whipping cream (35%)
3 tbsp	crushed dried rosehips
⅓ cup	unsalted butter, softened
1½ cups	icing sugar
pinch	salt

VARIATION

LEMON CREAM SANDWICH COOKIES
Replace rosehip-infused cream with 1 tbsp each lemon juice and whipping cream; stir 1 tsp grated lemon zest into filling.

53

MINI LEMON SCONES
WITH STRAWBERRIES AND CREAM

opposite

HANDS-ON TIME	TOTAL TIME	MAKES
25 MINUTES	40 MINUTES	ABOUT 24 PIECES

STRAWBERRIES

2 cups	sliced hulled strawberries
1 tbsp	granulated sugar
1 tsp	grated lemon zest

SCONES

2½ cups	all-purpose flour
2 tbsp	granulated sugar
1 tbsp	grated lemon zest
2½ tsp	baking powder
½ tsp	each baking soda and salt
½ cup	cold butter, cubed
1 cup	buttermilk
1	egg

TOPPING

1	egg, lightly beaten
2 tsp	granulated sugar
1	bottle (170 g) Devonshire cream (or 1 cup whipped cream)

STRAWBERRIES In bowl, combine strawberries, sugar and lemon zest; cover and refrigerate until chilled. *(Make-ahead: Refrigerate for up to 6 hours.)*

SCONES Meanwhile, in large bowl, whisk together flour, sugar, lemon zest, baking powder, baking soda and salt. Using pastry blender or 2 knives, cut in butter until mixture resembles coarse crumbs. Whisk buttermilk with egg; add to flour mixture, stirring with fork to make soft dough.

Using lightly floured hands, press dough into ball. On floured work surface, knead gently 10 times. Pat into scant ¾-inch (2 cm) thick round. Using 1¾-inch (4.5 cm) floured round or fluted cookie cutter, cut out rounds, pressing scraps together as necessary. Arrange, 1 inch (2.5 cm) apart on parchment paper–lined rimless baking sheets.

TOPPING Brush tops of scones with egg; sprinkle with sugar. Bake, 1 sheet at a time, in 400°F (200°C) oven until golden, about 12 minutes. Let cool on pans on racks. *(Make-ahead: Store in airtight container for up to 24 hours, or wrap in plastic wrap and freeze in airtight container for up to 2 weeks.)* Serve with strawberry mixture and Devonshire cream.

NUTRITIONAL INFORMATION, PER PIECE: about 135 cal, 3 g pro, 8 g total fat (5 g sat. fat), 14 g carb (1 g dietary fibre), 37 mg chol, 162 mg sodium. % RDI: 3% calcium, 5% iron, 7% vit A, 15% vit C, 15% folate.

VARIATION

MINI CHOCOLATE SCONES
Reduce flour to 2 cups. Add ½ cup cocoa powder, sifted. Increase sugar in scones to ¼ cup.

THE PERFECT CUP OF TEA
To make the perfect cup of tea, fill kettle with fresh, cold water and bring to boil. Meanwhile, warm clean teapot by rinsing with hot tap water; drain. Place 2 tsp loose tea or 1 tea bag in teapot for every 2 cups tea. When water comes to boil, immediately pour into the pot. Cover teapot and let steep for 5 minutes. Remove tea bags (if using); stir and pour tea (through strainer if using loose tea).

MINI LEMON SCONES WITH STRAWBERRIES AND CREAM

BABY SHOWER

A shower welcomes the soon-to-arrive baby, who is full of potential and possibilities, and fetes the new mother. Everyone will enjoy an easy assortment of finger foods, dips and, of course, a party cake. It will be the first of many cakes celebrating the little one.

MENU FOR 16

CREAMY HERBES DE PROVENCE DIP **p.58**

ROASTED VEGETABLE HUMMUS **p.58**

MINI CHEDDAR AND ONION GALETTE BITES **p.59**

MINI SMOKED SALMON QUICHES **p.60**

WHITE CHOCOLATE CHEESECAKE DIP **p.61**

PITCHER COSMOPOLITANS **p.61**

BABY SLEEPER CAKE **p.63**

CREAMY HERBES DE PROVENCE DIP

HANDS-ON TIME	TOTAL TIME	MAKES
10 MINUTES	10 MINUTES	1½ CUPS

½ cup	cream cheese, softened
½ cup	sour cream
½ cup	light mayonnaise
½ tsp	Dijon mustard
½ tsp	herbes de Provence
¼ tsp	each garlic powder and onion powder
pinch	each salt and pepper
dash	hot pepper sauce
1 tbsp	chopped fresh chives

In bowl, beat together cream cheese, sour cream, mayonnaise and mustard until smooth. Add herbes de Provence, garlic powder, onion powder, salt, pepper and hot pepper sauce; mix well. Stir in chives. *(Make-ahead: Cover and refrigerate for up to 24 hours.)*

NUTRITIONAL INFORMATION, PER 1 TBSP: about 41 cal, 1 g pro, 4 g total fat (2 g sat. fat), 1 g carb (0 g dietary fibre), 9 mg chol, 51 mg sodium. % RDI: 1% calcium, 1% iron, 3% vit A, 1% folate.

ROASTED VEGETABLE HUMMUS

HANDS-ON TIME	TOTAL TIME	MAKES
15 MINUTES	1¼ HOURS	2 CUPS

2	large carrots, chopped
4	shallots, quartered
4	cloves garlic (peel-on)
¼ cup	extra-virgin olive oil
1 cup	rinsed drained canned chickpeas
¼ cup	tahini
2 tbsp	lemon juice
¼ tsp	salt

On rimmed baking sheet, toss together carrots, shallots, garlic and 1 tbsp of the oil. Bake in 400°F (200°C) oven, stirring twice, until tender, 35 to 40 minutes. Let cool. Squeeze garlic from skins; discard skins.

In food processor, pulse carrots, shallots and garlic until finely chopped. Add chickpeas, tahini, lemon juice, salt and remaining oil; pulse until smooth. Add up to 3 tbsp water, 1 tbsp at a time, until mixture is spreadable. *(Make-ahead: Refrigerate in airtight container for up to 2 days.)*

NUTRITIONAL INFORMATION, PER 1 TBSP: about 37 cal, 1 g pro, 3 g total fat (trace sat. fat), 3 g carb (1 g dietary fibre), 0 mg chol, 39 mg sodium. % RDI: 1% calcium, 2% iron, 10% vit A, 2% vit C, 3% folate.

MINI CHEDDAR AND ONION GALETTE BITES

p.56

HANDS-ON TIME	**TOTAL TIME**	**MAKES**
1 HOUR	2 HOURS	24 PIECES

GALETTE PASTRY In bowl, whisk together flour, cornmeal, salt and thyme; using pastry blender or 2 knives, cut in butter until mixture resembles coarse crumbs. Whisk ice water with sour cream; drizzle over flour mixture, tossing with fork until dough comes together and adding up to 2 tsp more ice water if necessary. Shape into disc. Wrap in plastic wrap; refrigerate until chilled, about 30 minutes. *(Make-ahead: Refrigerate for up to 24 hours.)*

FILLING While pastry is chilling, in large skillet, heat butter with oil over medium-low heat; cook onions, sugar, salt and pepper, stirring often, until onion is very soft and light golden, 45 to 60 minutes. Scrape into bowl; let cool. Stir in egg yolk, Cheddar and sour cream. Set aside.

ASSEMBLY On lightly floured work surface, roll out pastry to 11- × 7-inch (28 × 18 cm) rectangle. Trim edges to straighten, if necessary. Cut into 6 squares. Spoon filling onto centre of each. Fold corners over filling so points meet in centre but do not touch. Transfer to parchment paper–lined baking sheet. *(Make-ahead: Freeze until firm. Transfer to airtight container and freeze for up to 2 weeks. Bake from frozen, adding 5 minutes to cook time.)*

Whisk egg yolk with 1 tbsp water; brush over pastry. Bake in top and bottom thirds of 425°F (220°C) oven, switching and rotating pans halfway through, until golden, about 20 minutes. *(Make-ahead: Let cool. Refrigerate in airtight container for up to 24 hours; reheat in 350°F/180°C oven for about 15 minutes.)*

Cut each galette diagonally into quarters. Serve warm.

NUTRITIONAL INFORMATION, PER PIECE: about 58 cal, 1 g pro, 4 g total fat (2 g sat. fat), 4 g carb (trace dietary fibre), 26 mg chol, 43 mg sodium. % RDI: 2% calcium, 1% iron, 4% vit A, 5% folate.

GALETTE PASTRY

½ cup	all-purpose flour
2 tbsp	cornmeal
pinch	each salt and dried thyme
¼ cup	cold unsalted butter, cubed
2 tbsp	ice water (approx)
2 tsp	sour cream

FILLING

1½ tsp	each butter and vegetable oil
3 cups	thinly sliced onions
½ tsp	granulated sugar
¼ tsp	salt
pinch	pepper
1	egg yolk
½ cup	shredded extra-old Cheddar cheese
3 tbsp	sour cream
1	egg yolk

59

MINI SMOKED SALMON QUICHES

p.56

HANDS-ON TIME	TOTAL TIME	MAKES
25 MINUTES	2¼ HOURS	24 PIECES

PASTRY

1¼ cups	all-purpose flour
pinch	salt
¼ cup	each cold butter and lard, cubed
2 tbsp	ice water (approx)
4 tsp	sour cream

FILLING

4 tsp	finely chopped fresh dill
3 tbsp	chopped smoked salmon
1	egg
¼ cup	milk
¼ tsp	Dijon mustard
pinch	each salt and pepper

PASTRY In bowl, whisk flour with salt. Using pastry blender or 2 knives, cut in butter and lard until mixture resembles fine crumbs with a few larger pieces.

Whisk 2 tbsp ice water with sour cream; drizzle over flour mixture, stirring briskly with fork to form ragged dough and adding up to 1 tbsp more ice water if necessary. Shape into disc. Wrap in plastic wrap; refrigerate until chilled, about 30 minutes. *(Make-ahead: Refrigerate for up to 24 hours.)*

On lightly floured work surface, roll out pastry to scant ⅛-inch (3 mm) thickness. Using 2¾-inch (7 cm) round cookie cutter, cut out 24 circles, rerolling scraps as necessary. Fit into 24 wells of ¾-inch (2 cm) deep mini-tart or muffin pans. Prick all over with fork; freeze until firm, about 20 minutes.

Bake in 350°F (180°C) oven until light golden, about 15 minutes. If dough has puffed while baking, gently press with fingertip. Let cool in pan on rack.

FILLING Sprinkle dill and salmon in pastry shells. Whisk together egg, milk, mustard, salt and pepper; pour into shells; do not overfill. Bake until knife inserted in centres comes out clean, about 20 minutes. Let cool on racks for 5 minutes. Remove from pans. *(Make-ahead: Let cool for 30 minutes; refrigerate in airtight container for up to 24 hours or freeze for up to 2 weeks. Thaw before reheating in 350°F/180°C oven for 10 minutes.)*

NUTRITIONAL INFORMATION, PER PIECE: about 68 cal, 1 g pro, 5 g total fat (2 g sat. fat), 5 g carb (trace dietary fibre), 16 mg chol, 34 mg sodium. % RDI: 1% calcium, 2% iron, 2% vit A, 7% folate.

VARIATION

MINI SMOKED SALMON AND GOAT CHEESE QUICHES
Substitute 2 tbsp goat cheese for the dill.

WHITE CHOCOLATE CHEESECAKE DIP

HANDS-ON TIME
15 MINUTES

TOTAL TIME
1¼ HOURS

MAKES
2 CUPS

In heatproof bowl set over saucepan of hot (not boiling) water, heat chocolate with cream, stirring gently, until melted and smooth. Let cool to room temperature.

In separate bowl, beat cream cheese with sugar until fluffy; beat in lime zest. Stir in chocolate mixture and liqueur. Refrigerate for 1 hour. *(Make-ahead: Refrigerate in airtight container for up to 2 days. Let stand at room temperature to soften.)* Serve with fruit.

NUTRITIONAL INFORMATION, PER 1 TBSP: about 47 cal, 1 g pro, 4 g total fat (2 g sat. fat), 2 g carb (0 g dietary fibre), 9 mg chol, 27 mg sodium. % RDI: 1% calcium, 1% iron, 3% vit A.

85 g	white chocolate (3 oz), coarsely chopped
⅓ cup	10% cream
1	pkg (250 g) cream cheese, softened
1 tbsp	granulated sugar
2 tsp	grated lime zest
1 tsp	orange-flavoured liqueur or lime juice
	sliced fresh fruit

PITCHER COSMOPOLITANS

In pitcher, stir together 1½ cups vodka, ½ cup cranberry juice, ¼ cup orange-flavoured liqueur and 2 tbsp lime juice. Top with ice; stir until well chilled.

Garnish each glass with frozen cranberries and a sliced lime, if desired. Strain cocktail into glasses.

MAKES 8 SERVINGS

NUTRITIONAL INFORMATION, PER SERVING: about 139 cal, trace pro, 0 g total fat (0 g sat. fat), 7 g carb (trace dietary fibre), 0 mg chol, 1 mg sodium. % RDI: 1% iron, 8% vit C.

VARIATION

NONALCOHOLIC COSMOPOLITANS
Omit vodka and orange liqueur. Increase cranberry juice to 2 cups and lime juice to ¼ cup. Add 1 cup ginger ale and ½ cup orange juice. Top with ice.

3" (8 cm)

3" (8 cm)

2" (5 cm)

BABY SLEEPER CAKE

BABY SLEEPER CAKE

opposite

HANDS-ON TIME	**TOTAL TIME**	**MAKES**
45 MINUTES	3 HOURS	18 SERVINGS

CAKE In large bowl, beat butter until fluffy, about 2 minutes. Beat in sugar, ¼ cup at a time, beating well after each addition. Beat in eggs, 1 at a time, beating well after each. Beat in vanilla.

Whisk together cake-and-pastry flour, all-purpose flour, baking powder and salt; stir into butter mixture, alternating with milk, making 4 additions of flour mixture and 3 of milk. Scrape into greased parchment paper–lined 13- × 9-inch (3.5 L) cake pan.

Bake in 350°F (180°C) oven until cake tester inserted in centre comes out clean, about 35 minutes. Let cool in pan on rack for 10 minutes. Turn out onto rack; peel off paper. Let cool completely.

ICING In large bowl, beat butter with salt until smooth. Beat in icing sugar, alternating with cream, making 3 additions of sugar and 2 of cream. Beat in vanilla.

ASSEMBLY Using measurements in photo as guide, cut out neck and leg openings from cake; discard neck. Trim off rounded cut edge of each leg piece; discard rounded pieces.

Place trimmed edge of each large leg piece against cake to form sleeves; attach with some of the icing.

Spread about 1 cup of the icing over top and sides of cake to seal in crumbs. Refrigerate until firm, about 30 minutes.

Remove ⅓ cup icing to small bowl. Tint remaining icing desired colour. Spread over top and sides of cake. Tint reserved icing a darker shade; spoon into piping bag. Using darker icing, decorate edges and surface of cake. Decorate with candies as desired. Refrigerate until firm, about 30 minutes.

NUTRITIONAL INFORMATION, PER SERVING: about 475 cal, 4 g pro, 23 g total fat (14 g sat. fat), 65 g carb (1 g dietary fibre), 101 mg chol, 176 mg sodium, 66 mg potassium. % RDI: 5% calcium, 9% iron, 21% vit A, 17% folate.

CAKE

1 cup	unsalted butter, softened
2 cups	granulated sugar
4	eggs, room temperature
1 tsp	vanilla
1½ cups	cake-and-pastry flour
1½ cups	all-purpose flour
1 tbsp	baking powder
¼ tsp	salt
1 cup	milk

ICING

1 cup	unsalted butter, softened
pinch	salt
4 cups	icing sugar
¼ cup	whipping cream (35%) or milk
½ tsp	vanilla

63

SEASONAL SUNDAY SUPPER

If breakfast is the most important meal of the day, then Sunday supper is the most important meal of the week. It's family time, a little ritual that doesn't have to be complicated or difficult to be valuable. Choose ingredients that highlight the best of spring: fresh greens, newly sprouted chives and morel mushrooms.

65

MENU FOR 4 TO 6

MIXED GREENS
WITH ORANGE CHIVE DRESSING p.66

GREEN BEANS AMANDINE p.67

FAN POTATOES p.67

CHICKEN WITH MOREL SAUCE p.68

MINI CARROT CAKE TRIFLES p.71

MIXED GREENS
WITH ORANGE CHIVE DRESSING

HANDS-ON TIME	TOTAL TIME	MAKES
20 MINUTES	20 MINUTES	6 SERVINGS

3	oranges
3 tbsp	vegetable oil
1 tbsp	chopped fresh chives
½ tsp	Dijon mustard
¼ tsp	each salt and pepper
half	bulb fennel, cored
5 cups	torn mixed salad greens

Cut off zest and pith from oranges; working over bowl, cut between membrane and pulp to release segments into bowl. Squeeze membrane to release juices.

Transfer 2 tbsp of the orange juice to separate bowl; whisk in oil, chives, mustard, salt and pepper. (Reserve remaining juice for another use.)

Using knife or mandoline, thinly slice fennel lengthwise; place in large salad bowl and toss with 2 tbsp of the orange juice mixture.

Add salad greens, orange segments and remaining orange juice mixture; toss to coat.

NUTRITIONAL INFORMATION, PER SERVING: about 97 cal, 2 g pro, 7 g total fat (1 g sat. fat), 9 g carb (2 g dietary fibre), 0 mg chol, 122 mg sodium, 308 mg potassium. % RDI: 5% calcium, 4% iron, 11% vit A, 58% vit C, 27% folate.

TIP FROM THE TEST KITCHEN

Toss greens with the dressing at the very last minute to keep them crisp. If you let them sit in the dressing too long, they'll get soggy.

GREEN BEANS AMANDINE

p.64

HANDS-ON TIME
15 MINUTES

TOTAL TIME
20 MINUTES

MAKES
4 TO 6 SERVINGS

In skillet, toast almonds over medium-high heat just until golden, about 4 minutes. Remove to small bowl; set aside.

Add butter, salt and ¾ cup water to skillet; bring to boil. Add beans; reduce heat to simmer, cover and cook until bright green, about 3 minutes.

Uncover and simmer, turning beans often, until tender and no liquid remains, about 8 minutes. Toss with almonds.

⅔ cup	sliced almonds
2 tbsp	butter
¼ tsp	salt
450 g	green beans, trimmed

NUTRITIONAL INFORMATION, PER EACH OF 6 SERVINGS: about 116 cal, 4 g pro, 9 g total fat (3 g sat. fat), 7 g carb (3 g dietary fibre), 10 mg chol, 126 mg sodium, 161 mg potassium. % RDI: 5% calcium, 6% iron, 8% vit A, 10% vit C, 10% folate.

FAN POTATOES

p.64

HANDS-ON TIME
15 MINUTES

TOTAL TIME
1½ HOURS

MAKES
6 SERVINGS

Cutting almost but not all the way through, cut deep slits, ¼-inch (5 mm) apart, crosswise, in each potato.

Mix together flour, salt, pepper and paprika; roll each potato in mixture. Place, uncut side down, in ovenproof dish or roasting pan. Spoon butter over top; sprinkle with thyme.

Bake in 375°F (190°C) oven until tender, fanned out, golden and crisp, about 1¼ hours. Before serving, drizzle with any butter in pan.

6	white or yellow-fleshed potatoes (about 1 kg total), peeled
2 tbsp	all-purpose flour
1 tsp	salt
½ tsp	each pepper and paprika
3 tbsp	butter, melted
1 tsp	chopped fresh thyme

NUTRITIONAL INFORMATION, PER SERVING: about 165 cal, 3 g pro, 6 g total fat (4 g sat. fat), 26 g carb (2 g dietary fibre), 15 mg chol, 429 mg sodium, 409 mg potassium. % RDI: 1% calcium, 4% iron, 6% vit A, 15% vit C, 8% folate.

CHICKEN
WITH MOREL SAUCE

opposite

HANDS-ON TIME	TOTAL TIME	MAKES
25 MINUTES	1½ HOURS	4 TO 6 SERVINGS

1½ cups	sodium-reduced chicken broth
1	pkg (14 g) dried morel mushrooms
1	whole chicken (2 kg), cut into pieces
1 tsp	each salt and pepper
¼ cup	all-purpose flour
2 tbsp	vegetable oil
¼ cup	butter
⅓ cup	chopped shallots
2	cloves garlic, minced
1 cup	dry sherry
½ cup	whipping cream (35%)
1	sprig fresh thyme
2 tbsp	chopped fresh parsley

In small saucepan, bring broth to boil. Remove from heat. Add mushrooms; let stand for 30 minutes. Using slotted spoon, remove mushrooms to bowl. Strain broth through fine-mesh sieve into bowl with mushrooms.

Meanwhile, sprinkle chicken pieces with salt and pepper; dredge in flour, shaking off excess.

In large skillet or Dutch oven, heat oil over medium heat; working in batches, cook chicken, turning occasionally, until browned. Remove to plate. Drain fat from pan.

In same skillet, melt butter over medium heat; cook shallots and garlic until softened, about 2 minutes. Add sherry, stirring and scraping up any browned bits. Bring to boil; cook for 2 minutes.

Add cream, thyme and broth with mushrooms. Return chicken and any accumulated juices to skillet; bring to boil. Reduce heat and simmer until juices run clear when chicken is pierced and sauce is thickened, about 45 minutes. Sprinkle with parsley.

NUTRITIONAL INFORMATION, PER EACH OF 6 SERVINGS (WITHOUT SKIN): about 428 cal, 33 g pro, 20 g total fat (10 g sat. fat), 28 g carb (3 g dietary fibre), 146 mg chol, 690 mg sodium, 545 mg potassium. % RDI: 4% calcium, 19% iron, 16% vit A, 8% vit C, 20% folate.

CHICKEN WITH MOREL SAUCE

MINI CARROT CAKE TRIFLES

MINI CARROT CAKE TRIFLES

opposite

HANDS-ON TIME
1¼ HOURS

TOTAL TIME
16¾ HOURS

MAKES
12 SERVINGS

CREAM CHEESE CUSTARD In large bowl, whisk together egg yolks, ½ cup of the milk, the sugar and cornstarch. In heavy-bottomed saucepan, heat remaining milk and three-quarters of the cream cheese over medium heat, whisking, just until smooth and bubbles form around edge; gradually whisk into egg yolk mixture. Return to saucepan; cook over medium heat, stirring, until thick enough to mound on spoon, 6 to 8 minutes. Strain through fine-mesh sieve into clean bowl; stir in vanilla. Place plastic wrap directly on surface. Refrigerate until chilled, about 4 hours. *(Make-ahead: Refrigerate for up to 24 hours.)*

CARROT CAKE While custard is chilling, in large bowl, whisk together flour, baking powder, cinnamon, salt, baking soda and nutmeg. In separate bowl, beat together eggs, granulated sugar, brown sugar, oil and vanilla; stir into flour mixture just until moistened. Stir in carrots. Scrape into 2 parchment paper–lined 8- × 4-inch (1.5 L) loaf pans.

Bake in 350°F (180°C) oven until cake tester inserted in centres comes out clean, 40 to 45 minutes. Let cool completely in pans. *(Make-ahead: Cover with plastic wrap; store at room temperature for up to 24 hours.)* Remove from pans; cut into ¾-inch (2 cm) cubes.

TOPPING While cake is baking, in skillet, cook brown sugar, butter and cinnamon over medium heat, stirring, until melted; stir in walnuts. Cook, stirring, until walnuts are toasted and coated, about 4 minutes; let cool slightly. Reserve 12 pieces for garnish; coarsely chop remaining walnuts. Drain pineapple, reserving ½ cup of the juice and saving remaining juice for another use. Coarsely chop pineapple.

ASSEMBLY In each of twelve 1½-cup glasses, add scant ½ cup of the cake; drizzle 1 tsp of the reserved pineapple juice into each glass. Top each with scant 1 tbsp of the pineapple and 2 tsp of the chopped walnuts. Spoon rounded 2 tbsp of the custard into each. Repeat layers once. Cover and refrigerate for 12 hours. *(Make-ahead: Refrigerate for up to 24 hours.)*

Beat remaining quarter package cream cheese with granulated sugar until fluffy; slowly beat in cream until stiff peaks form. Spoon over trifles; top with reserved walnuts.

NUTRITIONAL INFORMATION, PER SERVING: about 722 cal, 11 g pro, 43 g total fat (13 g sat. fat), 76 g carb (2 g dietary fibre, 54 g sugar), 201 mg chol, 398 mg sodium, 340 mg potassium. % RDI: 18% calcium, 18% iron, 56% vit A, 6% vit C, 34% folate.

CREAM CHEESE CUSTARD

6	egg yolks
3 cups	milk
¾ cup	granulated sugar
¼ cup	cornstarch
1	pkg (250 g) cream cheese, cubed and softened
1 tsp	vanilla

CARROT CAKE

2 cups	all-purpose flour
2 tsp	each baking powder and cinnamon
¾ tsp	salt
½ tsp	each baking soda and nutmeg
3	eggs
¾ cup	each granulated sugar and packed brown sugar
¾ cup	vegetable oil
1 tsp	vanilla
2 cups	grated peeled carrots (about 2 large)

TOPPING

¼ cup	packed brown sugar
2 tbsp	butter
¼ tsp	cinnamon
1½ cups	walnut halves
1	can (400 mL) pineapple chunks
2 tbsp	granulated sugar
1 cup	whipping cream (35%)

SUMMER

FATHER'S DAY COOKOUT p.74

IT'S A PARADE p.82

CANADA DAY MAKE-AHEAD MENU p.90

CANADA DAY BARBECUE p.100

GARDEN PARTY GRILL p.108

A DAY AT THE COTTAGE p.116

BLOCK PARTY p.124

FAMILY REUNION PICNIC p.132

MARKET DAY p.140

SEASONAL SUNDAY SUPPER p.148

FATHER'S DAY COOKOUT

Hey, Dad, drop those tongs and step away from the grill! You've got the rest of the summer to refine your secret ribs recipe and to master low-and-slow smoking technique. Today, it's our turn. We're making dinner for you, with some backyard barbecue favourites and southern-style treats. Happy Father's Day.

MENU FOR 8

TEXAS BARBECUE BRISKET **p.76**

SMASHED POTATO SALAD **p.77**

JALAPEÑO BAKED BEANS **p.78**

FRIED OKRA **p.79**

NEGRONI SPRITZER **p.79**

BUTTER TART ICE CREAM **p.81**

TEXAS BARBECUE BRISKET

p.74

HANDS-ON TIME
10 MINUTES

TOTAL TIME
5 HOURS

MAKES
8 TO 10 SERVINGS

1 tbsp	chili powder
1 tbsp	smoked paprika
1 tbsp	kosher salt or coarse sea salt
2 tsp	granulated sugar
1 tsp	each ground cumin and pepper
2.2 kg	beef brisket
1 tbsp	vegetable oil
half	onion, finely chopped
2	cloves garlic, minced
2 cups	dark ale or sodium-reduced beef broth
¼ cup	packed brown sugar
¼ cup	Worcestershire sauce
¼ cup	cider vinegar
1 tbsp	salt
2 tsp	dry mustard
2 tbsp	tomato paste

Mix together chili powder, paprika, kosher salt, granulated sugar, cumin and pepper; rub all over brisket. Let stand for 1 hour. *(Make-ahead: Wrap with plastic wrap and refrigerate up to 1 day.)*

In small saucepan, heat oil over medium heat; cook onion and garlic until soft and translucent. Stir in ale, brown sugar, Worcestershire sauce, vinegar, salt and dry mustard (if using beef broth, reduce salt to 1½ tsp); bring to boil. Reduce heat and simmer for 10 minutes.

Place brisket in roasting pan; cover loosely with foil. Roast in 300°F (150°C) oven, basting with sauce every 30 minutes after first hour, until falling-apart tender, about 3 hours. Transfer to plate; skim fat off juices in pan. Add juices to remaining sauce. Set aside. *(Make-ahead: Refrigerate brisket and sauce separately up to 1 day.)*

Prepare barbecue for indirect grilling (see below). Soak 4 cups wood chips for smoking in water for 30 minutes. For gas barbecue, seal soaked chips in foil packet; poke several holes in top. Place over lit burner; close lid. For charcoal barbecue, place soaked chips directly on coals. Place brisket on greased grill over drip pan. Close lid and grill, basting with some of the remaining sauce every 15 minutes (without allowing too much smoke to escape), until dark brown and crisp, about 1 hour. Thinly slice across the grain before serving.

During final 15 minutes of cook time, in saucepan over medium-high heat, whisk remaining sauce with tomato paste; simmer until thickened, about 10 minutes. Serve with brisket.

NUTRITIONAL INFORMATION, PER EACH OF 10 SERVINGS: about 355 cal, 35 g pro, 18 g total fat (6 g sat. fat), 12 g carb (1 g dietary fibre), 89 mg chol, 1,323 mg sodium, 506 mg potassium. % RDI: 3% calcium, 31% iron, 6% vit A, 5% vit C, 6% folate.

TIP FROM THE TEST KITCHEN

Indirect grilling is a useful technique for traditional low-and-slow barbecuing; the meat cooks slowly and evenly because it's not over the direct flame. On a gas barbecue, set a foil drip pan under 1 grill of a 2-burner barbecue or under the centre grill of 3-burner barbecue. Use the burners adjacent to the drip pan and place the meat above the pan. On a charcoal grill, centre a drip pan under the cooking grill and arrange hot charcoal on either side.

SMASHED POTATO SALAD

HANDS-ON TIME
10 MINUTES

TOTAL TIME
1¾ HOURS

MAKES
8 SERVINGS

Place eggs in saucepan; cover with at least 1 inch (2.5 cm) cold water. Cover and bring to boil over high heat; remove from heat and let stand for 20 minutes.

Meanwhile, in large saucepan of boiling salted water, cook potatoes until fork-tender, about 15 minutes. Drain and coarsely chop into chunks. Place in large bowl.

Peel and chop eggs. Add to potatoes along with onion, celery and pickles, breaking up slightly with potato masher.

In small bowl, whisk together mayonnaise, mustard, vinegar, salt, pepper and paprika. Add to potatoes, mixing well. Refrigerate until chilled, about 1 hour.

NUTRITIONAL INFORMATION, PER SERVING: about 208 cal, 4 g pro, 13 g total fat (2 g sat. fat), 20 g carb (2 g dietary fibre), 75 mg chol, 634 mg sodium, 315 mg potassium. % RDI: 3% calcium, 6% iron, 5% vit A, 12% vit C, 11% folate.

3	eggs
750 g	potatoes (about 4 large), peeled
half	Vidalia onion or sweet onion, finely chopped
2	ribs celery, diced
½ cup	diced gherkin pickles
½ cup	mayonnaise
2 tbsp	Dijon mustard
1 tbsp	cider vinegar
¾ tsp	salt
½ tsp	pepper
¼ tsp	paprika

77

JALAPEÑO BAKED BEANS

HANDS-ON TIME	TOTAL TIME	MAKES
15 MINUTES	3 HOURS	10 TO 12 SERVINGS

500 g	dried pinto beans
2	white onions, chopped
6	strips bacon, chopped
4	jalapeño peppers, seeded and finely chopped
5	cloves garlic, minced
1 cup	chopped fresh cilantro
2 cups	dark beer
1 cup	chopped canned or ripe tomatoes
1¼ tsp	salt

In saucepan, pour enough water to come at least 3 inches (8 cm) above beans; bring to boil. Boil for 5 minutes; remove from heat. Cover and let stand for 1 hour. (Or soak beans overnight in 3 times their volume of water.) Drain.

In large saucepan, bring beans, 10 cups water and half of the onions to boil. Reduce heat to medium; simmer, adding more water if necessary to keep beans covered, until beans are tender, 1 to 1½ hours. Set aside.

In Dutch oven or large heavy-bottomed saucepan, cook bacon over medium-high heat until fat begins to render, 2 to 3 minutes. Add remaining onions; cook until lightly browned, about 8 minutes.

Add jalapeño peppers, garlic and cilantro; cook for 2 minutes.

Add beans with cooking liquid, beer, tomatoes and salt; bring to boil. Reduce heat to medium; simmer, stirring occasionally, until thickened, 45 to 60 minutes.

NUTRITIONAL INFORMATION, PER EACH OF 12 SERVINGS: about 214 cal, 10 g pro, 6 g total fat (3 g sat. fat), 31 g carb (9 g dietary fibre), 8 mg chol, 348 mg sodium. % RDI: 6% calcium, 21% iron, 2% vit A, 15% vit C, 79% folate.

FRIED OKRA

HANDS-ON TIME
15 MINUTES

TOTAL TIME
15 MINUTES

MAKES
8 SERVINGS

Trim tops and tails off okra. Cut each into thirds; set aside.

In large bowl, whisk together cornmeal, flour, baking powder and egg; stir in buttermilk until smooth.

Meanwhile, in deep skillet, pour enough oil to come 1 inch (2.5 cm) up side; heat to 375°F (190°C). Stir okra into buttermilk mixture. Working in batches and using fork or fingers to shake off excess batter, transfer okra to skillet; cook until crisp and golden brown, about 3 minutes. Season with salt to taste.

500 g	fresh okra
½ cup	cornmeal
½ cup	all-purpose flour
1 tsp	baking powder
1	egg
1 cup	buttermilk
	vegetable oil or lard for frying
	salt

79

NUTRITIONAL INFORMATION, PER SERVING: about 171 cal, 5 g pro, 9 g total fat (1 g sat. fat), 18 g carb (3 g dietary fibre), 26 mg chol, 75 mg sodium, 259 mg potassium. % RDI: 9% calcium, 6% iron, 5% vit A, 15% vit C, 28% folate.

NEGRONI SPRITZER

Cut 2 oranges in half. Slice 1 of the halves; place in pitcher. Juice remaining orange halves to make about ½ cup juice; add to pitcher. Mash slices gently with spoon.

Add 1¼ cups gin, 6 oz soda water (about ¾ cup), 5 oz Campari (about ⅔ cup) and 4 oz sweet vermouth (about ½ cup); stir to combine. Add 4 cups ice cubes.

MAKES 6 SERVINGS

NUTRITIONAL INFORMATION, PER SERVING: about 219 cal, 0 g pro, 0 g total fat (0 g sat. fat), 16 g carb (0 g dietary fibre), 0 mg chol, 12 mg sodium. % RDI: 1% calcium, 1% iron, 1% vit A, 27% vit C, 5% folate.

BUTTER TART ICE CREAM

BUTTER TART ICE CREAM

opposite

HANDS-ON TIME
45 MINUTES

TOTAL TIME
6½ HOURS

MAKES
ABOUT 4 CUPS

In large heavy-bottomed saucepan, whisk egg yolks with granulated sugar until combined. Whisk in 1½ cups of the cream, the milk and vanilla. Cook over medium heat, stirring frequently, until thick enough to coat back of spoon and distinct trail remains after finger is drawn across back of spoon, 10 to 15 minutes (do not boil).

Strain through fine-mesh sieve into 9-inch (2.5 L) square cake pan; place plastic wrap directly on surface of custard. Refrigerate until chilled, about 1½ hours. *(Make-ahead: Refrigerate in airtight container, with plastic wrap directly on surface, for up to 24 hours.)*

While custard is chilling, in saucepan, cook brown sugar and butter over medium heat, stirring, until butter is melted and sugar is dissolved, about 4 minutes. Stir in remaining cream. Scrape into heatproof bowl; let cool to room temperature, about 1½ hours.

Process custard in ice cream machine according to manufacturer's instructions. Spoon one-third of the ice cream into large airtight freezer-safe container; drizzle with one-third of the brown sugar mixture and sprinkle with one-third of the cookies. Using tip of knife, swirl together. Repeat layers twice, swirling between each. Freeze until firm, 4 to 6 hours.

NUTRITIONAL INFORMATION, PER ½ CUP: about 497 cal, 5 g pro, 33 g total fat (18 g sat. fat), 47 g carb (trace dietary fibre, 41 g sugar), 237 mg chol, 150 mg sodium, 159 mg potassium. % RDI: 12% calcium, 7% iron, 34% vit A, 14% folate.

6	egg yolks
⅔ cup	granulated sugar
1¾ cups	whipping cream (35%)
1½ cups	milk
1 tsp	vanilla
¾ cup	packed dark brown sugar
⅓ cup	butter
¾ cup	chopped shortbread cookies

81

IT'S A PARADE

Happy Pride, everyone! Invite your friends to drop by for a cocktail and nibbles; it's the time to recognize diversity and enjoy one of summer's most colourful events. We all love a good party, so let's join in the fun.

83

MENU FOR 8

ORANGE-SPICED OLIVES **p.84**

MARINATED MOZZARELLA **p.84**

ASSORTED CROSTINI **p.85**

ASPARAGUS WITH HERBED DIPPING SAUCE **p.87**

SHRIMP AND PANCETTA SKEWERS **p.87**

CHEESE AND CHARCUTERIE PLATTERS **p.88**

GIN CHILLER **p.89**

ORANGE FIZZ **p.89**

PEACH TEA **p.89**

ORANGE-SPICED OLIVES

HANDS-ON TIME	**TOTAL TIME**
10 MINUTES	10 MINUTES

MAKES
2 CUPS

3 tbsp	olive oil
3	cloves garlic, sliced
1	jar (375 mL) green olives, drained
1	jar (375 mL) Kalamata olives, drained
3	strips orange zest
¼ tsp	fennel seeds
pinch	hot pepper flakes
2 tbsp	orange juice

In saucepan, heat oil over medium heat; cook garlic until starting to soften, about 2 minutes.

Add green olives, Kalamata olives, orange zest, fennel seeds and hot pepper flakes; cook until warmed through, about 3 minutes. Remove from heat; stir in orange juice. *(Make-ahead: Refrigerate in airtight container for up to 5 days; let stand at room temperature for 1 hour before serving.)*

NUTRITIONAL INFORMATION, PER 2 TBSP: about 64 cal, trace pro, 7 g total fat (1 g sat. fat), 2 g carb (1 g dietary fibre, trace sugar), 0 mg chol, 416 mg sodium, 13 mg potassium. % RDI: 1% calcium, 1% iron, 1% vit A, 2% vit C.

84

MARINATED MOZZARELLA

HANDS-ON TIME	**TOTAL TIME**
10 MINUTES	10 MINUTES

MAKES
ABOUT 2 CUPS

1	pkg (200 g) mini fresh mozzarella balls, drained
1 tbsp	olive oil
1 tsp	white balsamic vinegar or lemon juice
4	thin strips lemon zest
¼ tsp	each salt and pepper
2	leaves fresh basil, torn

In bowl, combine mozzarella balls, oil, vinegar, lemon zest, salt and pepper. *(Make-ahead: Refrigerate in airtight container for up to 24 hours; let stand at room temperature for 15 minutes.)* Stir in basil.

NUTRITIONAL INFORMATION, PER ¼ CUP: about 86 cal, 4 g pro, 8 g total fat (4 g sat. fat), 1 g carb (trace dietary fibre, trace sugar), 18 mg chol, 156 mg sodium, 3 mg potassium. % RDI: 14% iron, 4% vit A, 5% vit C.

CROSTINI BAR

HANDS-ON TIME 15 MINUTES   **TOTAL TIME** 15 MINUTES   **MAKES** 15 PIECES

p.86

Crostini are the ultimate cocktail party food. Serve them garnished with an array of flavourful combinations or set up all the ingredients in pretty bowls and have guests top their own.

To make crostini, cut fifteen ¼-inch (5 mm) thick slices from a baguette. Arrange slices on a baking sheet; drizzle with 1 tsp olive oil; bake in 400°F (200°C) oven until crisp and light golden, about 6 minutes. Cut 1 garlic clove in half; rub tops of crostini with cut sides of garlic halves. Set aside. *(Make-ahead: Store in airtight container for up to 24 hours.)*

PESTO WHITE BEAN

HANDS-ON TIME 15 MINUTES

TOTAL TIME 15 MINUTES

MAKES 15 PIECES

1 cup	drained canned white kidney beans or cannellini beans
½	clove garlic, chopped
pinch	each salt and pepper
15	crostini (see recipe, above)
1 tbsp	pesto
5	cherry tomatoes, cut in thirds

In food processor, purée together beans, garlic, salt and pepper until smooth. *(Make-ahead: Refrigerate in airtight container for up to 24 hours.)* Spread over crostini. Dot with pesto; top with tomato wedge.

NUTRITIONAL INFORMATION, PER PIECE: about 39 cal, 2 g pro, 1 g total fat (trace sat. fat), 6 g carb (1 g dietary fibre, trace sugar), 0 mg chol, 89 mg sodium, 52 mg potassium. % RDI: 1% calcium, 3% iron, 1% vit A, 2% vit C, 5% folate.

PEAS AND PROSCIUTTO

HANDS-ON TIME 15 MINUTES

TOTAL TIME 15 MINUTES

MAKES 15 PIECES

2 tsp	olive oil
2	shallots, chopped
3	cloves garlic, chopped
1 cup	frozen peas
pinch	each salt and pepper
¼ cup	soft goat cheese
15	crostini (see recipe, above)
3 slices	prosciutto, coarsely chopped

In skillet, heat oil over medium heat; cook shallots and garlic until softened, about 2 minutes. Add peas, salt and pepper; cook until warmed through, about 5 minutes.

In food processor, purée pea mixture until smooth, about 1 minute, Add goat cheese; purée until smooth. *(Make-ahead: Refrigerate in airtight container for up to 24 hours.)* Spread over crostini; top with prosciutto.

NUTRITIONAL INFORMATION, PER PIECE: about 55 cal, 3 g pro, 2 g total fat (1 g sat. fat), 6 g carb (1 g dietary fibre, 1 g sugar), 5 mg chol, 137 mg sodium, 44 mg potassium. % RDI: 1% calcium, 4% iron, 3% vit A, 2% vit C, 5% folate.

ASPARAGUS AND RICOTTA

HANDS-ON TIME 15 MINUTES

TOTAL TIME 15 MINUTES

MAKES 15 PIECES

8	spears asparagus, trimmed
½ cup	ricotta cheese
2 tsp	chopped fresh chives
½ tsp	grated lemon zest
1 tbsp	lemon juice
¼ tsp	salt
pinch	pepper
½ cup	thinly sliced radishes
15	crostini (see recipe, above)

In saucepan of boiling salted water, cook asparagus for 1 minute; drain. Immediately chill in ice water; drain and pat dry. Slice diagonally into 1-inch (2.5 cm) long pieces.

Combine ricotta, chives, lemon zest, 2 tsp of the lemon juice, half of the salt and the pepper; set aside. *(Make-ahead: Refrigerate asparagus and ricotta mixture in separate airtight containers for up to 24 hours.)*

Toss together asparagus, radishes and remaining lemon juice and salt. Top crostini with ricotta mixture, then asparagus mixture.

NUTRITIONAL INFORMATION, PER PIECE: about 40 cal, 2 g pro, 2 g total fat (1 g sat. fat), 5 g carb (1 g dietary fibre, trace sugar), 4 mg chol, 144 mg sodium, 46 mg potassium. % RDI: 2% calcium, 2% iron, 2% vit A, 3% vit C, 9% folate.

85

CLOCKWISE, FROM TOP LEFT: GIN CHILLER; PESTO WHITE BEAN CROSTINI, AND PEAS AND PROSCIUTTO CROSTINI; AND MARINATED MOZZARELLA AND ORANGE-SPICED OLIVES

ASPARAGUS
WITH HERBED DIPPING SAUCE

HANDS-ON TIME	**TOTAL TIME**	**MAKES**
15 MINUTES	15 MINUTES	6 TO 8 SERVINGS

In large saucepan of boiling salted water, cook asparagus until tender-crisp, about 1 minute; drain. Immediately chill in ice water; drain and pat dry.

Stir together crème fraîche, chives, mustard, lemon juice and pepper. Serve with asparagus. *(Make-ahead: Refrigerate sauce and asparagus in separate airtight containers for up to 24 hours.)*

NUTRITIONAL INFORMATION, PER EACH OF 8 SERVINGS: about 71 cal, 2 g pro, 6 g total fat (4 g sat. fat), 2 g carb (1 g dietary fibre, 1 g sugar), 25 mg chol, 149 mg sodium, 105 mg potassium. % RDI: 1% calcium, 4% iron, 15% vit A, 7% vit C, 30% folate.

1	bunch asparagus, trimmed
½ cup	crème fraîche
2 tbsp	chopped fresh chives
1 tbsp	grainy mustard
1 tsp	lemon juice
¼ tsp	pepper

SHRIMP AND PANCETTA SKEWERS

p.82

HANDS-ON TIME	**TOTAL TIME**	**MAKES**
15 MINUTES	40 MINUTES	16 PIECES

In bowl, combine garlic, orange zest, orange juice and hot pepper flakes; add shrimp and toss to coat. Cover and refrigerate for 30 minutes. *(Make-ahead: Refrigerate for up to 24 hours.)*

Wrap each shrimp with piece of pancetta; thread onto metal or soaked wooden skewer. Place on greased grill over medium heat; close lid and grill, turning once, until pancetta is crisp and shrimp are pink and opaque throughout, about 4 minutes.

NUTRITIONAL INFORMATION, PER PIECE: about 29 cal, 4 g pro, 1 g total fat (trace sat. fat), 1 g carb (0 g dietary fibre, trace sugar), 28 mg chol, 80 mg sodium, 35 mg potassium. % RDI: 1% calcium, 3% iron, 1% vit A, 2% vit C, 1% folate.

2	cloves garlic, minced
1 tsp	grated orange zest
2 tbsp	orange juice
pinch	hot pepper flakes, crushed
16	jumbo shrimp (about 340 g total), peeled and deveined
8	thin slices pancetta, halved crosswise

CHEESE AND CHARCUTERIE PLATTERS

There are good reasons platters of cheeses and cured meats appear—and then disappear— at almost every cocktail party. For hosts, they're no-fuss options that don't require any work once they're set out. For guests, they're tasty finger food that's easy to hold in one hand with a drink in the other. But there is an art to creating an interesting, crowd-pleasing combination; for more on cheese platters, see page 215, and for charcuterie, see page 212.

GIN CHILLER
p.86

HANDS-ON TIME 5 MINUTES

TOTAL TIME 5 MINUTES

MAKES 1 SERVING

	ice cubes
1½ oz	gin (about 3 tbsp)
1 oz	simple syrup (about 2 tbsp; see recipe below)
1½ oz	carbonated water (about 3 tbsp)
3	thin slices cucumber
3	drained canned whole lychees (in syrup)

Fill cocktail shaker with ice. Add gin and simple syrup; shake vigorously. Strain into glass; top with carbonated water. Stir in cucumber and lychees.

NUTRITIONAL INFORMATION, PER SERVING: about 211 cal, trace pro, 0 g total fat (0 g sat. fat), 31 g carb (1 g dietary fibre, 30 g sugar), 0 mg chol, 22 mg sodium, 20 mg potassium. % RDI: 1% calcium, 1% iron, 3% vit C.

SIMPLE SYRUP
To make simple syrup, bring equal parts sugar and water to boil. Reduce heat and simmer, stirring, until sugar is dissolved, about 1 minute. Let cool completely before using.

ORANGE FIZZ

HANDS-ON TIME 5 MINUTES

TOTAL TIME 5 MINUTES

MAKES 1 SERVING

5 oz	chilled sparkling white wine, such as Prosecco (about ⅔ cup)
1 oz	orange-flavoured liqueur (about 2 tbsp)
2 tbsp	frozen raspberries
quarter	orange, thinly sliced

In glass, stir together wine, liqueur, raspberries and orange slices.

NUTRITIONAL INFORMATION, PER SERVING: about 240 cal, 1 g pro, trace total fat (0 g sat. fat), 20 g carb (2 g dietary fibre, 19 g sugar), 0 mg chol, 11 mg sodium, 196 mg potassium. % RDI: 3% calcium, 4% iron, 1% vit A, 35% vit C, 6% folate.

PEACH TEA

HANDS-ON TIME 20 MINUTES

TOTAL TIME 3 HOURS

MAKES 6 TO 8 SERVINGS

4	bags white tea
5 cups	boiling water
½ cup	granulated sugar
1	piece (1½ inches/4 cm) fresh ginger, peeled and sliced
1	pkg (600 g) frozen peach slices
2 cups	ice water
½ cup	peach nectar
¼ cup	torn fresh mint

In large heatproof measure or bowl, steep tea in boiling water for 6 minutes. Discard bags.

Meanwhile, in saucepan, bring sugar, ginger and ½ cup water to boil. Reduce heat to medium-low; simmer, stirring, until fragrant and sugar is dissolved, 5 to 6 minutes. Add to tea; let cool. Cover and refrigerate until cold, about 2 hours. Strain into large pitcher. *(Make-ahead: Refrigerate for up to 24 hours.)*

Stir in peaches, ice water, peach nectar and mint.

NUTRITIONAL INFORMATION, PER EACH OF 8 SERVINGS: about 87 cal, 1 g pro, trace total fat (0 g sat. fat), 22 g carb (2 g dietary fibre, 21 g sugar), 0 mg chol, 3 mg sodium, 178 mg potassium. % RDI: 1% calcium, 4% iron, 4% vit A, 18% vit C, 3% folate.

89

CANADA DAY MAKE-AHEAD MENU

Celebrate Canada Day with a tasty make-ahead
meal that leaves you more time to feel patriotic.
We've had fun creating this menu, with a red-and-white
theme that starts with a colourful appetizer inspired
by Tuscan bread salad and finishes with a
show-stopping Raspberry Lemon Cream Cake.

MENU FOR 10

GRILLED PANZANELLA BITES **p.92**

MAPLE BUTTERMILK GRILLED CHICKEN **p.93**

STEAKHOUSE SLIDERS **p.94**

GRILLED BALSAMIC VEGETABLES **p.95**

HERBED MINI POTATO SKEWERS **p.96**

TANGY SUMMER COLESLAW **p.96**

LEMONY RED PEPPER AND
ASPARAGUS PASTA SALAD **p.97**

RASPBERRY LEMON CREAM CAKE **p.99**

GRILLED PANZANELLA BITES

HANDS-ON TIME	TOTAL TIME	MAKES
25 MINUTES	2½ HOURS	10 TO 12 SERVINGS

⅓ cup	olive oil
¼ cup	red wine vinegar or white wine vinegar
2	cloves garlic, minced
½ tsp	salt
¼ tsp	pepper
1 cup	mini pearl bocconcini
½ cup	finely chopped red onion
1	large baguette, diagonally sliced ½-inch (1 cm) thick
4 cups	halved grape tomatoes
½ cup	chopped fresh basil

In bowl, whisk together ¼ cup of the oil, the vinegar, garlic, salt and pepper. Add bocconcini and onion; cover and refrigerate for 2 hours. *(Make-ahead: Refrigerate for up to 24 hours.)*

Brush baguette slices with remaining oil. Place on greased grill over medium heat; grill, turning occasionally, until crisp and golden, about 5 minutes.

Meanwhile, add tomatoes and basil to bocconcini mixture; toss to combine. Serve on toasted baguette slices.

NUTRITIONAL INFORMATION, PER EACH OF 12 SERVINGS: about 187 cal, 6 g pro, 10 g total fat (3 g sat. fat), 18 g carb (2 g dietary fibre, 2 g sugar), 11 mg chol, 276 mg sodium, 149 mg potassium. % RDI: 10% calcium, 7% iron, 6% vit A, 10% vit C, 14% folate.

VARIATION
VILLAGE SALAD BITES
Omit salt. Replace bocconcini with ¾ cup crumbled feta cheese. Replace basil with mint. Add ⅓ cup chopped Kalamata olives with tomatoes.

MAPLE BUTTERMILK
GRILLED CHICKEN

p.90

HANDS-ON TIME
45 MINUTES

TOTAL TIME
2¾ HOURS

MAKES
10 TO 12 SERVINGS

In large bowl, combine buttermilk, onions, garlic, pepper, cinnamon and hot pepper flakes. Add chicken, turning to coat. Cover and refrigerate for 2 hours. *(Make-ahead: Refrigerate for up to 24 hours.)*

Remove chicken from marinade; discard marinade. Sprinkle chicken with salt. Place on greased grill over medium-high heat; close lid and grill, turning occasionally, until instant-read thermometer inserted into thickest part reads 165°F (74°C), about 35 minutes.

Continue grilling, brushing with maple syrup, until glossy and coated, about 5 minutes.

NUTRITIONAL INFORMATION, PER EACH OF 12 SERVINGS: about 113 cal, 10 g pro, 5 g total fat (2 g sat. fat), 6 g carb (trace dietary fibre, 5 g sugar), 34 mg chol, 149 mg sodium, 157 mg potassium. % RDI: 3% calcium, 2% iron, 2% vit A, 2% folate.

2 cups	buttermilk
2	green onions, chopped
4	cloves garlic, minced
½ tsp	pepper
¼ tsp	each cinnamon and hot pepper flakes
20	small bone-in skin-on chicken pieces (about 1.125 kg total)
½ tsp	salt
¼ cup	maple syrup

93

STEAKHOUSE SLIDERS

HANDS-ON TIME	TOTAL TIME	MAKES
25 MINUTES	30 MINUTES	12 SLIDERS

HORSERADISH SAUCE

¼ cup	light mayonnaise
1 tbsp	each Dijon mustard and prepared horseradish
pinch	pepper

SLIDERS

1 tsp	vegetable oil
2	cloves garlic, minced
1	pkg (227 g) cremini mushrooms, cut in ¼-inch (5 mm) pieces
1	egg, lightly beaten
2 tbsp	prepared steak sauce (such as HP)
1 tbsp	Dijon mustard
1 tsp	onion powder
½ tsp	pepper
¼ tsp	salt
pinch	cayenne pepper
450 g	lean ground beef

GRILLED ONIONS

2	small cooking onions, cut crosswise in ½-inch (1 cm) slices
1 tsp	vegetable oil
pinch	salt
12	mini-hamburger (slider) buns

HORSERADISH SAUCE In bowl, stir together mayonnaise, mustard, horseradish and pepper. *(Make-ahead: Cover and refrigerate for up to 5 days.)*

SLIDERS In nonstick skillet, heat oil over medium-high heat; cook garlic, stirring, until fragrant, about 1 minute. Add mushrooms; cook, stirring, until golden and no liquid remains, about 8 minutes. Let cool for 5 minutes. *(Make-ahead: Let cool completely. Cover and refrigerate for up to 24 hours.)*

In bowl, stir together mushroom mixture, egg, steak sauce, mustard, onion powder, pepper, salt and cayenne pepper. Mix in beef. Shape into twelve 2½-inch (6 cm) wide patties. *(Make-ahead: Cover and refrigerate for up to 24 hours.)*

Place patties on greased grill over medium heat; grill, turning once, until no longer pink inside, about 5 minutes.

GRILLED ONIONS Thread onion slices onto metal or soaked wooden skewers. Brush both sides with oil; sprinkle with salt. Place on greased grill over medium heat; close lid and grill, turning occasionally, until golden and softened, about 8 minutes. Transfer to plate; separate into rings and keep warm.

ASSEMBLY Place patties in buns; garnish with horseradish sauce and onion rings.

NUTRITIONAL INFORMATION, PER SERVING: about 173 cal, 10 g pro, 9 g total fat (3 g sat. fat), 15 g carb (1 g dietary fibre, 3 g sugar), 46 mg chol, 278 mg sodium, 236 mg potassium. % RDI: 3% calcium, 11% iron, 3% vit A, 2% vit C, 16% folate.

94

GRILLED BALSAMIC VEGETABLES

HANDS-ON TIME
25 MINUTES

TOTAL TIME
2½ HOURS

MAKES
10 TO 12 SERVINGS

BALSAMIC MARINADE In bowl, combine vinegar, garlic, honey, salt and pepper; slowly whisk in oil until combined.

VEGETABLES Cut each zucchini in half crosswise; cut lengthwise into ½-inch (1 cm) thick slices. Place in large dish. Cut onion into ½-inch (1 cm) thick rounds; add to dish.

Core and seed sweet peppers; cut into large chunks and add to dish. Remove stems and gills from mushrooms; cut caps into quarters and add to dish. Pour marinade over vegetables; cover and let stand at room temperature for 2 hours, tossing occasionally.

Place vegetables on greased grill over medium-high heat; close lid and grill, basting frequently with marinade, until tender, about 12 minutes. Serve sprinkled with parsley.

NUTRITIONAL INFORMATION, PER EACH OF 12 SERVINGS: about 97 cal, 2 g pro, 7 g total fat (1 g sat. fat), 9 g carb (2 g dietary fibre, 4 g sugar), 0 mg chol, 41 mg sodium, 309 mg potassium. % RDI: 2% calcium, 4% iron, 10% vit A, 60% vit C, 10% folate.

BALSAMIC MARINADE

⅓ cup	balsamic vinegar
3	cloves garlic, pressed or grated
2 tsp	liquid honey
¼ tsp	each salt and pepper
½ cup	olive oil

VEGETABLES

3	large green and/or yellow zucchini (about 675 g total)
1	large red onion
2	sweet red, orange and/or yellow peppers
4	portobello mushrooms
¼ cup	chopped fresh flat-leaf parsley

95

HERBED MINI POTATO SKEWERS

HANDS-ON TIME	**TOTAL TIME**	**MAKES**
30 MINUTES	40 MINUTES	10 TO 12 SERVINGS

30	mini yellow-fleshed potatoes or mini white potatoes, scrubbed (about 675 g total)
30	mini red potatoes, scrubbed (about 675 g total)
⅔ cup	butter, melted
2	cloves garlic, pressed or grated
1 tbsp	finely chopped fresh parsley
2 tsp	finely chopped fresh rosemary
¼ tsp	each salt and pepper

In large saucepan of boiling salted water, cook yellow-fleshed and red potatoes until tender, about 15 minutes. Drain and let cool slightly. *(Make-ahead: Cover and refrigerate for up to 24 hours.)*

Combine butter, garlic, parsley, rosemary, salt and pepper. Alternating colours, thread potatoes onto metal skewers. Brush with some of the butter mixture.

Place skewers on greased grill over medium-high heat; close lid and grill, turning and brushing frequently with butter mixture, until potatoes are hot and golden, about 8 minutes.

NUTRITIONAL INFORMATION, PER EACH OF 12 SERVINGS: about 142 cal, 2 g pro, 7 g total fat (4 g sat. fat), 19 g carb (2 g dietary fibre, 1 g sugar), 18 mg chol, 310 mg sodium, 417 mg potassium. % RDI: 1% calcium, 6% iron, 6% vit A, 23% vit C, 6% folate.

TANGY SUMMER COLESLAW

HANDS-ON TIME	**TOTAL TIME**	**MAKES**
15 MINUTES	2¼ HOURS	10 TO 12 SERVINGS

¼ cup	cider vinegar
1 tbsp	lemon juice
2 tsp	granulated sugar
½ tsp	salt
¼ tsp	pepper
⅓ cup	extra-virgin olive oil
10 cups	shredded green cabbage
1½ cups	thinly sliced radishes
half	Vidalia onion, thinly sliced
2 tbsp	chopped fresh parsley

In large bowl, whisk together vinegar, lemon juice, sugar, salt and pepper until sugar is dissolved, 1 minute. Whisk in oil until combined. Add cabbage, radishes, onion and parsley; toss. Cover and refrigerate for 2 hours. *(Make-ahead: Refrigerate for up to 24 hours.)*

NUTRITIONAL INFORMATION, PER EACH OF 12 SERVINGS: about 78 cal, 1 g pro, 6 g total fat (1 g sat. fat), 6 g carb (1 g dietary fibre, 4 g sugar), 0 mg chol, 114 mg sodium, 204 mg potassium. % RDI: 3% calcium, 4% iron, 2% vit A, 38% vit C, 15% folate.

VARIATION
TROPICAL COLESLAW
Substitute lime juice for the vinegar and fresh cilantro for the parsley. Add 1 cup diced pineapple and 1 mango, peeled and diced.

96

LEMONY RED PEPPER
AND ASPARAGUS PASTA SALAD

HANDS-ON TIME	**TOTAL TIME**	**MAKES**
15 MINUTES	6¼ HOURS	10 TO 12 SERVINGS

LEMON DRESSING In small bowl, combine lemon zest, lemon juice, honey, garlic, mustard, salt and pepper; slowly whisk in oil until combined. Set aside.

SALAD In large saucepan of boiling lightly salted water, cook pasta according to package directions until al dente, adding asparagus for last 2 minutes. Drain and rinse with cold water; drain again. Transfer to large bowl.

Pour dressing over pasta mixture. Add red peppers and chives; toss to combine. Cover and refrigerate for 6 hours. *(Make-ahead: Refrigerate for up to 24 hours.)*

NUTRITIONAL INFORMATION, PER EACH OF 12 SERVINGS: about 209 cal, 6 g pro, 7 g total fat (1 g sat. fat), 32 g carb (3 g dietary fibre, 3 g sugar), 0 mg chol, 386 mg sodium, 136 mg potassium. % RDI: 2% calcium, 13% iron, 9% vit A, 62% vit C, 55% folate.

LEMON DRESSING

1 tbsp	grated lemon zest
¼ cup	lemon juice
2 tsp	liquid honey
1	clove garlic, pressed or grated
1 tsp	Dijon mustard
¾ tsp	salt
¼ tsp	pepper
⅓ cup	extra-virgin olive oil

SALAD

450 g	farfalle
1	bunch asparagus (450 g), cut in 1½-inch (4 cm) pieces
1	jar (370 mL) roasted red peppers, drained and sliced
½ cup	chopped fresh chives or sliced green onions

97

RASPBERRY LEMON CREAM CAKE

RASPBERRY LEMON CREAM CAKE

opposite

HANDS-ON
55 MINUTES

TOTAL TIME
6¾ HOURS

MAKES
12 SERVINGS

SPONGE CAKE Line bottom of 10-inch (3 L) springform pan with parchment paper; grease side. Set aside.

Set eggs in bowl of warm (100°F/40°C) water for 5 minutes.

In electric stand mixer on medium-high speed, beat eggs until foamy. Gradually beat in sugar until pale yellow and mixture falls in ribbons when beaters are lifted, about 10 minutes. Fold in lemon zest and vanilla.

Sift together flour, baking powder and salt; sift one-third over egg mixture and fold in. Repeat twice. Transfer one-quarter to bowl; fold in butter. Fold back into remaining batter. Pour into prepared pan.

Bake in 325°F (160°C) oven until cake springs back when lightly touched in centre, 45 to 50 minutes. Let cool in pan on rack for 10 minutes. Remove side of pan; let cake cool on rack. *(Make-ahead: Wrap in plastic wrap and store for up to 24 hours, or overwrap with heavy-duty foil and freeze for up to 2 weeks.)*

LEMON CREAM In small bowl, sprinkle gelatin over 3 tbsp water; set aside.

In heatproof bowl, whisk together eggs, egg yolks, sugar, lemon zest and lemon juice. Set over saucepan of simmering water; cook, stirring frequently, until translucent and thick enough to softly mound on spoon, about 20 minutes.

Strain into large bowl. Stir in gelatin mixture until melted. Place plastic wrap directly on surface; refrigerate, stirring every 10 minutes, until cool and thick enough to mound on spoon, about 1 hour.

In bowl, whip cream; fold one-third into lemon mixture. Fold in remaining cream. Fold in 2⅓ cups of the raspberries; set aside.

ASSEMBLY Line bottom and side of same springform pan with waxed or parchment paper. Cut cake horizontally into thirds. Place top cake layer, cut side up, in pan. Spread with half of the lemon cream. Top with middle cake layer, remaining lemon cream and remaining cake layer, cut side down. Cover and refrigerate until set, about 4 hours. *(Make-ahead: Refrigerate for up to 24 hours.)*

Remove side of pan. Sprinkle top with icing sugar. Arrange remaining raspberries around top edge.

NUTRITIONAL INFORMATION, PER SERVING: about 404 cal, 8 g pro, 19 g total fat (11 g sat. fat), 52 g carb (3 g dietary fibre), 221 mg chol, 107 mg sodium. % RDI: 5% calcium, 9% iron, 21% vit A, 25% vit C, 25% folate.

SPONGE CAKE

6	eggs
1 cup	granulated sugar
1 tbsp	grated lemon zest
1 tsp	vanilla
1 cup	all-purpose flour
½ tsp	baking powder
pinch	salt
⅓ cup	butter, melted

99

LEMON CREAM

1	pkg unflavoured gelatin
3	eggs
2	egg yolks
1¼ cups	granulated sugar
1 tbsp	grated lemon zest
⅔ cup	lemon juice
1⅓ cups	whipping cream (35%)
3 cups	raspberries
1 tbsp	icing sugar

CANADA DAY BARBECUE

Ours is a multicultural country,
and here's a combination of satisfying barbecued
dishes to match. This menu includes Asian,
Mediterranean and North American flavours,
all working well together. Isn't diversity delicious?

MENU FOR 8

BRINED MAPLE MUSTARD PORK CHOPS **p.102**

CHAR SIU–STYLE RIBS **p.103**

KALE AND CABBAGE SLAW **p.103**

GRILLED HONEY-GARLIC CHICKEN WINGS **p.104**

GRILLED RADICCHIO **p.104**

CURRIED POTATO SALAD **p.105**

AVOCADO COCO LIME POPS **p.107**

BRINED MAPLE MUSTARD PORK CHOPS

HANDS-ON TIME	TOTAL TIME	MAKES
20 MINUTES	2½ HOURS	6 TO 8 SERVINGS

BRINED PORK CHOPS

2 tbsp	each brown sugar and coarse salt
1 cup	boiling water
6	fresh sage leaves
2	cloves garlic, crushed
1 tsp	black peppercorns
2 cups	ice water
4	boneless pork loin chops (¾-inch/2 cm thick, about 550 g total)

MAPLE MUSTARD GLAZE

⅓ cup	apple jelly
1 tbsp	grainy mustard
1 tbsp	maple syrup
¼ tsp	pepper

BRINED PORK CHOPS In large, shallow dish, dissolve brown sugar and salt in boiling water. Add sage, garlic and black peppercorns. Stir in ice water; let cool completely, about 15 minutes. *(Make-ahead: Cover and refrigerate for up to 3 days.)*

Add pork chops to brine. Cover and refrigerate for 2 hours. Remove pork chops from brine; pat dry. Discard brine. *(Make-ahead: Cover and refrigerate for up to 24 hours.)*

MAPLE MUSTARD GLAZE While pork chops are brining, in small saucepan, stir together apple jelly, mustard, maple syrup and pepper. Bring to boil; reduce heat and simmer, stirring, until mixture is thickened and coats back of spoon, about 5 minutes.

Place chops on greased grill over medium heat; close lid and grill, turning once, until juices run clear when pork is pierced and just a hint of pink remains inside, about 6 minutes. Brush with glaze during last 2 minutes.

NUTRITIONAL INFORMATION, PER SERVING: about 133 cal, 17 g pro, 2 g total fat (1 g sat. fat), 12 g carb (trace dietary fibre, 7 g sugar), 34 mg chol, 188 mg sodium, 229 mg potassium. % RDI: 1% calcium, 4% iron, 2% vit C, 1% folate.

102

CHAR SIU-STYLE RIBS

p.100

HANDS-ON TIME
15 MINUTES

TOTAL TIME
14 HOURS

MAKES
ABOUT 24 RIBS

In blender, purée shallots, hoisin sauce, garlic, grenadine, honey, ginger, cooking wine, soy sauce, pepper and five-spice powder; set aside. *(Make-ahead: Cover and refrigerate for up to 2 days.)*

Remove membrane from underside of ribs, if attached. Rub ½ cup of the sauce all over ribs. Cover and refrigerate for 12 to 24 hours.

Place ribs, bone side down, in roasting pan; cover pan with foil. Roast in 350°F (180°C) oven until meat is fork-tender, about 1¾ hours. Brush with pan drippings. *(Make-ahead: Let cool completely. Cover and refrigerate for up to 24 hours. Reheat on medium-low grill, turning once, about 10 minutes.)*

Place ribs on greased grill over medium heat; grill, brushing all over with remaining sauce until caramelized, about 5 to 8 minutes.

NUTRITIONAL INFORMATION, PER RIB: about 177 cal, 12 g pro, 11 g total fat (4 g sat. fat), 6 g carb (trace dietary fibre, 4 g sugar), 47 mg chol, 192 mg sodium, 159 mg potassium. % RDI: 2% calcium, 4% iron, 2% vit C, 1% folate.

2	shallots, chopped
½ cup	hoisin sauce
10	cloves garlic
3 tbsp	grenadine
2 tbsp	liquid honey
1	piece (1½ inches/4 cm) fresh ginger, sliced
2 tbsp	Chinese cooking wine or dry sherry
2 tbsp	sodium-reduced soy sauce
½ tsp	each pepper and five-spice powder
2.25 kg	pork back ribs (about 2 racks)

103

KALE AND CABBAGE SLAW

HANDS-ON TIME
15 MINUTES

TOTAL TIME
4¼ HOURS

MAKES
12 SERVINGS

In large bowl, whisk together oil, lemon juice, vinegar, honey, garlic, salt and pepper. Stir in kale, cabbage and red pepper; toss to combine. Cover and refrigerate for 4 hours. *(Make-ahead: Refrigerate for up to 24 hours.)*

NUTRITIONAL INFORMATION, PER SERVING: about 71 cal, 2 g pro, 5 g total fat (1 g sat. fat), 7 g carb (2 g dietary fibre, 3 g sugar), 0 mg chol, 115 mg sodium, 267 mg potassium. % RDI: 7% calcium, 6% iron, 34% vit A, 107% vit C, 20% folate.

¼ cup	extra-virgin olive oil
2 tbsp	each lemon juice and white wine vinegar
2 tsp	liquid honey
1	clove garlic, minced
½ tsp	each salt and pepper
6 cups	thinly sliced stemmed kale
6 cups	shredded napa cabbage
1	red pepper, cored, seeded and thinly sliced

GRILLED HONEY-GARLIC CHICKEN WINGS

HANDS-ON TIME	10 MINUTES
TOTAL TIME	30 MINUTES
MAKES	ABOUT 24 WINGS

900 g	chicken wings and/or drumettes
¼ tsp	each salt and pepper
¼ cup	liquid honey
4	cloves garlic, minced
2 tbsp	sodium-reduced soy sauce

Sprinkle wings with salt and pepper. Place wings on greased rack set over foil-lined rimmed baking sheet. Bake in 325°F (165°C) oven until juices run clear when chicken is pierced, about 20 minutes. *(Make-ahead: Cover and refrigerate for up to 24 hours. Reheat on grill over medium heat before continuing.)*

Meanwhile, in bowl, stir together honey, garlic and soy sauce.

Place wings on greased grill over medium-high heat; close lid and grill, turning and brushing with honey mixture often, until browned, about 5 minutes.

NUTRITIONAL INFORMATION, PER WING: about 53 cal, 4 g pro, 3 g total fat (1 g sat. fat), 3 g carb (0 g dietary fibre, 3 g sugar), 12 mg chol, 86 mg sodium, 33 mg potassium. % RDI: 1% iron, 1% vit A.

GRILLED RADICCHIO

HANDS-ON TIME	20 MINUTES
TOTAL TIME	20 MINUTES
MAKES	8 SERVINGS

4 heads	radicchio
6 tbsp	olive oil
1 tsp	coarse sea salt
½ tsp	pepper
2 tbsp	balsamic vinegar

Leaving cores intact, cut radicchio in half (cut large heads into quarters); thread onto metal skewers. Brush with half of the oil; sprinkle with half each of the salt and pepper.

Place skewers on greased grill over medium-high heat. Close lid and grill, turning often, until radicchio is wilted and lightly browned and centres are softened, about 10 minutes. Transfer to platter. Drizzle with vinegar and remaining oil; sprinkle with remaining salt and pepper.

NUTRITIONAL INFORMATION, PER SERVING: about 113 cal, 1 g pro, 10 g total fat (1 g sat. fat), 5 g carb (1 g dietary fibre), 0 mg chol, 307 mg sodium. % RDI: 2% calcium, 5% iron, 10% vit C, 16% folate.

CURRIED POTATO SALAD

p.100

HANDS-ON TIME
20 MINUTES

TOTAL TIME
6 HOURS

MAKES
12 SERVINGS

In Dutch oven or large saucepan, pour enough cold salted water to come at least 1 inch (2.5 cm) above potatoes; bring to boil. Reduce heat to medium-high; uncover and cook, adding extra water as needed to keep potatoes covered, until tender, about 45 minutes. Drain and let cool slightly; peel. *(Make-ahead: Let cool completely; cover and refrigerate for up to 1 day.)* Cut into ¾-inch (2 cm) chunks. Let cool completely, about 30 minutes.

Meanwhile, in skillet over medium heat, cook curry powder, mustard seeds, coriander seeds and turmeric until fragrant and lightly toasted, about 4 minutes. Transfer to bowl.

In small saucepan of boiling water, cook peas until heated through, about 30 seconds. Drain and rinse with cold water; drain again.

In large bowl, stir together mayonnaise, sour cream, cilantro, green onions, lemon juice, honey, salt and pepper. Stir in curry mixture until well combined. Stir in potatoes and peas; cover and refrigerate for 4 hours. *(Make-ahead: Cover and refrigerate for up to 24 hours.)*

2.5 kg	white potatoes (4 to 6 large potatoes)
4 tsp	each curry powder and mustard seeds
1 tbsp	coriander seeds
2 tsp	turmeric
1 cup	frozen peas
¾ cup	each light mayonnaise and light sour cream
⅓ cup	chopped fresh cilantro
2	green onions, thinly sliced
4 tsp	lemon juice
2 tsp	liquid honey
1 tsp	salt
½ tsp	pepper

105

NUTRITIONAL INFORMATION, PER SERVING: about 225 cal, 5 g pro, 8 g total fat (2 g sat. fat), 36 g carb (3 g dietary fibre, 4 g sugar), 10 mg chol, 660 mg sodium, 646 mg potassium. % RDI: 4% calcium, 9% iron, 5% vit A, 35% vit C, 13% folate.

AVOCADO COCO LIME POPS

AVOCADO COCO LIME POPS

opposite

HANDS-ON TIME
10 MINUTES

TOTAL TIME
4 HOURS

MAKES
10 TO 12 POPS

In blender, purée together avocados, coconut milk, maple syrup, lime zest and lime juice until smooth. Pour into ice pop moulds and insert wooden sticks in the middle. Freeze 4 hours or until firm. *(Make-ahead: Freeze for up to 2 weeks.)*

Before serving, run moulds under lukewarm running water. Unmould; dip top third of ice pops in chocolate, sprinkle with Graham crackers. Let stand until firm, about 20 seconds.

NUTRITIONAL INFORMATION, PER SERVING: about 215 cal, 2 g pro, 14 g total fat (5 g sat. fat), 22 g carb (4 g dietary fibre), 2 mg chol, 32 mg sodium.

3	ripe avocados, pitted and peeled
1	can (400 mL) light coconut milk
⅓ cup	maple syrup
2 tsp	lime zest
¼ cup	lime juice (about 3 limes)
½ cup	chopped white chocolate (about 75 g), melted
¼ cup	crumbled Graham crackers

107

GARDEN PARTY GRILL

Sweep the patio, get out the croquet set,
and serve a selection of grilled dishes with a fresh,
contemporary twist: jerk chicken wings, grilled
radishes, edamame and sriracha-lime shrimp.

MENU FOR 10

GRILLED RADISHES
WITH CREAMY CILANTRO DIP **p.111**

GRILLED SESAME EDAMAME **p.111**

GRILLED JERK CHICKEN WINGS **p.112**

GRILLED SHRIMP
WITH SRIRACHA-LIME COCKTAIL SAUCE **p.114**

GRILLED BACON AND FETA MINI PIZZAS **p.114**

TEA SANGRIA **p.115**

GARDEN MARTINIS **p.115**

GRILLED RADISHES WITH CREAMY CILANTRO DIP

GRILLED RADISHES
WITH CREAMY CILANTRO DIP

opposite

HANDS-ON TIME
15 MINUTES

TOTAL TIME
15 MINUTES

MAKES
10 SERVINGS

CREAMY CILANTRO DIP In small bowl, whisk together mayonnaise, sour cream, cilantro, mint, lime juice and pepper. Set aside. *(Make-ahead: Cover and refrigerate for up to 24 hours.)*

RADISHES In bowl, toss together radishes, butter, lime juice, honey and pepper. Place on lightly greased grill over medium-high heat; close lid and grill, turning once, until tender and slightly charred, about 5 minutes. Return to bowl; toss with salt. Serve warm with dip.

NUTRITIONAL INFORMATION, PER SERVING: about 69 cal, 1 g pro, 6 g total fat (2 g sat. fat), 3 g carb (1 g dietary fibre, 2 g sugar), 7 mg chol, 117 mg sodium, 111 mg potassium. % RDI: 2% calcium, 1% iron, 3% vit A, 8% vit C, 4% folate.

CREAMY CILANTRO DIP

¼ cup	each mayonnaise and sour cream
2 tbsp	chopped fresh cilantro
1 tbsp	finely chopped fresh mint
½ tsp	lime juice
pinch	pepper

RADISHES

20	large radishes, halved lengthwise
1 tbsp	butter, melted
2 tsp	lime juice
1 tsp	liquid honey
pinch	pepper
¼ tsp	salt

111

GRILLED SESAME EDAMAME

p.108

HANDS-ON TIME
15 MINUTES

TOTAL TIME
15 MINUTES

MAKES
12 SERVINGS

Thread edamame onto metal or soaked wooden skewers; brush with sesame oil. Place on grill over medium-high heat; close lid and grill, turning once, until tender and slightly charred, 6 to 8 minutes. Remove from skewers; toss with sesame seeds and salt. Serve warm.

NUTRITIONAL INFORMATION, PER SERVING: about 33 cal, 3 g pro, 2 g total fat (trace sat. fat), 2 g carb (2 g dietary fibre, 1 g sugar), 0 mg chol, 66 mg sodium, 135 mg potassium. % RDI: 2% calcium, 4% iron, 3% vit C, 30% folate.

500 g	frozen whole edamame (in shell), thawed
2 tsp	sesame oil
1½ tsp	sesame seeds
½ tsp	sea salt

GRILLED JERK CHICKEN WINGS

opposite

HANDS-ON TIME	**TOTAL TIME**	**MAKES**
25 MINUTES	3 HOURS	ABOUT 24 WINGS

4	green onions, chopped
2 tbsp	lime juice
1 tbsp	sodium-reduced soy sauce
1 tbsp	vegetable oil
1	jalapeño pepper, seeded and chopped
2	cloves garlic, chopped
1 tbsp	chopped fresh thyme
2 tsp	ground allspice
1 tsp	each packed brown sugar and salt
½ tsp	each ground ginger and pepper
¼ tsp	each cinnamon and nutmeg
900 g	chicken wings and/or drumettes

In food processor, purée together green onions, lime juice, soy sauce, oil, jalapeño pepper, garlic, thyme, allspice, brown sugar, salt, ginger, pepper, cinnamon and nutmeg until smooth. Scrape into large bowl; add wings and toss to coat. Cover and refrigerate for 2 hours. *(Make-ahead: Refrigerate for up to 24 hours.)*

Place wings on greased rack set over foil-lined rimmed baking sheet. Bake in 350°F (180°C) oven until juices run clear when chicken is pierced, about 30 minutes. *(Make-ahead: Refrigerate in airtight container for up to 24 hours. Reheat on grill over medium heat before continuing.)*

Place wings on greased grill over medium-high heat; close lid and grill, turning once, until browned and crisp, 6 to 8 minutes.

NUTRITIONAL INFORMATION, PER WING: about 63 cal, 5 g pro, 4 g total fat (1 g sat. fat), 1 g carb (trace dietary fibre, trace sugar), 16 mg chol, 137 mg sodium, 50 mg potassium. % RDI: 1% calcium, 3% iron, 1% vit A, 2% vit C, 1% folate.

GRILLED JERK CHICKEN WINGS AND GRILLED BACON AND FETA MINI PIZZAS

GRILLED SHRIMP
WITH SRIRACHA-LIME COCKTAIL SAUCE

HANDS-ON TIME	**TOTAL TIME**	**MAKES**
15 MINUTES	15 MINUTES	12 SERVINGS

SRIRACHA-LIME COCKTAIL SAUCE

¾ cup	tomato-based chili sauce or ketchup
2 tbsp	drained prepared horseradish
1 tbsp	each lime juice and sriracha
pinch	each salt and pepper

SHRIMP

450 g	jumbo shrimp (21 to 24 count), peeled (tail-on) and deveined
1 tsp	olive oil
pinch	each salt and pepper

SRIRACHA-LIME COCKTAIL SAUCE In small bowl, whisk together chili sauce, horseradish, lime juice, sriracha, salt and pepper. Set aside. *(Make-ahead: Cover and refrigerate for up to 3 days.)*

SHRIMP In bowl, toss together shrimp, oil, salt and pepper. Place on greased grill over medium-high heat; close lid and grill, turning once, until pink and opaque throughout, 4 to 5 minutes. Serve with cocktail sauce.

NUTRITIONAL INFORMATION, PER SERVING: about 54 cal, 7 g pro, 1 g total fat (trace sat. fat), 4 g carb (1 g dietary fibre, 2 g sugar), 60 mg chol, 319 mg sodium, 126 mg potassium. % RDI: 1% calcium, 7% iron, 2% vit A, 3% vit C, 3% folate.

GRILLED BACON AND
FETA MINI PIZZAS

p.113

HANDS-ON TIME	**TOTAL TIME**	**MAKES**
20 MINUTES	20 MINUTES	12 MINI PIZZAS

4	strips bacon
12	mini pita breads
4 tsp	red pepper jelly
¼ cup	thinly sliced red onion
¼ cup	crumbled feta cheese

In skillet, cook bacon over medium heat, turning once, until crisp, about 8 minutes. Transfer to paper towel–lined plate to drain. Chop bacon; set aside. *(Make-ahead: Refrigerate in airtight container for up to 24 hours.)*

Place pitas on rimmed baking sheet. Spread jelly over tops; sprinkle with bacon, red onion and feta.

Using metal spatula, carefully transfer pitas to greased grill over medium heat; close lid and grill until warm, about 4 minutes.

NUTRITIONAL INFORMATION, PER MINI PIZZA: about 60 cal, 2 g pro, 2 g total fat (1 g sat. fat), 8 g carb (trace dietary fibre, 1 g sugar), 5 mg chol, 152 mg sodium, 34 mg potassium. % RDI: 2% calcium, 3% iron, 4% folate.

TEA SANGRIA

HANDS-ON TIME	TOTAL TIME	MAKES
15 MINUTES	4½ HOURS	10 SERVINGS

In large heatproof liquid measure or bowl, steep tea bags in boiling water for 5 minutes; discard tea bags. Stir in sugar until dissolved. Let cool to room temperature. Cover and refrigerate until chilled, about 2 hours. *(Make-ahead: Refrigerate for up to 24 hours.)*

Pour into pitcher; stir in lemon juice, lime juice, cherries, apple and orange. Refrigerate until chilled, about 2 hours. *(Make-ahead: Refrigerate for up to 4 hours.)* Stir in frozen grapes just before serving.

NUTRITIONAL INFORMATION, PER SERVING: about 133 cal, 1 g pro, trace total fat (trace sat. fat), 35 g carb (2 g dietary fibre, 30 g sugar), 0 mg chol, 11 mg sodium, 309 mg potassium. % RDI: 2% calcium, 3% iron, 1% vit A, 30% vit C, 9% folate.

5	black tea bags
8 cups	boiling water
¾ cup	granulated sugar
¼ cup	each lemon juice and lime juice
2 cups	cherries, pitted and halved
1	apple, quartered, cored and thinly sliced
1	orange, thinly sliced
4 cups	frozen seedless green grapes

GARDEN MARTINIS

HANDS-ON TIME	TOTAL TIME	MAKES
10 MINUTES	10 MINUTES	10 SERVINGS

In large pitcher, using muddler or handle of wooden spoon, muddle aquavit with cucumber.

Add grape juice, elderflower liqueur and lime juice; stir in ice cubes. Pour into chilled martini glasses and garnish with dill.

NUTRITIONAL INFORMATION, PER SERVING: about 295 cal, 1 g pro, trace total fat (trace sat. fat), 26 g carb (trace dietary fibre, 24 g sugar), 0 mg chol, 12 mg sodium, 115 mg potassium. % RDI: 1% calcium, 2% iron, 23% vit C, 1% folate.

2½ cups	aquavit or gin, chilled
half	English cucumber, thinly sliced
3 cups	white grape juice, chilled
1⅓ cups	elderflower liqueur, chilled
⅔ cup	lime juice
4 cups	ice cubes
	fresh dill sprigs

A DAY AT THE COTTAGE

We get it. You want to spend the day at the lake, not in the kitchen or in front of the barbecue. These flavourful, easy recipes—for breakfast, lunch and dinner—keep the gang well-fed and happy, so you can focus on what's important: a nap in the hammock, a swim before dinner and a sunset you'll never forget.

117

ALL-DAY MENU FOR 4

BARBECUED BREAKFAST PACKETS **p.118**

BACON AND ONION GRILLED CHEESE **p.119**

MARINATED CHICKPEA SALAD **p.119**

MOROCCAN CHICKEN WITH GRILLED VEGETABLES **p.120**

GRILLED FRUIT WITH HONEYED CRÈME FRAÎCHE **p.123**

APPLE MINT ICED TEA **p.123**

BARBECUED BREAKFAST PACKETS

p.116

HANDS-ON TIME	**TOTAL TIME**	**MAKES**
20 MINUTES	35 MINUTES	4 SERVINGS

1	large sweet potato (about 450 g total)
1 tbsp	butter, melted
1 tsp	smoked paprika
½ tsp	garlic powder
¼ tsp	each salt and pepper
2	green onions, thinly sliced
⅓ cup	thinly sliced ham
¼ cup	diced roasted sweet red pepper
4	eggs
¼ cup	chopped fresh basil

Using fork, prick sweet potato all over. Microwave on high, turning once halfway through, until tender, about 5 minutes. Let cool slightly. *(Make-ahead: Wrap and refrigerate for up to 24 hours.)* Peel and cut into ⅛-inch (3 mm) thick slices.

Meanwhile, combine butter, paprika, garlic powder and half each of the salt and pepper.

Lightly grease four 12-inch (30 cm) lengths of heavy-duty foil. In centre of each sheet, arrange sweet potato slices in circle, overlapping slightly; drizzle with butter mixture. Divide green onions, ham and red pepper over top.

Bring up sides of foil to create bowl. Crack egg into each packet. Bring together 2 long sides of foil and fold to seal, leaving room inside for expansion; fold in remaining sides to seal.

Carefully slide packets onto grill over medium-low heat; close lid and grill just until eggs are set, about 8 minutes. Averting hands and face to avoid steam, open packets; sprinkle with basil and remaining salt and pepper.

NUTRITIONAL INFORMATION, PER SERVING: about 217 cal, 12 g pro, 10 g total fat (4 g sat. fat), 21 g carb (4 g dietary fibre, 9 g sugar), 242 mg chol, 405 mg sodium, 599 mg potassium. % RDI: 7% calcium, 14% iron, 192% vit A, 57% vit C, 21% folate.

VARIATION
CHEESY BARBECUED BREAKFAST PACKETS
Omit paprika, garlic powder and red pepper. Substitute white potato for the sweet potato. Sprinkle with ¼ cup shredded Cheddar before adding eggs.

118

BACON AND ONION GRILLED CHEESE

HANDS-ON TIME
25 MINUTES

TOTAL TIME
25 MINUTES

MAKES
4 SERVINGS

Thread onion rounds onto metal or soaked wooden skewers. Brush with 1 tsp of the oil; sprinkle with salt and pepper. Place onion and bacon on greased grill over medium-high heat; close lid and grill, turning occasionally, until bacon is heated through, about 4 minutes, and onion is softened, about 7 minutes.

Top 4 of the bread slices with Cheddar, bacon, tomato and onion. Sandwich with remaining bread.

Brush both sides of sandwiches with remaining oil. Return to grill over medium heat; close lid and grill, turning once, until Cheddar is melted, about 5 minutes.

NUTRITIONAL INFORMATION, PER SERVING: about 401 cal, 21 g pro, 15 g total fat (6 g sat. fat), 45 g carb (8 g dietary fibre, 10 g sugar), 29 mg chol, 721 mg sodium, 427 mg potassium. % RDI: 23% calcium, 20% iron, 8% vit A, 12% vit C, 35% folate.

1	small sweet onion, cut in scant ½-inch (1 cm) thick rounds
1 tbsp	olive oil
pinch	each salt and pepper
4	slices back bacon
8	thick slices multigrain bread
4	slices Cheddar cheese
1	tomato, thinly sliced

MARINATED CHICKPEA SALAD

p.121

HANDS-ON TIME
10 MINUTES

TOTAL TIME
2¼ HOURS

MAKES
4 SERVINGS

In bowl, whisk together lemon juice, oil, coriander, pepper, cayenne pepper and salt. Stir in chickpeas, cucumber and onion. Cover and refrigerate for 2 hours. *(Make-ahead: Refrigerate for up to 24 hours.)* Stir in cilantro.

NUTRITIONAL INFORMATION, PER SERVING: about 199 cal, 6 g pro, 8 g total fat (1 g sat. fat), 27 g carb (5 g dietary fibre, 6 g sugar), 0 mg chol, 279 mg sodium, 226 mg potassium. % RDI: 4% calcium, 11% iron, 1% vit A, 17% vit C, 31% folate.

3 tbsp	lemon juice
2 tbsp	extra-virgin olive oil
¾ tsp	ground coriander
¼ tsp	pepper
pinch	each cayenne pepper and salt
1	can (540 mL) chickpeas, drained and rinsed
1	baby cucumber, quartered lengthwise and sliced
⅓ cup	diced red onion
¼ cup	chopped fresh cilantro

MOROCCAN CHICKEN
WITH GRILLED VEGETABLES

opposite

HANDS-ON TIME	TOTAL TIME	MAKES
30 MINUTES	2¾ HOURS	4 SERVINGS

MOROCCAN CHICKEN

⅓ cup	Greek yogurt
1 tbsp	each tahini and lemon juice
2	cloves garlic, minced
2 tsp	minced fresh ginger
1 tsp	ground coriander
½ tsp	ground cumin
¼ tsp	cinnamon
pinch	each salt and pepper
450 g	boneless skinless chicken breasts

GRILLED VEGETABLES

2 tbsp	each lemon juice and olive oil
1	clove garlic, minced
1 tsp	minced fresh ginger
¼ tsp	each salt and pepper
pinch	cinnamon
1	small red onion, cut in ½-inch (1 cm) thick rounds
1	zucchini, cut lengthwise in ½-inch (1 cm) thick slices
2	portobello mushrooms, stems and gills removed
1	sweet red pepper, seeded and quartered
2 tbsp	chopped fresh cilantro

MOROCCAN CHICKEN In bowl, combine yogurt, tahini, lemon juice, garlic, ginger, coriander, cumin, cinnamon, salt and pepper.

Add chicken to bowl; toss to coat. Cover and refrigerate for 2 hours. *(Make-ahead: Refrigerate for up to 24 hours.)*

Place chicken on greased grill over medium-high heat; close lid and grill, turning occasionally, until no longer pink inside, about 8 minutes. Let stand for 3 minutes before slicing.

GRILLED VEGETABLES In bowl, combine lemon juice, oil, garlic, ginger, salt, pepper and cinnamon.

Thread onion rounds onto metal or soaked wooden skewers. Place onion, zucchini, mushrooms and red pepper on greased grill over medium-high heat; close lid and grill, basting frequently with lemon mixture, until tender, about 7 minutes. Cut mushrooms in half. Place on platter along with remaining grilled vegetables; sprinkle with cilantro. Serve with sliced chicken.

NUTRITIONAL INFORMATION, PER SERVING: about 288 cal, 31 g pro, 13 g total fat (3 g sat. fat), 14 g carb (4 g dietary fibre, 5 g sugar), 74 mg chol, 229 mg sodium, 946 mg potassium. % RDI: 8% calcium, 13% iron, 14% vit A, 92% vit C, 17% folate.

MOROCCAN CHICKEN WITH GRILLED VEGETABLES AND MARINATED CHICKPEA SALAD

GRILLED FRUIT WITH HONEYED CRÈME FRAÎCHE

GRILLED FRUIT
WITH HONEYED CRÈME FRAÎCHE

opposite

HANDS-ON TIME
15 MINUTES

TOTAL TIME
15 MINUTES

MAKES
4 SERVINGS

HONEYED CRÈME FRAÎCHE Stir together crème fraîche, honey and vanilla. *(Make-ahead: Cover and refrigerate for up to 24 hours.)*

GRILLED FRUIT In small bowl, combine butter, bourbon and honey. Place peaches, pineapple and mango on greased grill over medium heat; close lid and grill, brushing with butter mixture and turning frequently, until softened and caramelized, about 5 minutes.

Arrange pineapple rings on 4 dessert plates; top with peaches and mango. Spoon crème fraîche mixture over top; sprinkle with mint.

NUTRITIONAL INFORMATION, PER SERVING: about 257 cal, 2 g pro, 12 g total fat (8 g sat. fat), 37 g carb (4 g dietary fibre, 31 g sugar), 40 mg chol, 49 mg sodium, 367 mg potassium. % RDI: 3% calcium, 6% iron, 22% vit A, 63% vit C, 7% folate.

HONEYED CRÈME FRAÎCHE

¼ cup	crème fraîche
2 tsp	liquid honey
½ tsp	vanilla

GRILLED FRUIT

2 tbsp	butter, melted
1 tbsp	each bourbon and liquid honey
4	small firm ripe peaches, halved and pitted
4	pineapple rings (½-inch/1 cm thick)
1	large mango, peeled and cut in 4 wedges
2 tbsp	chopped fresh mint

123

APPLE MINT ICED TEA

In large heatproof measuring cup or bowl, steep 3 bags mint herbal tea in 8 cups boiling water for 4 minutes. Discard bags. Meanwhile, in saucepan, bring 1 cup water, 3 tbsp liquid honey and 2 Granny Smith apples, cored and thinly sliced, to boil. Reduce heat to medium-low; simmer for 5 minutes to combine flavours. Add to tea; let cool to room temperature, about 30 minutes. Refrigerate until cold, about 2 hours. Strain through cheesecloth into pitcher, pressing solids gently so beverage remains clear. Serve over ice.

MAKES 8 SERVINGS

NUTRITIONAL INFORMATION, PER SERVING: about 27 cal, 0 g pro, 0 g total fat (0 g sat. fat), 7 g carb (0 g dietary fibre), 0 mg chol, 3 mg sodium. % RDI: 1% calcium, 1% iron, 1% folate.

BLOCK PARTY

There's nothing like sharing a meal with
your neighbours to build community spirit on your street.
Have them over for a summery Caribbean-themed
meal of grilled chicken, salt fish and our take on rice
and peas. And if the party gets bigger, all of these
recipes can be easily doubled or tripled.

125

MENU FOR 8

GRILLED CARIBBEAN CHICKEN p.126

SPICY CUCUMBER SALAD p.126

COOKUP RICE p.127

SALT FISH CAKES p.128

SPLIT PEA FRITTERS p.129

TAMARIND DIP p.130

MANGO SAUCE p.130

GINGER BEER SHANDY p.131

RUM PUNCH p.131

PITCHER LIME SQUASH p.131

GRILLED CARIBBEAN CHICKEN

p.124

HANDS-ON TIME	**TOTAL TIME**	**MAKES**
50 MINUTES	5 HOURS	8 SERVINGS

2	chickens (about 3.5 kg total)
¼ cup	vegetable oil
1	onion, chopped
2	cloves garlic, chopped
1	piece (2 inches/5 cm) fresh ginger, chopped
2 tsp	chopped fresh thyme
1 tsp	each ground coriander and hot pepper sauce
½ tsp	each ground cloves and ground allspice
¾ tsp	salt
½ tsp	pepper

Cut chickens into 10 pieces each.

In food processor, pulse together oil, onion, garlic and ginger until chunky paste. Transfer to large shallow glass baking dish; stir in thyme, coriander, hot pepper sauce, cloves and allspice. Add chicken; rub paste all over. Cover and refrigerate for 4 hours. *(Make-ahead: Refrigerate for up to 24 hours.)*

Sprinkle chicken with salt and pepper. Place on greased grill over medium-high heat; close lid and grill, turning once, until juices run clear when chicken is pierced, about 40 minutes for thighs and legs and 20 minutes for breasts.

NUTRITIONAL INFORMATION, PER SERVING: about 428 cal, 38 g pro, 29 g total fat (7 g sat. fat), 2 g carb (1 g dietary fibre), 139 mg chol, 339 mg sodium. % RDI: 2% calcium, 10% iron, 7% vit A, 2% vit C, 5% folate.

SPICY CUCUMBER SALAD

p.124

HANDS-ON TIME	**TOTAL TIME**	**MAKES**
10 MINUTES	1¾ HOURS	8 SERVINGS

3	English cucumbers
½ tsp	salt
2 tbsp	lime juice
1 tsp	minced seeded hot red pepper
½ tsp	granulated sugar
pinch	pepper
¼ cup	chopped fresh cilantro

Peel and seed cucumbers; slice crosswise into ¼-inch (5 mm) thick slices. Place in colander set over bowl; sprinkle with salt. Let stand for 30 minutes. Drain and gently squeeze out liquid.

In bowl, toss together cucumbers, lime juice, hot pepper, sugar and pepper; cover and refrigerate for 1 hour. *(Make-ahead: Refrigerate for up to 24 hours.)* Stir in cilantro.

NUTRITIONAL INFORMATION, PER SERVING: about 12 cal, 1 g pro, trace total fat (0 g sat. fat), 2 g carb (1 g dietary fibre), 0 mg chol, 73 mg sodium. % RDI: 1% calcium, 1% iron, 1% vit A, 8% vit C, 5% folate.

COOKUP RICE

p.124

HANDS-ON TIME
20 MINUTES

TOTAL TIME
2¼ HOURS

MAKES
8 SERVINGS

Soak peas overnight in 2 cups cold water. (Or use quick-soak method: bring peas and 2 cups water to boil; boil gently for 2 minutes. Remove from heat, cover and let stand for 1 hour.) Drain.

In saucepan, cover peas again with 3 times their new volume of water and bring to boil. Reduce heat, cover and simmer until tender, about 40 minutes. Drain, reserving cooking liquid.

In Dutch oven or large heavy-bottomed saucepan, cook salt pork over medium heat, stirring, until golden, about 5 minutes. Transfer to paper towel–lined plate; set aside. Drain all but 1 tbsp fat from pan.

In same Dutch oven, cook half of the green onions, the carrot, onion, garlic, hot pepper, thyme sprigs, cinnamon stick, salt and pepper until onion is softened and golden, about 5 minutes.

Return pork to pan. Stir in rice; cook, stirring, for 1 minute.

In large glass measure, whisk together coconut milk, enough of the reserved cooking liquid and water (if needed) to make 4 cups; stir into rice mixture.

Add peas; bring to boil. Reduce heat, cover and simmer until rice is tender and no liquid remains, 15 to 18 minutes. Remove from heat; let stand, covered, for 5 minutes. Discard hot pepper, thyme and cinnamon; stir in remaining green onions.

NUTRITIONAL INFORMATION, PER SERVING: about 380 cal, 7 g pro, 20 g total fat (13 g sat. fat), 44 g carb (3 g dietary fibre), 10 mg chol, 285 mg sodium. % RDI: 4% calcium, 16% iron, 16% vit A, 3% vit C, 15% folate.

¼ cup	dried pigeon peas
115 g	cubed salt pork
3	green onions, chopped
1	carrot, diced
1	onion, finely chopped
2	cloves garlic, minced
1	hot red pepper, halved and seeded
2	sprigs fresh thyme
1	cinnamon stick
¼ tsp	each salt and pepper
2 cups	long-grain rice, rinsed
1	can (400 mL) coconut milk

127

SALT FISH CAKES

HANDS-ON TIME	**TOTAL TIME**	**MAKES**
40 MINUTES	12¾ HOURS	8 SERVINGS

115 g	salt cod pieces
1	yellow-fleshed potato, peeled and chopped
1	small onion, minced
2	cloves garlic, minced
2	eggs
½ cup	all-purpose flour
1 tsp	chopped fresh thyme
¼ tsp	each salt and pepper
½ cup	dry bread crumbs
	vegetable oil

In bowl in refrigerator, soak salt cod in cold water for 12 hours, changing water twice. Taste cod; if still too salty, continue changing water and soaking for up to 4 hours. Drain, rinse and coarsely chop. Set aside.

In saucepan of boiling salted water, cover and cook potato until fork-tender, about 10 minutes. Drain and return to pan over medium heat; cook, stirring, for 1 minute. Transfer to bowl and mash. Add onion, garlic, 1 egg, ¼ cup of the flour, the thyme, salt, pepper and cod; stir to combine. Form mixture, by 2 tbsp, into 2-inch (5 cm) long logs.

In shallow dish, whisk remaining egg. Place remaining flour in separate shallow bowl; place bread crumbs in another shallow bowl. Coat fish cakes in flour, then egg, then bread crumbs, turning to coat all over. *(Make-ahead: Cover and refrigerate for up to 24 hours.)*

In wok, Dutch oven or large saucepan, pour enough oil to come 2 inches (5 cm) up side. Heat until deep-fryer thermometer reads 375°F (190°C) or 1-inch (2.5 cm) cube of white bread turns golden in 30 seconds. Working in batches, deep-fry fish, turning once, until golden, 4 to 5 minutes. Drain on paper towel–lined tray.

NUTRITIONAL INFORMATION, PER SERVING: about 155 cal, 12 g pro, 6 g total fat (1 g sat. fat), 13 g carb (1 g dietary fibre), 68 mg chol, 812 mg sodium. % RDI: 4% calcium, 8% iron, 2% vit A, 3% vit C, 13% folate.

SPLIT PEA FRITTERS

HANDS-ON TIME
20 MINUTES

TOTAL TIME
20 MINUTES

MAKES
8 SERVINGS

In bowl, whisk together ground peas, baking powder, cumin, salt and pepper. Whisk in hot pepper sauce and ¾ cup water; beat until thick, about 1 minute.

In wok, Dutch oven or large saucepan, pour enough oil to come 2 inches (5 cm) up side. Heat until deep-fryer thermometer reads 375°F (190°C) or 1-inch (2.5 cm) cube of white bread turns golden in 30 seconds. Working in batches, drop batter by heaping 1 tbsp into hot oil; cook, turning once, until golden brown, 4 to 5 minutes. Drain on paper towel–lined tray.

NUTRITIONAL INFORMATION, PER SERVING: about 129 cal, 5 g pro, 7 g total fat (1 g sat. fat), 13 g carb (2 g dietary fibre), 0 mg chol, 166 mg sodium. % RDI: 2% calcium, 6% iron, 18% folate.

1 cup	ground dried split peas
½ tsp	each baking powder, ground cumin and salt
¼ tsp	pepper
½ tsp	hot pepper sauce
	vegetable oil

129

TIP FROM THE TEST KITCHEN

Ground split peas are available in West Indian grocery stores and some specialty food shops. If you can't find them, finely grind split dried yellow peas in a spice or coffee grinder.

TAMARIND DIP

HANDS-ON TIME	TOTAL TIME	MAKES
15 MINUTES	15 MINUTES	ABOUT 1 CUP

¼ cup	tamarind pulp
1 tsp	cumin seeds
1 tbsp	vegetable oil
1	small onion, minced
1	clove garlic, minced
1 tbsp	granulated sugar
2 tsp	minced fresh ginger
¼ tsp	each salt and pepper

Break up tamarind in 1 cup warm water; soak for 5 minutes. Press through fine-mesh sieve; discard fibrous pulp and seeds.

Meanwhile, in saucepan, toast cumin seeds over medium heat until popping, about 2 minutes; transfer to bowl.

In same saucepan, heat oil over medium heat; cook onion, garlic, sugar, ginger, salt and pepper, stirring occasionally, until softened and golden, about 7 minutes. Stir in tamarind mixture and cumin; bring to boil; cook for 2 minutes. *(Make-ahead: Refrigerate in airtight container for up to 2 days.)*

NUTRITIONAL INFORMATION, PER 1 TBSP: about 18 cal, trace pro, 1 g total fat (trace sat. fat), 3 g carb (trace dietary fibre), 0 mg chol, 37 mg sodium. % RDI: 1% iron.

MANGO SAUCE

HANDS-ON TIME	TOTAL TIME	MAKES
25 MINUTES	25 MINUTES	ABOUT 1 CUP

1	mango, peeled, pitted and chopped
1	small shallot, minced
2	cloves garlic, minced
¼ cup	cider vinegar
2 tbsp	packed brown sugar
1 tbsp	minced fresh ginger
2	whole cloves
1	cinnamon stick
¼ tsp	salt

In saucepan, bring mango, shallot, garlic, vinegar, brown sugar, ginger, cloves, cinnamon and salt to boil. Reduce heat, cover and simmer until mango is tender, about 15 minutes. Discard cloves and cinnamon.

In blender, purée mango mixture until smooth. *(Make-ahead: Refrigerate in airtight container for up to 2 days.)*

NUTRITIONAL INFORMATION, PER 1 TBSP: about 17 cal, trace pro, 0 g total fat (0 g sat. fat), 4 g carb (trace dietary fibre), 0 mg chol, 37 mg sodium. % RDI: 1% iron, 1% vit A, 5% vit C.

GINGER BEER SHANDY

Half fill glass with ice (if using). Squeeze lime over top, twisting zest to release oils. Add lager and ginger beer, stirring to combine.

MAKES 1 SERVING

NUTRITIONAL INFORMATION, PER SERVING: about 177 cal, 1 g pro, trace total fat (0 g sat. fat), 37 g carb (0 g dietary fibre), 0 mg chol, 10 mg sodium. % RDI: 1% calcium, 1% iron, 5% vit C, 6% folate.

	ice cubes (optional)
1	lime quarter
4 oz	lager (about ½ cup)
4 oz	ginger beer (about ½ cup)

RUM PUNCH

In glass, stir together coconut water, rum, guava juice and lime juice. Add ice.

MAKES 1 SERVING

NUTRITIONAL INFORMATION, PER SERVING: about 220 cal, 1 g pro, 12 g total fat (10 g sat. fat), 7 g carb (1 g dietary fibre), 0 mg chol, 8 mg sodium. % RDI: 2% calcium, 14% iron, 20% vit C, 7% folate.

2 oz	coconut water, pineapple juice or soursop juice (about ¼ cup)
1½ oz	rum (about 3 tbsp)
1 oz	guava juice or mango juice (about 2 tbsp)
½ oz	lime juice (about 1 tbsp)
	ice cubes

PITCHER LIME SQUASH

In microwaveable measure, microwave lime juice with honey on high for 30 seconds; whisk until honey is dissolved. Let cool.

Pour carbonated water over ice cubes in pitcher; stir in lime mixture.

MAKES 8 SERVINGS

NUTRITIONAL INFORMATION, PER SERVING: about 53 cal, trace pro, 0 g total fat (0 g sat. fat), 15 g carb (0 g dietary fibre), 0 mg chol, 3 mg sodium. % RDI: 3% calcium, 1% iron, 20% vit C, 2% folate.

1¼ cups	lime juice (about 6 limes)
⅓ cup	liquid honey
2	bottles (750 mL each carbonated water
	ice cubes

FAMILY REUNION PICNIC

They're all coming for the picnic: favourite aunts, the nephews who are growing up quickly and even the cousin you rarely see. Between the laughs and the debates, this is a chance to reinforce the connections you share. Here's an adaptable, expandable menu for the all-ages, all-tastes, mixed-up crew that is your extended family.

133

MENU FOR 8 TO 10

**GRILLED SAUSAGES
WITH ASSORTED TOPPINGS p.134**

THAI DEVILLED EGGS p.136

GRILLED GARAM MASALA CORN p.136

WILD RICE AND LENTIL SALAD p.137

MEDITERRANEAN KALE SALAD p.138

CHAI MANGO LEMONADE p.138

GRILLED SAUSAGE BAR

When you're hosting a group, putting out a mix of grilled sausages, buns and topping options is an easy way to satisfy a range of tastes and appetites. Let your guests serve themselves, customizing their own meals and enjoying as much or as little as they like. Here's how:

- Grill a variety of sausages, such as bratwurst, veggie, turkey, sweet Italian and lamb.

- Offer a medley of toppings, including the recipes here, plus a variety of mustards, bottled sauces and pickles.

- Serve with paratha, naan, halved pitas, kaiser rolls, French rolls and oval crusty buns.

KIMCHI SLAW

HANDS-ON TIME 5 MINUTES
TOTAL TIME 5 MINUTES
MAKES 6 SERVINGS

1 tbsp	seasoned rice vinegar
1 tsp	granulated sugar
1 tsp	sesame oil
⅔ cup	thinly sliced carrot
⅔ cup	thinly sliced seeded English cucumber
¼ cup	packed kimchi, drained and thinly sliced
3 tbsp	light mayonnaise
¼ tsp	sriracha sauce

In bowl, whisk together vinegar, sugar and oil until sugar is dissolved. Toss with carrot, cucumber and kimchi.

Combine mayonnaise with sriracha; drizzle over slaw just before serving.

NUTRITIONAL INFORMATION, PER SERVING: about 48 cal, trace pro, 3 g total fat (1 g sat. fat), 4 g carb (1 g dietary fibre, 3 g sugar), 3 mg chol, 206 mg sodium, 63 mg potassium. % RDI: 1% calcium, 1% iron, 24% vit A, 3% vit C, 2% folate.

TOMATILLO SALSA

HANDS-ON TIME 10 MINUTES
TOTAL TIME 10 MINUTES
MAKES 6 SERVINGS

8	canned or fresh tomatillos
1	avocado, pitted, peeled and chopped
half	small red onion, diced
1	jalapeño pepper, minced
1	clove garlic, minced
2 tbsp	chopped fresh cilantro
2 tbsp	extra-virgin olive oil
2 tbsp	lime juice
pinch	each salt and pepper

Chop tomatillos; drain in colander.

In bowl, combine tomatillos, avocado, onion, jalapeño pepper, garlic, cilantro, oil, lime juice, salt and pepper. *(Make-ahead: Refrigerate in airtight container for up to 24 hours. Drain before using.)*

NUTRITIONAL INFORMATION, PER SERVING: about 116 cal, 1 g pro, 10 g total fat (1 g sat. fat), 8 g carb (3 g dietary fibre, 3 g sugar), 0 mg chol, 6 mg sodium, 319 mg potassium. % RDI: 1% calcium, 4% iron, 1% vit A, 18% vit C, 16% folate.

TOMATO CURRY TOPPING

HANDS-ON TIME 10 MINUTES

TOTAL TIME 15 MINUTES

MAKES 6 SERVINGS

1 tbsp	vegetable oil
1	onion, chopped
2	cloves garlic, finely chopped
2 tsp	Massaman curry powder or other hot curry powder
1 can	(400 mL) diced tomatoes
2 tsp	each packed brown sugar and tomato paste
pinch	each salt and pepper

In saucepan, heat oil over medium heat; cook onion until beginning to soften, about 5 minutes.

Add garlic and curry powder; cook until fragrant, about 1 minute. Stir in tomatoes, brown sugar, tomato paste, salt and pepper; cook over medium-low heat until reduced to 2 cups, about 5 minutes.

NUTRITIONAL INFORMATION, PER SERVING:
about 50 cal, 1 g pro, 3 g total fat (trace sat. fat), 7 g carb (1 g dietary fibre, 4 g sugar), 0 mg chol, 89 mg sodium, 188 mg potassium. % RDI: 3% calcium, 7% iron, 1% vit A, 18% vit C, 3% folate.

OKONOMIYAKI TOPPING

HANDS-ON TIME 45 MINUTES

TOTAL TIME 45 MINUTES

MAKES 6 SERVINGS

2 tbsp	butter
2	sweet onions, thinly sliced
2¼ tsp	granulated sugar
pinch	each salt and pepper
3 tbsp	ketchup
1 tbsp	Worcestershire sauce
1 tsp	sodium-reduced soy sauce
¼ tsp	Dijon mustard
¼ cup	each bonito flakes and sliced nori

In large skillet, melt butter over medium heat; cook onions, 2 tsp sugar, the salt and pepper, stirring occasionally, until onions are tender and golden, about 40 minutes.

Meanwhile, in small bowl, whisk together ketchup, Worcestershire sauce, soy sauce, remaining sugar and the mustard until sugar is dissolved. *(Make-ahead: Cover and refrigerate for up to 5 days.)* Just before serving, drizzle sauce over onions; sprinkle with bonito flakes and nori.

NUTRITIONAL INFORMATION, PER SERVING:
about 87 cal, 1 g pro, 4 g total fat (2 g sat. fat), 13 g carb (1 g dietary fibre, 9 g sugar), 10 mg chol, 182 mg sodium, 200 mg potassium. % RDI: 3% calcium, 4% iron, 6% vit A, 13% vit C, 12% folate.

TZATZIKI

HANDS-ON TIME 5 MINUTES

TOTAL TIME 5 MINUTES

MAKES 6 SERVINGS

½ cup	shredded cucumber
¼ tsp	salt
½ cup	Greek-style plain yogurt
2 tbsp	frozen chopped spinach, thawed and squeezed dry
2	cloves garlic, minced
2 tbsp	chopped fresh dill
2 tsp	lemon juice
pinch	pepper
⅓ cup	crumbled feta cheese

Mix cucumber with pinch of the salt; let stand for 10 minutes. Squeeze out moisture.

In small bowl, mix together cucumber, yogurt, spinach, garlic, dill, lemon juice, pepper and remaining salt. *(Make-ahead: Cover and refrigerate for up to 2 days.)* Garnish with feta.

NUTRITIONAL INFORMATION, PER SERVING:
about 56 cal, 3 g pro, 4 g total fat (3 g sat. fat), 3 g carb (trace dietary fibre, 2 g sugar), 16 mg chol, 138 mg sodium, 108 mg potassium. % RDI: 9% calcium, 1% iron, 4% vit A, 3% vit C, 4% folate.

135

THAI DEVILLED EGGS

p.139

HANDS-ON TIME	**TOTAL TIME**	**MAKES**
30 MINUTES	30 MINUTES	20 PIECES

10	eggs
½ cup	light mayonnaise
2 tsp	Thai red curry paste
1 tsp	chili garlic sauce
2	green onions, finely chopped
1 tbsp	chopped roasted unsalted peanuts
20	fresh cilantro leaves

In large saucepan, pour enough cold water to come at least 1 inch (2.5 cm) above eggs; bring to boil. Remove from heat; cover and let stand for 10 minutes. Drain and rinse under cold water until cool, about 2 minutes; drain again. *(Make-ahead: Refrigerate for up to 2 days.)*

Peel off shells. Cut eggs in half lengthwise; scoop yolks into bowl. Set whites on platter; cover and set aside.

Using whisk, smash egg yolks until fine. Stir in mayonnaise, curry paste and garlic sauce until smooth; stir in green onions.

Using piping bag fitted with 1-inch (2.5 cm) plain tip (or plastic bag with corner snipped off), pipe yolk mixture into hollows of whites. Sprinkle with peanuts; garnish with cilantro.

NUTRITIONAL INFORMATION, PER PIECE: about 61 cal, 3 g pro, 5 g total fat (1 g sat. fat), 1 g carb (trace dietary fibre, 1 g sugar), 94 mg chol, 73 mg sodium, 40 mg potassium. % RDI: 1% calcium, 3% iron, 5% vit A, 7% folate.

GRILLED GARAM MASALA CORN

p.139

HANDS-ON TIME	**TOTAL TIME**	**MAKES**
20 MINUTES	20 MINUTES	10 SERVINGS

⅔ cup	butter, softened
2	green onions, minced
2	cloves garlic, minced
2 tsp	garam masala
½ tsp	pepper
pinch	each cinnamon and salt
10	corn cobs, husked

In small bowl, stir together butter, green onions, garlic, garam masala, pepper, cinnamon and salt. *(Make-ahead: Cover and refrigerate for up to 5 days. Let soften at room temperature for 15 minutes.)*

Place corn on greased grill over medium-high heat; close lid and grill, turning occasionally, for 7 minutes. Continue grilling, brushing occasionally with butter mixture, until grill-marked and tender, 12 to 15 minutes.

NUTRITIONAL INFORMATION, PER SERVING: about 242 cal, 4 g pro, 14 g total fat (8 g sat. fat), 31 g carb (4 g dietary fibre, 4 g sugar), 33 mg chol, 109 mg sodium, 320 mg potassium. % RDI: 1% calcium, 7% iron, 14% vit A, 13% vit C, 26% folate.

WILD RICE AND LENTIL SALAD

p.132

HANDS-ON TIME	**TOTAL TIME**	**MAKES**
5 MINUTES	1 HOUR	8 TO 10 SERVINGS

In saucepan, bring rice and 4 cups water to boil; reduce heat, cover and simmer until most of the rice is split and tender, about 45 minutes. Remove from heat; let stand, covered, for 5 minutes. Drain.

Meanwhile, in large bowl, whisk together coriander, cumin, turmeric, sugar, cinnamon, salt and pepper; whisk in vinegar and oil. Stir in lentils, red onion, parsley, currants and rice. *(Make-ahead: Refrigerate in airtight container for up to 2 days.)* Stir in almonds.

NUTRITIONAL INFORMATION, PER EACH OF 10 SERVINGS: about 199 cal, 7 g pro, 8 g total fat (1 g sat. fat), 26 g carb (4 g dietary fibre, 5 g sugar), 0 mg chol, 159 mg sodium, 316 mg potassium. % RDI: 3% calcium, 18% iron, 3% vit A, 10% vit C, 44% folate.

1 cup	wild rice, rinsed
1 tsp	each ground coriander and ground cumin
½ tsp	each turmeric and granulated sugar
¼ tsp	each cinnamon, salt and pepper
¼ cup	each vinegar and extra-virgin olive oil
1	can (540 mL) lentils, drained and rinsed
1 cup	diced red onion
½ cup	chopped fresh parsley
¼ cup	currants
½ cup	sliced almonds, toasted

137

MEDITERRANEAN KALE SALAD

opposite

HANDS-ON TIME	TOTAL TIME	MAKES
10 MINUTES	2¼ HOURS	8 TO 10 SERVINGS

3 tbsp	extra-virgin olive oil
2 tbsp	balsamic vinegar
1 tsp	liquid honey
2	cloves garlic, minced
½ tsp	pepper
pinch	salt
10 cups	stemmed kale, thinly sliced
2 cups	cherry tomatoes, halved
1 can	(400 mL) water-packed artichoke hearts, drained, rinsed and thinly sliced
1 cup	shaved Pecorino-Romano cheese or Parmesan cheese (80 g)

In large bowl, whisk together oil, vinegar, honey, garlic, pepper and salt. Add kale, tomatoes and artichoke hearts; toss to coat.

Cover and refrigerate, tossing occasionally, until kale begins to soften slightly, about 2 hours. *(Make-ahead: Refrigerate for up to 24 hours.)*

Toss salad; sprinkle with Pecorino-Romano.

NUTRITIONAL INFORMATION, PER EACH OF 10 SERVINGS: about 125 cal, 6 g pro, 7 g total fat (2 g sat. fat), 12 g carb (3 g dietary fibre, 4 g sugar), 8 mg chol, 213 mg sodium, 476 mg potassium. % RDI: 18% calcium, 12% iron, 64% vit A, 145% vit C, 17% folate.

CHAI MANGO LEMONADE

opposite

HANDS-ON TIME	TOTAL TIME	MAKES
10 MINUTES	20 MINUTES	10 SERVINGS, OR 12 CUPS

6	bags chai tea
1 cup	granulated sugar
2 cups	mango nectar
2 cups	freshly squeezed lemon juice (6 to 8 lemons)
2 cups	ice cubes

In small saucepan, bring 1 cup water to boil; add tea bags. Remove from heat; let stand for 10 minutes. Gently press bags to release excess tea; discard bags. Stir in sugar and bring to boil; cook until sugar is dissolved, about 1 minute. Let cool.

In pitcher, stir together chai syrup, mango nectar, lemon juice, ice and 4 cups water. *(Make-ahead: Cover and refrigerate for up to 7 days.)*

NUTRITIONAL INFORMATION, PER SERVING: about 124 cal, 1 g pro, trace total fat (trace sat. fat), 32 g carb (1 g dietary fibre, 28 g sugar), 0 mg chol, 12 mg sodium, 91 mg potassium. % RDI: 1% calcium, 1% iron, 6% vit A, 43% vit C, 4% folate.

CLOCKWISE, FROM TOP: THAI DEVILLED EGGS; MEDITERRANEAN KALE SALAD;
CHAI MANGO LEMONADE; AND GRILLED GARAM MASALA CORN

MARKET DAY

Get 'em while they're fresh! Sweet and fragrant just-picked fruits, juicy berries and heirloom vegetable varieties you've never tried before—it's farmers' market season, when shopping for dinner is as much fun as eating it.

MENU FOR 4 TO 6

PORTUGESE SUMMER DAISY COCKTAIL **p.142**

SWISS CHARD, STRAWBERRY AND FETA SALAD
WITH HONEY VINAIGRETTE **p.142**

ZA'ATAR LAMB FLATBREAD
WITH PEA SHOOTS **p.143**

CORN AND ZUCCHINI SAUTÉ **p.144**

GRILLED VEGETABLES WITH CILANTRO CHIMICHURRI **p.145**

THE ULTIMATE PEACH PIE **p.147**

PORTUGUESE SUMMER DAISY COCKTAIL

HANDS-ON TIME	**TOTAL TIME**	**MAKES**	
5 MINUTES	5 MINUTES	1 SERVING	

1 oz	white Port (about 2 tbsp)
½ oz	orange-flavoured liqueur (about 1 tbsp)
4 oz	chilled sparkling white wine (about ½ cup)
	lemon twist

Pour Port and liqueur into chilled champagne flute; top with sparkling wine. Garnish with lemon twist.

NUTRITIONAL INFORMATION, PER SERVING: about 188 cal, trace pro, trace total fat (0 g sat. fat), 12 g carb (0 g dietary fibre, 10 g sugar), 0 mg chol, 9 mg sodium, 122 mg potassium. % RDI: 1% calcium, 4% iron.

SWISS CHARD, STRAWBERRY AND FETA SALAD
WITH HONEY VINAIGRETTE

HANDS-ON TIME	**TOTAL TIME**	**MAKES**	
10 MINUTES	10 MINUTES	4 SERVINGS	

3 tbsp	extra-virgin olive oil
2 tbsp	lemon juice
1 tsp	liquid honey
¼ tsp	each salt and pepper
6 cups	thinly sliced stemmed Swiss chard (about 1 small bunch)
1 cup	strawberries, hulled and cut in 8 wedges
½ cup	crumbled feta cheese
2 tbsp	pepitas, toasted

In large bowl, whisk together oil, lemon juice, honey, salt and pepper. Add Swiss chard, strawberries, feta and pepitas; toss to coat.

NUTRITIONAL INFORMATION, PER SERVING: about 187 cal, 5 g pro, 16 g total fat (5 g sat. fat), 7 g carb (2 g dietary fibre, 4 g sugar), 17 mg chol, 418 mg sodium, 224 mg potassium. % RDI: 11% calcium, 11% iron, 12% vit A, 53% vit C, 10% folate.

ZA'ATAR LAMB FLATBREAD
WITH PEA SHOOTS

p.140

HANDS-ON TIME	TOTAL TIME	MAKES
20 MINUTES	30 MINUTES	4 SERVINGS

FLATBREAD In nonstick skillet, heat ½ tsp of the oil over medium-high heat; cook lamb, breaking up with spoon, until browned, about 4 minutes. Stir in 4 tsp of the za'atar, the cumin, salt and pepper. Using slotted spoon, transfer lamb mixture to bowl. Set aside.

On lightly floured work surface, roll out or press dough into 16- x 8-inch (20 x 40 cm) oval. Transfer to greased large rimless baking sheet.

In small bowl, mix remaining oil with remaining za'atar; brush over top of dough. In separate small bowl, stir together ricotta, lemon zest and lemon juice; dollop over dough, spreading slightly with back of spoon. Sprinkle with lamb mixture. Bake on bottom rack of 500°F (260°C) oven until edge is beginning to brown, about 8 minutes.

Cut kernels from corn cob. Sprinkle over flatbread; bake on bottom rack of 500°F (260°C) oven until bottom is crisp and golden, about 10 minutes. Sprinkle with hot pepper flakes.

PEA SHOOT TOPPING Stir together pea shoots, lemon juice, oil and salt; sprinkle over flatbread.

NUTRITIONAL INFORMATION, PER SERVING: about 537 cal, 28 g pro, 21 g total fat (9 g sat. fat), 57 g carb (4 g dietary fibre, 5 g sugar), 56 mg chol, 684 mg sodium, 307 mg potassium. % RDI: 14% calcium, 36% iron, 21% vit A, 20% vit C, 14% folate.

FLATBREAD

1 tbsp	olive oil
250 g	ground lamb
2 tbsp	za'atar
1 tsp	ground cumin
¼ tsp	each salt and pepper
375 g	prepared pizza dough
1 cup	extra-smooth ricotta cheese
1 tsp	grated lemon zest
2 tbsp	lemon juice
1	cob corn, husked
¼ tsp	hot pepper flakes

PEA SHOOT TOPPING

2 cups	pea shoots, halved
1 tsp	lemon juice
1 tsp	olive oil
pinch	salt

143

TIP FROM THE TEST KITCHEN

Za'atar is a Middle Eastern spice blend that usually includes dried thyme, oregano or marjoram (different parts of the region use different herbs), as well as sesame seeds, sumac and salt. It's available in many grocery stores.

CORN AND ZUCCHINI SAUTÉ

HANDS-ON TIME
10 MINUTES

TOTAL TIME
10 MINUTES

MAKES
4 SERVINGS

1 tbsp	vegetable oil
3	green onions, sliced
1	zucchini, halved lengthwise and sliced
½ tsp	dried oregano
¼ tsp	each salt and pepper
2 cups	fresh or frozen corn kernels

144

In large skillet, heat oil over medium heat; cook green onions, stirring occasionally, until softened, about 3 minutes.

Add zucchini, oregano, salt and pepper. Cook, stirring occasionally, until zucchini is tender-crisp, about 3 minutes. Stir in corn; cook, stirring often, until hot, about 3 minutes.

NUTRITIONAL INFORMATION, PER SERVING: about 104 cal, 3 g pro, 4 g total fat (0 g sat. fat), 16 g carb (2 g dietary fibre), 0 mg chol, 150 mg sodium. % RDI: 2% calcium, 5% iron, 3% vit A, 10% vit C, 16% folate.

GRILLED VEGETABLES
WITH CILANTRO CHIMICHURRI

HANDS-ON TIME
30 MINUTES

TOTAL TIME
45 MINUTES

MAKES
4 SERVINGS

CILANTRO CHIMICHURRI In blender, purée together cilantro, oil, parsley, lemon zest, lemon juice, garlic, salt and pepper, scraping down side occasionally, until smooth. *(Make-ahead: Refrigerate in airtight container for up to 24 hours.)*

GRILLED VEGETABLES In large saucepan of boiling salted water, cook potatoes just until fork-tender, 7 to 10 minutes. Drain and transfer to paper towel–lined plate; let cool.

Trim tops and bottom of fennel bulb, leaving root ends intact. Halve bulb and remove core; cut each half into 4 wedges. Core peppers. Halve leeks lengthwise, leaving root ends intact; rinse well under running water, separating layers to remove grit. Drain well. *(Make-ahead: Refrigerate potatoes, fennel, peppers and leeks in separate airtight containers for up to 24 hours.)*

Brush potatoes, fennel, peppers, leeks and tomatoes with 3 tbsp of the chimichurri. Arrange vegetables on greased grill over medium-high heat, placing tomatoes along outer edge; close lid and grill until tomatoes begin to shrivel, about 10 minutes. Transfer tomatoes to platter.

Turn remaining vegetables; grill until tender and lightly charred, about 5 minutes. Transfer to platter; drizzle with remaining chimichurri. Serve hot or let cool to room temperature.

NUTRITIONAL INFORMATION, PER SERVING: about 446 cal, 8 g pro, 19 g total fat (3 g sat. fat), 67 g carb (9 g dietary fibre, 7 g sugar), 0 mg chol, 889 mg sodium, 1,476 mg potassium. % RDI: 10% calcium, 32% iron, 9% vit A, 187% vit C, 39% folate.

CILANTRO CHIMICHURRI

⅓ cup	packed fresh cilantro
⅓ cup	extra-virgin olive oil
3 tbsp	packed fresh parsley
1½ tsp	grated lemon zest
2 tbsp	lemon juice
2	cloves garlic
½ tsp	salt
¼ tsp	pepper

GRILLED VEGETABLES

3	large yellow-fleshed potatoes, scrubbed and cut in ½-inch (1 cm) thick slices
1	bulb fennel
340 g	mini sweet peppers (about 12)
4	leeks (white and light green parts only)
8	yellow and/or red cherry tomatoes on the vine

145

TIP FROM THE TEST KITCHEN

To remove the seeds and cores from mini sweet peppers, insert a paring knife into top of each pepper, cut a circle around stem and pull stem out with seeds and core attached.

THE ULTIMATE PEACH PIE

THE ULTIMATE PEACH PIE

opposite

HANDS-ON TIME
35 MINUTES

TOTAL TIME
2½ HOURS

MAKES
8 SERVINGS

PASTRY In large bowl, whisk together flour, cornmeal and salt. Using pastry blender or 2 knives, cut in butter and lard until mixture resembles fine crumbs.

In separate bowl, whisk ¼ cup ice water with sour cream; drizzle over flour mixture, stirring briskly with fork to form ragged dough and adding more ice water, 1 tbsp at a time, until dough comes together. Divide pastry in half; press into discs. Wrap each in plastic wrap; refrigerate until chilled, about 30 minutes. *(Make-ahead: Refrigerate for up to 3 days.)*

FILLING In bowl, toss together peaches, granulated sugar, flour, lemon juice and vanilla; set aside.

ASSEMBLY On lightly floured work surface, roll out 1 of the pastry discs to generous ⅛-inch (3 mm) thickness; fit pastry into 9-inch (23 cm) pie plate. Trim to fit, leaving ¾-inch (2 cm) overhang; flute rim. Spoon in peach mixture.

Roll out remaining pastry disc to scant ⅛-inch (3 mm) thickness. Using 2½-inch (6 cm) round pastry cutter, cut out about 24 circles, rerolling scraps as necessary. Cover pie with circles, overlapping slightly, using about 15 for outer ring, about 8 for inner ring and 1 in centre. Whisk egg yolk with 2 tsp water; brush over circles and rim. Sprinkle with coarse sugar (if using). Bake on rimmed baking sheet on bottom rack of 425°F (220°C) oven for 20 minutes.

Reduce heat to 350°F (180°C); bake until bottom is golden brown, peaches are tender and juice is thick and bubbly, 60 to 70 minutes. Let cool on rack.

NUTRITIONAL INFORMATION, PER SERVING: about 385 cal, 5 g pro, 19 g total fat (9 g sat. fat), 52 g carb (3 g dietary fibre, 30 g sugar), 43 mg chol, 158 mg sodium, 285 mg potassium. % RDI: 2% calcium, 11% iron, 11% vit A, 10% vit C, 20% folate.

147

PASTRY

2 cups	all-purpose flour
3 tbsp	cornmeal
½ tsp	salt
½ cup	cold butter, cubed
½ cup	cold lard, cubed
¼ cup	ice water (approx)
3 tbsp	sour cream

FILLING

6 cups	sliced pitted peeled firm ripe peaches
¾ cup	granulated sugar
¼ cup	all-purpose flour
1 tbsp	lemon juice
1 tsp	vanilla
1	egg yolk
2 tsp	coarse sugar (optional)

TIP FROM THE TEST KITCHEN

Make this pie year-round: Substitute 8 cups frozen sliced peaches (thawed, drained and patted dry) for the fresh fruit; increase the flour in the filling to ⅓ cup.

SEASONAL SUNDAY SUPPER

The song does not lie: Summer living is easy.
Time to slow down the pace—because the other truth
about summer in Canada is that it doesn't last long
enough. Make the most of the season with your family
and a light, fresh Sunday meal of quick-prep dishes.

149

MENU FOR 4

GRILLED CORN AND AVOCADO SALAD **p.150**

PISTACHIO-CRUSTED SALMON
WITH GARLIC RAPINI **p.151**

QUINOA TABBOULEH **p.151**

RHUBARB GINGER FOOL **p.153**

GRILLED CORN AND AVOCADO SALAD

HANDS-ON TIME
30 MINUTES

TOTAL TIME
30 MINUTES

MAKES
4 SERVINGS

DRESSING

2 tbsp	lemon juice
1 tbsp	vegetable oil
1 tbsp	finely chopped fresh mint (or ½ tsp dried mint)
½ tsp	chipotle hot pepper sauce
pinch	each salt, pepper and granulated sugar

SALAD

4	corn cobs, husked
1 tbsp	vegetable oil
1	rib celery, chopped
half	sweet red pepper, diced
¼ cup	diced red onion
half	avocado, pitted, peeled and diced

DRESSING In small bowl, whisk together lemon juice, oil, mint, hot pepper sauce, salt, pepper and sugar.

SALAD Brush corn with oil. Place on greased grill over medium-high heat; close lid and grill, turning frequently, until lightly grill-marked, 15 to 20 minutes. Let cool; slice kernels off cob.

Meanwhile, in large bowl, combine celery, red pepper and red onion; add dressing and toss to coat. *(Make-ahead: Refrigerate corn and celery mixture in separate airtight containers for up to 24 hours.)*

Add corn and avocado; toss gently to coat.

NUTRITIONAL INFORMATION, PER SERVING: about 212 cal, 4 g pro, 10 g total fat (1 g sat. fat), 33 g carb (5 g dietary fibre), 0 mg chol, 88 mg sodium. % RDI: 1% calcium, 7% iron, 11% vit A, 55% vit C, 30% folate.

PISTACHIO-CRUSTED SALMON
WITH GARLIC RAPINI

HANDS-ON TIME	**TOTAL TIME**	**MAKES**
15 MINUTES	20 MINUTES	4 SERVINGS

Place salmon on parchment paper–lined rimmed baking sheet; sprinkle with salt and pepper. Brush tops with mustard; sprinkle with pistachios, pressing firmly to adhere. Bake in 425°F (220°C) oven until fish flakes easily when tested with fork, 12 to 15 minutes.

Meanwhile, in large saucepan of boiling salted water, cook rapini until tender-crisp, about 2 minutes; drain. Transfer to bowl of ice water to chill; drain well.

In large skillet, heat oil over medium-high heat; sauté garlic until fragrant, about 1 minute. Add rapini; sauté until heated through, about 3 minutes. Serve with salmon.

NUTRITIONAL INFORMATION, PER SERVING: about 382 cal, 35 g pro, 24 g total fat (4 g sat. fat), 6 g carb (3 g dietary fibre, 1 g sugar), 84 mg chol, 390 mg sodium, 922 mg potassium. % RDI: 13% calcium, 15% iron, 45% vit A, 68% vit C, 53% folate.

4	skinless salmon fillets (each about 170 g)
pinch	each salt and pepper
2 tsp	Dijon mustard
¼ cup	shelled pistachios, toasted and coarsely ground
1	bunch rapini, trimmed
1 tbsp	olive oil
3	cloves garlic, minced

151

QUINOA TABBOULEH

HANDS-ON TIME	**TOTAL TIME**	**MAKES**
15 MINUTES	1 HOUR	6 SERVINGS

In saucepan, bring 1½ cups water to boil; add quinoa and return to boil. Reduce heat, cover and simmer until no liquid remains, about 15 minutes. Fluff with fork; transfer to large bowl. Let cool.

Add parsley, cucumber, green onions, mint and tomato.

Whisk together lemon juice, oil, salt and pepper; pour over quinoa mixture and toss to coat. Serve at room temperature, or cover and refrigerate for 1 hour.

NUTRITIONAL INFORMATION, PER SERVING: about 135 cal, 4 g pro, 6 g total fat (1 g sat. fat), 18 g carb (3 g dietary fibre, 1 g sugar), 0 mg chol, 112 mg sodium, 335 mg potassium. % RDI: 4% calcium, 24% iron, 13% vit A, 33% vit C, 18% folate.

¾ cup	quinoa, rinsed
1 cup	each chopped fresh parsley and chopped English cucumber
½ cup	chopped green onions
¼ cup	chopped fresh mint
1	tomato, seeded and chopped
3 tbsp	lemon juice
2 tbsp	extra-virgin olive oil
¼ tsp	each salt and pepper

RHUBARB GINGER FOOL

RHUBARB GINGER FOOL

opposite

HANDS-ON TIME	**TOTAL TIME**	**MAKES**
30 MINUTES	3½ HOURS	4 SERVINGS

In saucepan, cook rhubarb, all but 2 tbsp of the sugar and the marmalade over medium heat, stirring often, until rhubarb is broken down and mixture is thick and glossy, 15 to 20 minutes. Scrape into bowl; refrigerate until chilled, about 3 hours. *(Make-ahead: Cover and refrigerate for up to 24 hours.)*

In separate bowl, whip cream, remaining sugar and the vanilla until stiff peaks form.

Divide one-third of the rhubarb mixture among 4 small glasses. Top with half of the whipped cream, dividing evenly. Spoon another third of the rhubarb mixture over top. Repeat layers once with remaining whipped cream and rhubarb mixture. Using knife, lightly swirl layers. Sprinkle with cookie crumbs.

NUTRITIONAL INFORMATION, PER SERVING: about 395 cal, 3 g pro, 22 g total fat (13 g sat. fat), 50 g carb (2 g dietary fibre, 40 g sugar), 76 mg chol, 76 mg sodium, 392 mg potassium. % RDI: 13% calcium, 5% iron, 24% vit A, 17% vit C, 8% folate.

4 cups	sliced fresh rhubarb (½-inch/1 cm lengths)
⅔ cup	granulated sugar
4 tsp	ginger marmalade
1 cup	whipping cream (35%)
½ tsp	vanilla
4	gingersnap cookies, crumbled (about ½ cup total)

153

TIP FROM THE TEST KITCHEN

The cooked rhubarb mixture is also delicious
served warm with a scoop of ice cream.
Make a double batch and save
the extra for another day.

AUTUMN

SEAFOOD SUPPER **p.156**

MAKE-AHEAD THANKSGIVING **p.164**

THANKSGIVING FEAST **p.176**

GAME NIGHT **p.186**

HARVEST TABLE **p.192**

SEASONAL SUNDAY SUPPER **p.200**

SEAFOOD SUPPER

Lobster, scallops, mussels, and oysters—
this sophisticated supper for eight showcases
the best of Canada's world-renowned seafood.
Better yet, the menu features dishes that can
be made ahead of time, allowing you to
sit back and enjoy the catch.

157

MENU FOR 8

SURF AND TURF CAESAR p.158

OYSTERS ON THE HALF SHELL p.158

CREAMED CORN POTATOES p.161

CHEDDAR CHIVE BISCUITS p.161

WINE AND BACON STEAMED MUSSELS p.162

BOILED FRESH LOBSTERS
WITH SEASONED BUTTERS p.163

SURF AND TURF CAESAR

opposite

HANDS-ON TIME	**TOTAL TIME**	**MAKES**
10 MINUTES	15 MINUTES	8 SERVINGS

4	strips sodium-reduced bacon
8	large sea scallops (about 165 g total)
5 cups	tomato clam cocktail (such as Clamato)
1 cup	vodka
1 tbsp	Worcestershire sauce
1 tbsp	lime juice
2 tsp	prepared horseradish
1 tsp	hot pepper sauce
¼ tsp	pepper
	ice cubes

Arrange bacon on parchment paper–lined baking sheet; broil until some of the fat is rendered and edges begin to crisp but strips are still flexible, about 4 minutes. Transfer to paper towel–lined plate to drain.

Cut bacon in half lengthwise; wrap 1 piece around each scallop, securing ends with soaked toothpick. Arrange on parchment paper–lined baking sheet; broil, until scallops are opaque, 5 to 6 minutes. If toothpicks are charred, replace with stir sticks or long cocktail skewers.

In pitcher, stir together tomato cocktail, vodka, Worcestershire sauce, lime juice, horseradish, hot pepper sauce and pepper. *(Make-ahead: Cover and refrigerate for up to 1 day.)*

Fill old-fashioned glasses with ice; top with tomato cocktail mixture. Garnish with bacon-wrapped scallops.

NUTRITIONAL INFORMATION, PER SERVING: about 172 cal, 6 g pro, 2 g total fat (1 g sat. fat), 18 g carb (trace dietary fibre, 5 g sugar), 15 mg chol, 648 mg sodium, 279 mg potassium. % RDI: 4% calcium, 11% iron, 4% vit A, 12% vit C, 12% folate.

OYSTERS ON THE HALF SHELL

opposite

HANDS-ON TIME	**TOTAL TIME**	**MAKES**
15 MINUTES	15 MINUTES	8 SERVINGS

16	raw oysters
	hot pepper sauce
	lemon wedges
	grated fresh horseradish

Using stiff brush, scrub oysters under cold running water. Using thick cloth or glove, hold 1 oyster with curved part of shell down; insert oyster knife into small opening near hinge. Twist knife to break hinge; wipe blade clean. Reinsert knife and slide along underside of top shell to sever muscle; discard top shell, removing any grit or broken shell on oyster.

Keeping oyster level to retain juices, slide knife under oyster to sever bottom muscle. Repeat with remaining oysters, wiping knife clean between each.

Serve with hot pepper sauce, lemon wedges and horseradish.

NUTRITIONAL INFORMATION, PER SERVING: about 19 cal, 2 g pro, 1 g total fat (trace sat. fat), 1 g carb (0 g dietary fibre, 0 g sugar), 15 mg chol, 59 mg sodium, 44 mg potassium. % RDI: 1% calcium, 14% iron, 1% vit A, 2% vit C, 1% folate.

158

CLOCKWISE, FROM TOP LEFT: SURF AND TURF CAESAR;
WINE AND BACON STEAMED MUSSELS; AND OYSTERS ON THE HALF SHELL

CREAMED CORN POTATOES AND CHEDDAR CHIVE BISCUITS

CREAMED CORN POTATOES

opposite

HANDS-ON TIME	**TOTAL TIME**	**MAKES**
20 MINUTES	25 MINUTES	8 SERVINGS

In large nonstick or cast-iron skillet, melt butter over medium heat; cook potatoes, garlic and bay leaf, stirring often, until potatoes begin to brown, about 12 minutes.

Stir in corn, green onions, paprika, salt and pepper; cook, stirring often, for 7 minutes for frozen corn, 9 minutes for fresh.

Stir in cream; simmer until thickened, about 3 minutes. Discard bay leaf. *(Make-ahead: Cover and keep warm for up to 1 hour.)*

NUTRITIONAL INFORMATION, PER SERVING: about 201 cal, 5 g pro, 7 g total fat (4 g sat. fat), 34 g carb (3 g dietary fibre, 3 g sugar), 17 mg chol, 112 mg sodium, 748 mg potassium. % RDI: 4% calcium, 9% iron, 8% vit A, 30% vit C, 18% folate.

2 tbsp	butter
900 g	yellow-fleshed potatoes, peeled and cut in ½-inch (1 cm) cubes
1	clove garlic, minced
1	bay leaf
4 cups	frozen or fresh corn kernels
3	green onions, sliced
½ tsp	smoked paprika
¼ tsp	each salt and pepper
1 cup	10% cream

161

CHEDDAR CHIVE BISCUITS

opposite

HANDS-ON TIME	**TOTAL TIME**	**MAKES**
10 MINUTES	25 MINUTES	12 BISCUITS

In bowl, whisk together flour, baking powder, sugar, baking soda and salt. Using pastry blender or 2 knives, cut in butter until mixture resembles coarse crumbs with a few larger pieces. Using fork, stir in Cheddar and chives; stir in buttermilk to form soft dough.

On lightly floured work surface, gently knead dough 10 times; pat into ¾-inch (2 cm) thick round. Using floured 2½-inch (6 cm) round cutter, cut out 12 rounds, pressing scraps together as necessary.

Arrange biscuits on parchment paper–lined baking sheet. Whisk egg yolk with 2 tsp water; brush over tops of biscuits. Bake in 425°F (220°C) oven until golden, 12 to 14 minutes. *(Make-ahead: Store in airtight container for up to 4 hours.)*

NUTRITIONAL INFORMATION, PER BISCUIT: about 207 cal, 6 g pro, 12 g total fat (7 g sat. fat), 19 g carb (1 g dietary fibre, 2 g sugar), 42 mg chol, 346 mg sodium, 71 mg potassium. % RDI: 12% calcium, 9% iron, 10% vit A, 18% folate.

2¼ cups	all-purpose flour
2½ tsp	baking powder
2 tsp	granulated sugar
½ tsp	each baking soda and salt
½ cup	cold butter, cubed
1 cup	shredded extra-old Cheddar cheese
3 tbsp	finely chopped fresh chives
1 cup	buttermilk
1	egg yolk

WINE AND BACON STEAMED MUSSELS

p.159

HANDS-ON TIME	**TOTAL TIME**	**MAKES**
20 MINUTES	25 MINUTES	8 SERVINGS

2 kg	mussels
8	strips bacon, diced
1	large onion, diced
4	cloves garlic, minced
2½ cups	dry white wine
2	bay leaves
2 tbsp	tomato paste
¼ tsp	pepper
2 tbsp	chopped fresh parsley

Scrub mussels; remove any beards. Discard any mussels that do not close when tapped. Set aside. *(Make-ahead: Refrigerate for up to 4 hours.)*

In Dutch oven or large heavy-bottomed saucepan, cook bacon over medium heat, stirring occasionally, until crisp, about 5 minutes. Using slotted spoon, transfer to paper towel–lined plate to drain. Drain all but 1 tbsp fat from pan; cook onion, stirring occasionally, until softened, about 5 minutes. Add garlic; cook, stirring, until fragrant, about 1 minute.

Add wine and bay leaves; bring to simmer. Cook until reduced by half, about 5 minutes. Stir in tomato paste and pepper; return to boil.

Add mussels; cover with tight-fitting lid and steam until mussels open, about 5 minutes. Remove from heat; discard bay leaves and any mussels that do not open. Sprinkle with bacon and parsley.

NUTRITIONAL INFORMATION, PER SERVING: about 151 cal, 12 g pro, 6 g total fat (2 g sat. fat), 7 g carb (1 g dietary fibre, 2 g sugar), 29 mg chol, 297 mg sodium, 277 mg potassium. % RDI: 3% calcium, 22% iron, 5% vit A, 13% vit C, 15% folate.

BOILED FRESH LOBSTERS
WITH SEASONED BUTTERS

p.156

HANDS-ON TIME
15 MINUTES

TOTAL TIME
25 MINUTES

MAKES
8 SERVINGS

Fill stockpot with enough salted water to completely cover lobsters; bring to full boil over high heat. Plunge each lobster headfirst into water; cover and start timer when water returns to boil.

Reduce heat and simmer until lobsters are bright red and small legs easily come away when twisted and pulled, 8 to 10 minutes. Let cool enough to handle.

Using large chef's knife, cut each lobster in half lengthwise; remove and discard vein (if any) along top of tail. Using poultry shears, cut notch halfway up edge of large side of each claw. *(Make-ahead: Cover and keep warm for up to 1 hour.)*

4	live lobsters (each 565 g to 675 g)

NUTRITIONAL INFORMATION, PER SERVING: about 71 cal, 15 g pro, trace total fat (trace sat. fat), 1 g carb (0 g dietary fibre, 0 g sugar), 52 mg chol, 277 mg sodium, 257 mg potassium. % RDI: 4% calcium, 2% iron, 2% vit A, 3% folate.

163

LEMONY DILL BUTTER
Mash together ⅓ cup butter, softened, with 2 tbsp chopped fresh dill and 1 tsp grated lemon zest. *(Make-ahead: Wrap in plastic wrap and refrigerate for up to 3 days, or overwrap with foil and freeze for up to 2 months.)* Before serving, gently melt butter mixture.

MAKES ABOUT ⅓ CUP

SPICY GARLIC BUTTER
In small skillet, melt 2 tsp butter over medium heat. Add 3 cloves garlic, minced; and ½ tsp smoked paprika. Cook, stirring, until garlic is softened, about 2 minutes. Scrape into bowl; let cool to room temperature, about 5 minutes. Mash in ⅓ cup butter, softened, and 1 tsp hot pepper sauce. *(Make-ahead: Wrap in plastic wrap and refrigerate for up to 3 days, or overwrap with foil and freeze for up to 2 months.)* Before serving, gently melt butter mixture.

MAKES ABOUT ⅓ CUP

CURRIED GINGER BUTTER
In small skillet, melt 2 tsp butter over medium heat. Add 2 tbsp minced green onion, 1 tsp minced peeled fresh ginger and ½ tsp curry powder; cook, stirring, until ginger is softened, about 3 minutes. Scrape into bowl; let cool to room temperature, about 5 minutes. Mash in ⅓ cup butter, softened. *(Make-ahead: Wrap in plastic wrap and refrigerate for up to 3 days, or overwrap with foil and freeze for up to 2 months.)* Before serving, gently melt butter mixture.

MAKES ABOUT ⅓ CUP

MAKE-AHEAD THANKSGIVING

When life gets frantic, traditions are important. For many families, this holiday's familiar flavours—turkey and gravy, cranberry and squash—are touchstones. Preparing the meal doesn't have to be difficult or stressful; with our make-ahead Thanksgiving menu, you'll spend more time with your family and less time cooking.

165

MENU FOR 8 TO 10

**HERB-RUBBED ROAST TURKEY
WITH FRESH SAGE GRAVY** p.166

SMOOTH AND CREAMY MASHED POTATOES p.167

SAUSAGE, APPLE AND SAGE STUFFING p.168

SWISS CHARD WITH FRIZZLED ONIONS p.171

**ROASTED BUTTERNUT SQUASH
AND CHEDDAR GRATIN** p.172

RED WINE CRANBERRY JELLY p.173

MAPLE POTS DE CRÈME WITH WARM PEARS p.174

HERB-RUBBED ROAST TURKEY
WITH FRESH SAGE GRAVY

p.164

HANDS-ON TIME	TOTAL TIME	MAKES
30 MINUTES	4 HOURS	10 TO 12 SERVINGS

HERB-RUBBED ROAST TURKEY

5 tsp	olive oil
2 tsp	each sweet paprika, dried rosemary, dried thyme and dried sage
1 tsp	dried savory
½ tsp	each salt and pepper
1	turkey (about 5 kg)

FRESH SAGE GRAVY

½ cup	dry white wine
2 cups	sodium-reduced chicken broth
⅓ cup	all-purpose flour
2 tbsp	thinly sliced fresh sage

166

HERB-RUBBED ROAST TURKEY Whisk together oil, paprika, rosemary, thyme, sage, savory, salt and pepper. *(Make-ahead: Cover and store at room temperature for up to 48 hours.)*

Remove giblets and neck from turkey; place turkey neck in roasting pan. Twist wings and tuck behind back. Place turkey, breast side up, on rack in roasting pan; rub all over with oil mixture.

Roast in 325°F (160°C) oven, basting every 30 minutes and covering loosely with foil if skin browns too quickly, until instant-read thermometer inserted in thickest part of breast reads 170°F (77°C), about 3 hours.

Wearing oven mitts and using tongs, gently tip turkey to pour juices from cavity into roasting pan; reserve juices for gravy. Discard neck. Transfer turkey to platter; cover loosely with foil. Let stand for 45 minutes before carving.

FRESH SAGE GRAVY While turkey is resting, tilt roasting pan so juices collect at end. Skim fat from surface; discard. Pour juices into heatproof bowl. Set aside.

Add wine to roasting pan; bring to boil over medium-high heat. Cook, stirring and scraping up any browned bits from bottom of pan, for 1 minute.

In bowl, whisk broth with flour until smooth; whisk into roasting pan along with reserved turkey juices; bring to boil. Reduce heat and simmer, whisking often, until thickened, 5 to 8 minutes. Strain through fine-mesh sieve into heatproof bowl; stir in sage. Serve with turkey.

NUTRITIONAL INFORMATION, PER EACH OF 12 SERVINGS: about 332 cal, 57 g pro, 8 g total fat (2 g sat. fat), 3 g carb (1 g dietary fibre, trace sugar), 188 mg chol, 339 mg sodium, 835 mg potassium. % RDI: 3% calcium, 13% iron, 3% vit A, 2% vit C, 10% folate.

SMOOTH AND CREAMY MASHED POTATOES

p.169

HANDS-ON TIME
15 MINUTES

TOTAL TIME
30 MINUTES

MAKES
8 TO 10 SERVINGS

In large saucepan of boiling salted water, cook potatoes until fork-tender, about 15 minutes; drain well. Press potatoes through potato ricer. *(Make-ahead: Spread onto parchment paper–lined rimmed baking sheet; let cool. Cover and refrigerate for up to 24 hours. Continue with recipe, adding 8 minutes to cook time.)*

In large saucepan, heat together cream, butter, salt and pepper over medium heat until butter is melted. Add potatoes; cook, stirring frequently, until smooth and hot, about 4 minutes.

NUTRITIONAL INFORMATION, PER EACH OF 10 SERVINGS: about 226 cal, 5 g pro, 8 g total fat (5 g sat. fat), 36 g carb (2 g dietary fibre, 1 g sugar), 22 mg chol, 730 mg sodium, 751 mg potassium. % RDI: 5% calcium, 11% iron, 6% vit A, 47% vit C, 11% folate.

2.25 kg	russet potatoes, peeled and cut in chunks
1¼ cups	10% cream
¼ cup	butter
1 tsp	salt
¼ tsp	pepper

167

SAUSAGE, APPLE AND SAGE STUFFING

opposite

HANDS-ON TIME	TOTAL TIME	MAKES
25 MINUTES	1 HOUR	8 TO 10 SERVINGS

12 cups	cubed crusty French or Italian bread (about 1 loaf)
¼ cup	butter
1	pkg (500 g) fresh pork sausage, casings removed
2 cups	diced leeks (white and light green parts only)
1 cup	diced celery
2	sweet cooking apples (such as Gala), peeled, cored and diced
½ tsp	pepper
¼ tsp	salt
⅓ cup	chopped fresh parsley
3 tbsp	chopped fresh sage
1½ cups	sodium-reduced chicken broth
2	eggs

Arrange bread on rimmed baking sheet; toast in 350°F (180°C) oven until light golden, 10 to 12 minutes. Transfer to large bowl.

While bread is toasting, in large skillet, melt half of the butter over medium-high heat; cook sausage, breaking up with spoon, until browned, about 8 minutes. Using slotted spoon, remove to bowl with bread.

In same skillet, melt remaining butter over medium heat; cook leeks and celery, stirring occasionally, until beginning to soften, about 6 minutes. Add apples, pepper and salt; cook, stirring, until tender-crisp, about 4 minutes. Stir into bread mixture. Add parsley and sage.

In separate bowl, whisk broth with eggs; drizzle over bread mixture. Toss to coat.

Scrape into greased 13- × 9-inch (3 L) baking dish; cover with foil. *(Make-ahead: Refrigerate for up to 24 hours. Let stand at room temperature for 1 hour before continuing with recipe.)* Bake in 425°F (220°C) oven for 20 minutes; uncover and bake until top is browned, 10 to 15 minutes.

NUTRITIONAL INFORMATION, PER EACH OF 10 SERVINGS: about 345 cal, 14 g pro, 20 g total fat (8 g sat. fat), 28 g carb (2 g dietary fibre, 6 g sugar), 87 mg chol, 757 mg sodium, 293 mg potassium. % RDI: 5% calcium, 19% iron, 12% vit A, 10% vit C, 30% folate.

SMOOTH AND CREAMY MASHED POTATOES AND SAUSAGE, APPLE AND SAGE STUFFING

SWISS CHARD WITH FRIZZLED ONIONS AND ROASTED BUTTERNUT SQUASH AND CHEDDAR GRATIN

SWISS CHARD
WITH FRIZZLED ONIONS

opposite

HANDS-ON TIME
35 MINUTES

TOTAL TIME
35 MINUTES

MAKES
8 TO 10 SERVINGS

Cut Swiss chard stems into ½-inch (1 cm) lengths; coarsely chop Swiss chard leaves. Set aside.

In large bowl, sprinkle onion with cornstarch and pinch of the salt; toss to coat. Shake off any excess.

In cast-iron or heavy-bottomed skillet, pour enough vegetable oil to come ¼ inch (5 mm) up side; heat over medium heat. Working in batches, cook onions, stirring occasionally, until crisp and golden, 2 to 3 minutes. Using slotted spoon, remove to paper towel–lined plate to drain. *(Make-ahead: Store at room temperature for up to 2 hours.)*

In large nonstick skillet, heat olive oil over medium heat; cook garlic and hot pepper flakes, stirring often, until fragrant and edges of garlic are golden, about 2 minutes. Add Swiss chard stems, remaining salt and the pepper; cook, stirring occasionally, until tender-crisp, 8 to 10 minutes. Add half of the Swiss chard leaves; cook, stirring, until beginning to wilt, about 1 minute. Add remaining Swiss chard leaves; cook, stirring, until wilted, about 4 minutes.

In small bowl, whisk together lemon juice, mustard and honey. Stir into Swiss chard mixture. Scrape into bowl; top with onions.

3	bunches Swiss chard, stems and leaves separated
3 cups	thinly sliced onion (about 1 large)
¼ cup	cornstarch
½ tsp	salt
	vegetable oil for frying
2 tbsp	olive oil
6	cloves garlic, thinly sliced
pinch	hot pepper flakes
¼ tsp	pepper
1 tbsp	lemon juice
½ tsp	grainy mustard
½ tsp	liquid honey

171

NUTRITIONAL INFORMATION, PER EACH OF 10 SERVINGS: about 129 cal, 2 g pro, 10 g total fat (1 g sat. fat), 10 g carb (2 g dietary fibre, 3 g sugar), 0 mg chol, 254 mg sodium, 470 mg potassium. % RDI: 5% calcium, 14% iron, 46% vit A, 27% vit C, 5% folate.

ROASTED BUTTERNUT SQUASH AND CHEDDAR GRATIN

p.170

HANDS-ON TIME	**TOTAL TIME**	**MAKES**
20 MINUTES	1½ HOURS	8 TO 10 SERVINGS

1	large butternut squash (about 2 kg), peeled, seeded and cut in ¾-inch (2 cm) cubes
2 tsp	olive oil
1 tsp	salt
½ tsp	pepper
2 tbsp	butter
1 cup	diced leek (white and light green parts only)
2	cloves garlic, minced
1½ tsp	chopped fresh thyme
¼ cup	all-purpose flour
2 cups	milk
2 tsp	Dijon mustard
pinch	nutmeg
2 cups	shredded old Cheddar cheese

In large bowl, toss together squash, oil and ¼ tsp each of the salt and pepper; arrange in single layer on lightly greased foil-lined rimmed baking sheet. Roast on bottom rack of 450°F (230°C) oven, tossing once, until tender and edges are light golden, 20 to 25 minutes. Transfer to greased 8 cup (2 L) baking dish.

While squash is roasting, in large saucepan, melt butter over medium heat; cook leek, garlic and 1 tsp of the thyme, stirring often, until softened, about 5 minutes. Sprinkle with flour; cook, whisking constantly, for 1 minute. Whisk in milk, mustard, nutmeg and remaining salt and pepper; bring to boil. Reduce heat and simmer, stirring, until thick enough to coat back of spoon, about 5 minutes. Stir in 1 cup of the Cheddar.

Pour leek mixture over squash. *(Make-ahead: Cover and refrigerate for up to 24 hours. Let stand at room temperature for 1 hour before continuing with recipe.)* Sprinkle with remaining Cheddar and thyme. Cover and bake in 425°F (220°C) oven for 30 minutes; uncover and bake until top is browned, 10 to 15 minutes.

NUTRITIONAL INFORMATION, PER EACH OF 10 SERVINGS: about 219 cal, 9 g pro, 12 g total fat (7 g sat. fat), 21 g carb (3 g dietary fibre, 6 g sugar), 34 mg chol, 429 mg sodium, 515 mg potassium. % RDI: 26% calcium, 10% iron, 169% vit A, 37% vit C, 19% folate.

172

RED WINE CRANBERRY JELLY

HANDS-ON TIME
15 MINUTES

TOTAL TIME
12¼ HOURS

MAKES
ABOUT 6 CUPS

In saucepan, bring cranberry juice, cranberries, sugar, wine and thyme to boil; reduce heat, cover and simmer until cranberries begin to break down, about 3 minutes.

Strain through fine-mesh sieve, reserving cranberries; discard thyme. Line same sieve with 3 layers of cheesecloth. Strain juice mixture again; discard seeds.

In small saucepan, add ½ cup water; sprinkle gelatin over top. Let stand until absorbed, about 5 minutes. Cook over medium-low heat, stirring, until gelatin is melted. (Do not boil.) Stir into juice mixture. Stir in reserved cranberries.

Rinse 6-cup (1.5 L) jelly mould or deep bowl. (Do not dry.) Pour in cranberry mixture. Cover and refrigerate until set, about 12 hours. *(Make-ahead: Refrigerate for up to 3 days.)*

Dip mould into warm water for 5 seconds. Invert jelly onto serving platter, gently shaking to release.

NUTRITIONAL INFORMATION, PER 1 TBSP: about 17 cal, trace pro, trace total fat (0 g sat. fat), 4 g carb (trace dietary fibre, 4 g sugar), 0 mg chol, 1 mg sodium, 11 mg potassium. % RDI: 2% vit C.

3 cups	cranberry juice
3 cups	fresh or thawed frozen cranberries
1¼ cups	granulated sugar
1 cup	dry red wine
4	sprigs fresh thyme
3	pkg unflavoured gelatin

173

MAPLE POTS DE CRÈME
WITH WARM PEARS

opposite

HANDS-ON TIME	TOTAL TIME	MAKES
30 MINUTES	5¼ HOURS	8 SERVINGS

MAPLE CUSTARD

1½ cups	each whipping cream (35%) and milk
⅓ cup	maple syrup
4	egg yolks
2	eggs
½ cup	granulated sugar
½ tsp	maple extract

WARM PEAR TOPPING

2 tbsp	butter
2	firm ripe Bosc or Bartlett pears, peeled, cored and diced (about 2½ cups total)
2 tbsp	maple syrup

MAPLE CUSTARD In saucepan, heat together cream, milk and maple syrup over medium heat just until bubbles form around edge.

In bowl, whisk together egg yolks, eggs and sugar until smooth; slowly whisk in cream mixture. Strain through fine-mesh sieve into pitcher; stir in maple extract. Pour into eight 6-oz (175 mL) ramekins. Place ramekins in roasting pan; pour enough boiling water in pan to come 1 inch (2.5 cm) up sides. Cover pan with foil.

Bake in 325°F (160°C) oven until edges are lightly set yet centres still jiggle slightly, 30 to 35 minutes. Transfer ramekins to rack; let cool completely. Cover with plastic wrap and refrigerate until chilled, about 4 hours. *(Make-ahead: Refrigerate for up to 2 days.)*

WARM PEAR TOPPING While custard is chilling, in skillet, melt butter over medium-high heat; cook pears, stirring often, until browned and softened, about 6 minutes. Stir in maple syrup; cook, stirring, until pears are coated, about 1 minute. Scrape into bowl. Let cool to room temperature. Serve over custard.

NUTRITIONAL INFORMATION, PER SERVING: about 360 cal, 5 g pro, 23 g total fat (13 g sat. fat), 34 g carb (1 g dietary fibre, 30 g sugar), 213 mg chol, 80 mg sodium, 209 mg potassium. % RDI: 11% calcium, 6% iron, 27% vit A, 2% vit C, 12% folate.

174

MAPLE POTS DE CRÈME WITH WARM PEARS

THANKSGIVING FEAST

Here's a Thanksgiving feast that's casual but adventurous, an unforgettable combination of the season's best in dishes with just enough of a twist to keep every bite intriguing. And the big finish? A spectacular pumpkin dessert that will leave your guests truly impressed.

177

MENU FOR 12

JICAMA AND APPLE SPINACH SALAD
WITH HONEY-DIJON DRESSING **p.178**

BARBECUED PORK LOIN
STUFFED WITH BACON AND APPLES **p.180**

CREAMY MUSHROOM AND GRUYÈRE GRATIN **p.181**

SAUTÉED BRUSSELS SPROUTS
WITH SHAVED PARMESAN **p.182**

POTATO AND TURNIP MASH
WITH ROASTED GARLIC **p.182**

PUMPKIN CHEESECAKE
WITH WHITE CHOCOLATE ALMOND BARK **p.185**

JICAMA AND APPLE SPINACH SALAD
WITH HONEY-DIJON DRESSING

opposite

HANDS-ON TIME	**TOTAL TIME**	**MAKES**
20 MINUTES	20 MINUTES	12 SERVINGS

HONEY-DIJON DRESSING

3 tbsp	cider vinegar
2 tbsp	finely chopped fresh chives
1 tbsp	liquid honey
2 tsp	Dijon mustard
1	small clove garlic, grated or pressed
¼ tsp	each salt and pepper
⅓ cup	extra-virgin olive oil

SALAD

10	slices pancetta, chopped
2	pkg (each 142 g) baby spinach
2	Gala or Empire apples, cored and chopped
1	jicama (about 650 g), peeled and cut in ¼-inch (5 mm) wide sticks

HONEY-DIJON DRESSING In small bowl, whisk together vinegar, chives, honey, mustard, garlic, salt and pepper; gradually whisk in oil until combined. *(Make-ahead: Refrigerate in airtight container for up to 24 hours; whisk well before using.)*

SALAD In small skillet, cook pancetta over medium heat, stirring occasionally, until crisp, about 5 minutes. Using slotted spoon, transfer to paper towel–lined plate to drain.

In large bowl, toss together spinach, apples, jicama and dressing; top with pancetta.

NUTRITIONAL INFORMATION, PER SERVING: about 147 cal, 5 g pro, 10 g total fat (2 g sat. fat), 10 g carb (4 g dietary fibre, 5 g sugar), 18 mg chol, 349 mg sodium, 240 mg potassium. % RDI: 3% calcium, 8% iron, 23% vit A, 30% vit C, 24% folate.

VARIATION
FENNEL AND APPLE SPINACH SALAD
WITH HONEY-DIJON DRESSING
Substitute 1 bulb fennel, cored and thinly sliced, for the jicama.

178

JICAMA AND APPLE SPINACH SALAD WITH HONEY-DIJON DRESSING

BARBECUED PORK LOIN
STUFFED WITH BACON AND APPLES

📷 p.176

HANDS-ON TIME	**TOTAL TIME**	**MAKES**
45 MINUTES	2½ HOURS	12 SERVINGS

BACON AND APPLE STUFFING

4	strips sodium-reduced bacon
2	shallots, finely chopped
3	cloves garlic, minced
1	Gala or Empire apple, peeled, cored and cut in ½-inch (1 cm) chunks
1 tbsp	chopped fresh sage
2 tsp	chopped fresh thyme
¼ tsp	each salt and pepper
2 cups	diced (½-inch/1 cm) French or Italian bread
⅓ cup	sodium-reduced chicken broth

PORK LOIN

1	boneless pork loin roast (about 1.5 kg)
¼ tsp	each salt and pepper
½ cup	apple jelly
1 tbsp	grainy Dijon mustard

BACON AND APPLE STUFFING In large nonstick skillet, cook bacon over medium heat, turning once, until crisp, about 6 minutes. Transfer to paper towel–lined plate to drain; chop into bite-size pieces. Set aside.

Drain all but 2 tsp of fat from skillet; cook shallots and garlic over medium heat, stirring occasionally, until softened, about 2 minutes. Add apple, sage, thyme, salt and pepper; cook, stirring, just until apple is tender, about 4 minutes. Stir in bread. Drizzle with broth; cook, stirring, until absorbed, about 30 seconds. Scrape into bowl; stir in bacon. Let cool to room temperature. *(Make-ahead: Cover and refrigerate for up to 24 hours.)*

PORK LOIN Meanwhile, place roast, fat side up, on cutting board with short end facing you. Position knife horizontally ¾ inch (2 cm) from bottom of roast; cut 1 inch (2.5 cm) toward centre of pork. Lift up top half of pork; continue making shallow horizontal cuts deeper into roast, unrolling top of pork as you cut and keeping knife parallel to cutting board to maintain the same thickness, until pork unrolls to form flat rectangle. Sprinkle both sides with salt and pepper.

Spoon stuffing vertically along centre of pork. Working in same direction you unrolled, roll up pork tightly so that fat side is up and seam is facing down. Tie tightly with butcher's twine at 2-inch (5 cm) intervals.

Set foil drip pan under 1 rack of 2-burner barbecue or under centre rack of 3-burner barbecue. Heat adjacent burner(s) to medium heat (375°F/190°C). Place roast on greased grill over drip pan. Close lid and grill until instant-read thermometer inserted in centre reads 160°F (71°C) or juices run clear when pork is pierced and just a hint of pink remains inside, about 1½ hours.

In small saucepan, mix apple jelly with mustard; cook over medium heat, stirring, until slightly thickened, about 5 minutes. Brush jelly mixture over cooked roast. Increase grill heat to high; close lid. Grill until glaze is slightly browned, about 3 minutes. Cover loosely with foil; let stand for 10 minutes before slicing.

NUTRITIONAL INFORMATION, PER SERVING: about 265 cal, 31 g pro, 9 g total fat (4 g sat. fat), 15 g carb (1 g dietary fibre, 7 g sugar), 70 mg chol, 248 mg sodium, 473 mg potassium. % RDI: 2% calcium, 7% iron, 1% vit A, 3% vit C, 6% folate.

VARIATION

OVEN-ROASTED PORK LOIN STUFFED WITH BACON AND APPLES
Bake in 375°F (190°C) oven until instant-read thermometer inserted in centre reads 160°F (71°C) or juices run clear when pork is pierced and just a hint of pink remains inside, about 1½ hours. Brush with glaze; broil until slightly browned, about 4 minutes.

CREAMY MUSHROOM AND GRUYÈRE GRATIN

HANDS-ON TIME
35 MINUTES

TOTAL TIME
35 MINUTES

MAKES
12 SERVINGS

MUSHROOM GRATIN In large skillet, melt 2 tbsp of the butter over medium heat; cook leeks, garlic and half each of the salt and pepper, stirring occasionally, until leeks are softened, about 6 minutes. Scrape into bowl; set aside.

In same skillet, melt remaining butter over medium heat; cook cremini mushrooms, oyster mushrooms and remaining salt and pepper, stirring occasionally, until mushrooms are just tender and have released their juices, 5 to 8 minutes. Sprinkle with flour; cook, stirring, until light golden, about 2 minutes. Stir in leek mixture.

Whisk in broth, cream and mustard until smooth. Cook, whisking, until thickened, 3 to 5 minutes. Stir in chestnuts (if using), parsley, thyme and lemon juice. Spoon into 8-cup (2 L) casserole dish. *(Make-ahead: Let cool to room temperature; cover and refrigerate for up to 24 hours. To reheat, cover with foil and bake in 375°F/190°C oven until hot and bubbly, about 45 minutes; uncover and continue with recipe.)*

GRUYÈRE CRUMB TOPPING In bowl, stir together bread crumbs, Gruyère, butter and parsley; sprinkle over mushroom mixture. Broil until topping is golden, 2 to 4 minutes.

NUTRITIONAL INFORMATION, PER SERVING: about 191 cal, 8 g pro, 13 g total fat (8 g sat. fat), 14 g carb (3 g dietary fibre, 3 g sugar), 38 mg chol, 323 mg sodium, 429 mg potassium. % RDI: 11% calcium, 12% iron, 19% vit A, 12% vit C, 17% folate.

MUSHROOM GRATIN

5 tbsp	butter
1	bunch leeks (white and light green parts only), halved lengthwise and sliced crosswise
4	cloves garlic, minced
½ tsp	each salt and pepper
3	pkg (each 227 g) cremini or button mushrooms, sliced
227 g	oyster mushrooms, trimmed and torn
⅓ cup	all-purpose flour
1¼ cups	sodium-reduced chicken broth
½ cup	whipping cream (35%)
2 tbsp	grainy Dijon mustard
1	bag (100 g) prepared chestnuts, chopped (optional)
½ cup	chopped fresh parsley
1 tbsp	chopped fresh thyme
4 tsp	lemon juice

GRUYÈRE CRUMB TOPPING

2 cups	fresh bread crumbs
¾ cup	grated Gruyère cheese
2 tbsp	butter, melted
2 tbsp	chopped fresh parsley

POTATO AND TURNIP MASH
WITH ROASTED GARLIC

opposite

HANDS-ON TIME	TOTAL TIME	MAKES
35 MINUTES	1 HOUR	12 SERVINGS

1	head garlic
1 tsp	olive oil
8	large yellow-fleshed potatoes (about 2 kg total), peeled and cut in ¾-inch (2 cm) chunks
3	large white turnips (about 600 g total), peeled and cut in ¾-inch (2 cm) chunks
¾ cup	sour cream
⅓ cup	butter
3	green onions, sliced
1¼ tsp	each salt and pepper

Slice off top third of garlic head to expose cloves. Place garlic head on small square of foil; drizzle cut side with oil and fold foil over to seal. Bake in 375°F (190°C) oven until tender and golden, about 45 minutes. Let cool. Squeeze out cloves into bowl; mash until smooth. *(Make-ahead: Refrigerate in airtight container for up to 2 days.)*

Meanwhile, in large saucepan of boiling water, cook potatoes for 7 minutes. Add turnips; cook until potatoes and turnips are tender, about 10 minutes. Drain; return to pan. Mash potato mixture with garlic, sour cream, butter, green onions, salt and pepper until smooth. *(Make-ahead: Spoon into 13- × 9-inch/3 L baking dish. Let cool to room temperature; cover and refrigerate for up to 24 hours. To reheat, let stand at room temperature for 1 hour; cover with foil and bake in 375°F/190°C oven for 1 hour.)*

NUTRITIONAL INFORMATION, PER SERVING: about 204 cal, 4 g pro, 8 g total fat (5 g sat. fat), 31 g carb (3 g dietary fibre, 3 g sugar), 19 mg chol, 299 mg sodium, 563 mg potassium. % RDI: 5% calcium, 5% iron, 7% vit A, 27% vit C, 9% folate.

SAUTÉED BRUSSELS SPROUTS
WITH SHAVED PARMESAN

opposite

HANDS-ON TIME	TOTAL TIME	MAKES
25 MINUTES	25 MINUTES	12 SERVINGS

1.5 kg	brussels sprouts, trimmed and halved lengthwise
3 tbsp	butter
2 tsp	chopped fresh thyme
½ tsp	pepper
¼ tsp	salt
1 tbsp	lemon juice
⅓ cup	shaved Parmesan cheese

In large saucepan of boiling salted water, cook brussels sprouts just until tender, 5 to 8 minutes. Drain. *(Make-ahead: Rinse with cold water; drain. Refrigerate in airtight container for up to 24 hours.)*

In large skillet, melt butter over medium-high heat; sauté brussels sprouts, thyme, pepper and salt until brussels sprouts are golden, about 5 minutes. Stir in lemon juice. Transfer to serving dish; sprinkle with Parmesan.

NUTRITIONAL INFORMATION, PER SERVING: about 79 cal, 4 g pro, 4 g total fat (2 g sat. fat), 9 g carb (4 g dietary fibre, 2 g sugar), 9 mg chol, 414 mg sodium, 395 mg potassium. % RDI: 7% calcium, 11% iron, 12% vit A, 128% vit C, 34% folate.

POTATO AND TURNIP MASH WITH ROASTED GARLIC AND SAUTÉED BRUSSELS SPROUTS

PUMPKIN CHEESECAKE WITH WHITE CHOCOLATE ALMOND BARK

PUMPKIN CHEESECAKE
WITH WHITE CHOCOLATE ALMOND BARK

opposite

HANDS-ON TIME
45 MINUTES

TOTAL TIME
9 HOURS

MAKES
12 SERVINGS

PUMPKIN CHEESECAKE Scrape pumpkin purée into centre of a square of cheesecloth; wrap in a bundle, twisting top to seal. Place bundle in colander set over bowl. Place small plate and a heavy can (to help press liquids from purée) on top of bundle. Let drain for 1½ hours; discard liquid.

In bowl, stir together gingersnap crumbs, ground almonds, ¼ cup of the sugar and the butter until moistened. Scrape mixture into greased 9-inch (2.5 L) springform pan; press into bottom and about ¾ inch (2 cm) up side. Bake in 350°F (180°C) oven until set, 12 to 15 minutes. Let cool.

In large bowl, beat cream cheese until smooth. Gradually beat in remaining sugar, scraping down side of bowl twice, until light and smooth, about 3 minutes. On low speed, beat in eggs, 1 at a time, scraping down side of bowl often, just until smooth. Beat in pumpkin purée, cinnamon, ginger, vanilla, nutmeg, cloves and salt. Beat in sour cream. Pour over crust, smoothing top.

Bake on rimmed baking sheet in 300°F (150°C) oven until top is no longer shiny and edge is set yet centre still jiggles slightly, 2 to 2¼ hours.

Turn off oven; run knife around edge of cake. Let cool in oven for 1 hour. Transfer to rack; let cool completely. Refrigerate until chilled, at least 4 hours. *(Make-ahead: Cover and refrigerate for up to 2 days, or wrap in heavy-duty foil and freeze for up to 2 weeks.)*

Whip cream until stiff peaks form; spread over top of cheesecake.

WHITE CHOCOLATE ALMOND BARK While cheesecake is chilling, in heatproof bowl set over saucepan of hot (not boiling) water, melt chocolate, stirring until smooth. On parchment paper–lined baking sheet, spread all but 3 tbsp of the chocolate in ¹⁄₁₆-inch (2 mm) thick layer. Sprinkle almonds over top; drizzle with remaining chocolate. Refrigerate until firm, about 15 minutes. *(Make-ahead: Cover with plastic wrap; refrigerate for up to 24 hours.)* Break into 2-inch (5 cm) chunks. Arrange over top of cheesecake.

NUTRITIONAL INFORMATION, PER SERVING: about 613 cal, 12 g pro, 43 g total fat (23 g sat. fat), 49 g carb (2 g dietary fibre, 35 g sugar), 146 mg chol, 317 mg sodium, 392 mg potassium. % RDI: 19% calcium, 14% iron, 59% vit A, 2% vit C, 15% folate.

PUMPKIN CHEESECAKE

1 cup	pumpkin purée
1 cup	English-style gingersnap cookie crumbs (2 cups whole cookies)
½ cup	ground almonds
1¼ cups	granulated sugar
3 tbsp	butter, melted
2	pkg (each 250 g) cream cheese, softened
3	eggs
2 tsp	each cinnamon and ground ginger
1 tsp	vanilla
½ tsp	nutmeg
pinch	each ground cloves and salt
3 cups	sour cream
1 cup	whipping cream (35%)

WHITE CHOCOLATE ALMOND BARK

170 g	white chocolate (about 6 oz)
⅓ cup	sliced natural (skin-on) almonds, toasted

TIP FROM THE TEST KITCHEN

Make sure the cheesecake is fully chilled before slicing. After each slice, rinse your knife under hot water and dry it off well.

GAME NIGHT

It's down to the wire: your team, a tough opponent, one crucial battle. With all that tension, you and your fellow fans can't watch the big game without nibbling on something. But junk food? That's no way to win. Instead, serve these delicious homemade versions of classic game-night snacks.

MENU FOR 12

SPICY ROASTED POTATO SKINS **p.188**

CRISP CHEESE-STUFFED JALAPEÑOS **p.188**

TURKEY CHILI NACHOS **p.189**

SPICY HONEY-GARLIC BONELESS WINGS **p.191**

LIGHTENED-UP BLUE CHEESE DIP
WITH BAKED PITA CHIPS **p.191**

SPICY ROASTED POTATO SKINS

📷 p.186

HANDS-ON TIME	**TOTAL TIME**	**MAKES**
15 MINUTES	2 HOURS	24 PIECES

2	large russet potatoes (about 900 g total)
2 tbsp	olive oil
½ tsp	each chili powder and garlic powder
¼ tsp	each pepper and onion powder
pinch	salt
⅓ cup	finely grated Parmesan cheese
½ cup	0% plain Greek yogurt
2 tbsp	chopped fresh chives
1 tbsp	chopped fresh parsley
2 tsp	grainy Dijon mustard

Using fork, prick each potato several times. Bake in 350°F (180°C) oven until tender, about 1¼ hours. Let cool slightly.

Cut potatoes lengthwise; cut each half lengthwise. Scrape out flesh, leaving ¼-inch (5 mm) thick shell; reserve flesh for another use. Cut each piece crosswise diagonally into thirds. *(Make-ahead: Cover and refrigerate for up to 2 days.)*

Arrange potato pieces, skin side down, on parchment paper–lined rimmed baking sheet. Whisk together oil, chili powder, garlic powder, pepper, onion powder and salt; brush over tops of potato pieces. Sprinkle with Parmesan. Roast in 425°F (220°C) oven until golden and crisp, about 20 minutes.

Meanwhile, in small bowl, stir together yogurt, half of the chives, the parsley and mustard. Spoon small dollop onto each potato skin; sprinkle with remaining chives. Serve remaining yogurt mixture with potato skins.

NUTRITIONAL INFORMATION, PER PIECE: about 45 cal, 2 g pro, 2 g total fat (trace sat. fat), 6 g carb (1 g dietary fibre, trace sugar), 2 mg chol, 31 mg sodium, 149 mg potassium. % RDI: 3% calcium, 2% iron, 1% vit A, 7% vit C, 2% folate.

CRISP CHEESE-STUFFED JALAPEÑOS

HANDS-ON TIME	**TOTAL TIME**	**MAKES**
10 MINUTES	50 MINUTES	20 PIECES

10	jalapeño peppers
125 g	light soft garlic-and-herb cheese (such as Boursin)
⅓ cup	shredded light Cheddar-style cheese
2 tbsp	milk
2 tsp	lemon juice
½ tsp	dry mustard
¼ tsp	pepper
⅓ cup	panko bread crumbs
1 tbsp	olive oil

Cut jalapeños in half lengthwise; scrape out seeds and membranes, leaving stems intact. Mash together garlic-and-herb cheese, Cheddar-style cheese, milk, lemon juice, dry mustard and pepper; spoon into jalapeño halves. Arrange on rimmed baking sheet.

Toss panko with oil until moistened; sprinkle over jalapeño halves. *(Make-ahead: Cover and refrigerate for up to 24 hours.)*

Bake in 375°F (190°C) oven until jalapeños are soft and panko is golden, about 40 minutes.

NUTRITIONAL INFORMATION, PER PIECE: about 41 cal, 1 g pro, 4 g total fat (2 g sat. fat), 2 g carb (trace dietary fibre, 2 g sugar), 6 mg chol, 51 mg sodium, 20 mg potassium. % RDI: 1% calcium, 1% iron, 3% vit A, 5% vit C, 1% folate.

TURKEY CHILI NACHOS

p.186

HANDS-ON TIME
25 MINUTES

TOTAL TIME
25 MINUTES

MAKES
10 TO 12 SERVINGS

In skillet, heat oil over medium heat; cook onion, stirring often, until softened and light golden, about 8 minutes. Stir in garlic, cumin, paprika, salt, pepper and cayenne pepper; cook, stirring, until fragrant, about 30 seconds.

Stir in turkey; cook, breaking up with spoon, until no liquid remains and turkey is no longer pink, about 5 minutes. Stir in strained tomatoes, red pepper and half of the green onions; cook until heated through and thickened, about 5 minutes.

Layer chips and turkey mixture in lightly greased 13- × 9-inch (3 L) baking dish; sprinkle with mozzarella. Broil until mozzarella is melted and tips of chips are lightly charred, 60 to 90 seconds. Top with remaining green onions, the cilantro and lime juice.

NUTRITIONAL INFORMATION, PER EACH OF 12 SERVINGS: about 157 cal, 9 g pro, 5 g total fat (2 g sat. fat), 17 g carb (1 g dietary fibre, 2 g sugar), 32 mg chol, 286 mg sodium, 188 mg potassium. % RDI: 6% calcium, 11% iron, 3% vit A, 17% vit C, 4% folate.

2 tsp	olive oil
1	onion, chopped
2	cloves garlic, minced
1 tsp	each ground cumin and smoked paprika
¼ tsp	each salt and pepper
pinch	cayenne pepper
450 g	lean ground turkey
1½ cups	bottled strained tomatoes (passata)
half	sweet red pepper, diced
2	green onions, thinly sliced
200 g	baked tortilla chips (about 8 cups)
½ cup	shredded part-skim mozzarella cheese
¼ cup	chopped fresh cilantro
2 tsp	lime juice

189

LEFT: SPICY HONEY-GARLIC BONELESS WINGS; AND RIGHT: LIGHTENED-UP BLUE CHEESE DIP

SPICY HONEY-GARLIC BONELESS WINGS

opposite

HANDS-ON TIME	**TOTAL TIME**	**MAKES**
20 MINUTES	20 MINUTES	10 TO 12 SERVINGS

In small bowl, stir together honey, sesame oil, sesame seeds, garlic, hot pepper sauce, salt, pepper and ⅓ cup water. Set aside.

Sprinkle cornstarch over chicken; toss to coat. In large nonstick skillet, heat oil over medium-high heat; cook chicken, stirring occasionally, until light golden, about 5 minutes. Stir in honey mixture; cook, stirring occasionally, until sauce is thickened and coats chicken completely, and chicken is no longer pink inside, about 6 minutes.

Scrape into serving dish; sprinkle with green onions.

NUTRITIONAL INFORMATION, PER EACH OF 12 SERVINGS: about 166 cal, 18 g pro, 6 g total fat (1 g sat. fat), 10 g carb (trace dietary fibre, 8 g sugar), 44 mg chol, 166 mg sodium, 236 mg potassium. % RDI: 1% calcium, 4% iron, 1% vit A, 2% vit C, 2% folate.

⅓ cup	liquid honey
3 tbsp	sesame oil
2 tbsp	sesame seeds, toasted
3	cloves garlic, grated or pressed
5 tsp	hot pepper sauce (such as Frank's RedHot)
¼ tsp	each salt and pepper
2 tbsp	cornstarch
900 g	boneless skinless chicken breasts, cut in 1-inch (2.5 cm) chunks
2 tsp	olive oil
2	green onions, thinly sliced

191

LIGHTENED-UP BLUE CHEESE DIP

opposite

HANDS-ON TIME	**TOTAL TIME**	**MAKES**
10 MINUTES	10 MINUTES	1⅔ CUPS

In bowl, mash blue cheese with buttermilk until smooth with a few chunks. Stir in yogurt, lemon juice, honey, garlic, pepper, green onions and dill.

NUTRITIONAL INFORMATION, PER 1 TBSP: about 14 cal, 1 g pro, 1 g total fat (trace sat. fat), 1 g carb (0 g dietary fibre, 1 g sugar), 2 mg chol, 36 mg sodium, 9 mg potassium. % RDI: 2% calcium, 1% vit A, 1% folate.

BAKED PITA CHIPS

Cut 2 whole wheat pitas into 8 wedges each; arrange in single layer on rimmed baking sheet. Stir together 1 tbsp olive oil, ¼ tsp Italian herb seasoning and pinch salt; brush over pitas. Bake in 400°F (200°C) oven until crisp and golden, 6 to 8 minutes. *(Make-ahead: Store in airtight container for up to 24 hours.)*

⅓ cup	crumbled good-quality blue cheese, such as Roquefort
¼ cup	buttermilk
1 cup	0% plain Greek yogurt
1 tsp	each lemon juice and liquid honey
1	clove garlic, grated or pressed
¼ tsp	pepper
2	green onions, thinly sliced
1 tbsp	chopped fresh dill

HARVEST TABLE

Everyone is looking for a deeper connection with food, especially what's grown close to home. Whether you choose seasonal and local food because it tastes better or because it *feels* better, this menu is designed to show off the best of our country's bountiful autumn harvest.

193

MENU FOR 6

SPINACH SALAD
WITH APPLES AND GOAT CHEESE CROUTONS **p.194**

SLOW COOKER BALSAMIC-BRAISED POT ROAST **p.196**

ROASTED ONIONS AND APPLES WITH THYME **p.197**

CELERY ROOT GARLIC MASH **p.198**

THE ULTIMATE PECAN PIE **p.199**

SPINACH SALAD
WITH APPLES AND GOAT CHEESE CROUTONS

opposite

HANDS-ON TIME	TOTAL TIME	MAKES
30 MINUTES	30 MINUTES	6 SERVINGS

3 tbsp	butter
2	large heads Belgian endive
1¼ tsp	coarse salt
½ tsp	pepper
2	apples, cored and sliced
1	shallot, chopped
¼ cup	pomegranate juice
1 tbsp	cider vinegar
1 tsp	Dijon mustard
6 tbsp	olive oil
170 g	soft goat cheese
½ cup	finely chopped almonds
6	slices (½-inch/1 cm) baguette
4 cups	loosely packed baby spinach
⅓ cup	pomegranate seeds (optional)

Cut endive in half lengthwise; cut each half into 3 wedges. In large skillet, melt 2 tbsp of the butter over medium-high heat. Arrange endive wedges in single layer in skillet. Sprinkle with ¼ tsp each of the salt and pepper; cook until bottoms are golden, about 2 minutes. Turn and cook until softened, about 2 minutes. Remove to platter; set aside.

In same skillet, melt remaining butter. Add apples, shallot and ¼ tsp of the remaining salt. Cook, stirring, until apples begin to soften, about 2 minutes. Set aside.

Meanwhile, in small bowl, whisk together pomegranate juice, vinegar, mustard and remaining salt and pepper. Gradually whisk in olive oil; set aside.

In separate bowl, stir together goat cheese and almonds. Spread 2 tbsp onto each baguette slice. Arrange, cheese side up, on rimmed baking sheet; broil until cheese is bubbly and bread is golden, about 1 minute.

In large bowl, toss together spinach, apple mixture and half of the pomegranate juice mixture.

Arrange 2 pieces endive on each serving plate; top with spinach mixture and a baguette slice. Sprinkle with pomegranate seeds (if using) and drizzle with remaining pomegranate juice mixture.

NUTRITIONAL INFORMATION, PER SERVING: about 392 cal, 10 g pro, 31 g total fat (10 g sat. fat), 21 g carb (4 g dietary fibre, 9 g sugar), 28 mg chol, 568 mg sodium, 376 mg potassium. % RDI: 10% calcium, 16% iron, 33% vit A, 13% vit C, 33% folate.

194

SPINACH SALAD WITH APPLES AND GOAT CHEESE CROUTONS

SLOW COOKER
BALSAMIC-BRAISED POT ROAST

HANDS-ON TIME	**TOTAL TIME**	**MAKES**
15 MINUTES	8½ HOURS	6 TO 8 SERVINGS

1.85 kg	boneless beef pot roast (top or bottom blade or cross rib), trimmed
¾ tsp	salt
½ tsp	pepper
1	onion, thinly sliced
4	cloves garlic, minced
1	bay leaf
1 cup	sodium-reduced beef broth
½ cup	balsamic vinegar
2 tbsp	tomato paste
1 tbsp	each Dijon mustard, liquid honey and Worcestershire sauce
½ tsp	dried rosemary
⅓ cup	all-purpose flour
2 tbsp	chopped fresh parsley

Sprinkle beef with ½ tsp of the salt and ¼ tsp of the pepper. Set aside.

In slow cooker, combine onion, garlic and bay leaf. Arrange beef over top. Whisk together broth, vinegar, tomato paste, mustard, honey, Worcestershire sauce, rosemary and remaining salt and pepper; pour over beef. Cover and cook on low until beef is tender, 8 to 10 hours.

Transfer beef to cutting board; remove any butcher's twine.

Discard bay leaf. Skim fat from surface of cooking liquid. Whisk flour with ¼ cup water; whisk into slow cooker. Cover and cook on high until thickened, about 15 minutes. Stir in parsley.

Thinly slice beef across the grain; serve with sauce.

NUTRITIONAL INFORMATION, PER EACH OF 8 SERVINGS: about 467 cal, 46 g pro, 25 g total fat (10 g sat. fat), 12 g carb (1 g dietary fibre, 6 g sugar), 134 mg chol, 502 mg sodium, 492 mg potassium. % RDI: 4% calcium, 37% iron, 1% vit A, 7% vit C, 9% folate.

ROASTED ONIONS AND APPLES
WITH THYME

p.192

HANDS-ON TIME
20 MINUTES

TOTAL TIME
1¼ HOURS

MAKES
4 TO 6 SERVINGS

In large saucepan, bring apple juice to boil; cook until reduced to ⅓ cup, about 15 minutes. Whisk in butter and half of the salt. *(Make-ahead: Refrigerate in airtight container for up to 1 week. In saucepan, reheat over medium heat, whisking.)*

Cut each onion into 12 wedges. In large bowl, toss together onions, 1 tsp of the thyme and 4 tsp of the apple juice mixture. Spread on greased rimmed baking sheet. Cut each apple in half; core and cut each half into 4 wedges. In separate bowl, mix apples, 1 tsp of the remaining thyme and 4 tsp of the remaining apple juice mixture. Spread apple mixture on separate greased rimmed baking sheet; sprinkle with remaining salt.

Arrange 1 oven rack in top third of 425°F (220°C) oven and 1 oven rack in bottom third. Place onion mixture on top rack; bake for 10 minutes. Place apple mixture on bottom rack; bake for 20 minutes. Remove onion mixture and apple mixture from oven; sprinkle with remaining apple juice mixture. Bake until onions and apples are softened and slightly caramelized, about 30 minutes. Transfer onions and apples to serving bowl; sprinkle with pepper and remaining thyme.

NUTRITIONAL INFORMATION, PER EACH OF 6 SERVINGS: about 155 cal, 1 g pro, 6 g total fat (4 g sat. fat), 27 g carb (13 g dietary fibre), 15 mg chol, 200 mg sodium.

2 cups	apple juice
3 tbsp	unsalted butter
½ tsp	salt
3	onions
1 tbsp	chopped fresh thyme
3	apples
	pepper

197

CELERY ROOT GARLIC MASH

p.192

HANDS-ON TIME	**TOTAL TIME**	**MAKES**
15 MINUTES	35 MINUTES	6 TO 8 SERVINGS

1	celery root (about 1 kg), peeled and cut in 1-inch (2.5 cm) chunks
2	russet potatoes (about 500 g total), peeled and halved
8	cloves garlic
¼ cup	10% cream
¼ cup	butter, softened
1 tbsp	grainy Dijon mustard
¼ tsp	each salt and pepper

In large saucepan of boiling salted water, cook celery root, potatoes and garlic until tender, about 20 minutes. Drain and return to saucepan.

Mash until smooth; stir in cream, butter, mustard, salt and pepper until light and fluffy. *(Make-ahead: Let cool; refrigerate in airtight container for up to 24 hours.)*

NUTRITIONAL INFORMATION, PER EACH OF 8 SERVINGS: about 146 cal, 3 g pro, 7 g total fat (4 g sat. fat), 20 g carb (3 g dietary fibre), 18 mg chol, 709 mg sodium. % RDI: 6% calcium, 6% iron, 6% vit A, 17% vit C, 5% folate.

THE ULTIMATE PECAN PIE

HANDS-ON TIME
45 MINUTES

TOTAL TIME
3¼ HOURS

MAKES
12 SERVINGS

PASTRY In large bowl, whisk together flour, sugar and salt. Using pastry blender or 2 knives, cut in butter until mixture resembles coarse crumbs with a few larger pieces. Drizzle ice water over flour mixture, tossing with fork to form ragged dough and adding up to 1 tsp more ice water if necessary. Shape into disc; wrap in plastic wrap and refrigerate until chilled, about 1 hour. *(Make-ahead: Refrigerate for up to 3 days or freeze in airtight container for up to 1 month.)*

Let pastry stand at room temperature until slightly softened, about 5 minutes. On lightly floured work surface, roll out pastry to 12-inch (30 cm) circle; fit into 9-inch (23 cm) pie plate. Trim, leaving 1-inch (2.5 cm) overhang; fold under and flute edge. Prick bottom all over with fork. Refrigerate until firm, about 30 minutes.

PECAN FILLING In small saucepan, melt butter over medium heat; whisk in brown sugar until smooth. Remove from heat; whisk in honey, vinegar, vanilla and salt. Whisk in eggs.

Sprinkle pecans into pie shell; pour egg mixture over top. Bake on rimmed baking sheet in bottom third of 350°F (180°C) oven until filling is set, 50 to 60 minutes. Let cool completely in pan on rack.

NUTRITIONAL INFORMATION, PER SERVING: about 434 cal, 5 g pro, 29 g total fat (11 g sat. fat), 43 g carb (2 g dietary fibre, 31 g sugar), 87 mg chol, 121 mg sodium, 175 mg potassium. % RDI: 4% calcium, 11% iron, 15% vit A, 17% folate.

PASTRY

1¼ cups	all-purpose flour
1 tbsp	granulated sugar
¼ tsp	salt
½ cup	cold unsalted butter, cubed
¼ cup	ice water (approx)

PECAN FILLING

½ cup	unsalted butter
1 cup	packed brown sugar
½ cup	liquid honey
1 tbsp	cider vinegar
2 tsp	vanilla
¼ tsp	salt
3	eggs, lightly beaten
2 cups	pecan halves

199

TIP FROM THE TEST KITCHEN

Put the baking sheet in the oven while preheating—
the hot pan underneath the pie plate helps the
bottom crust cook to golden-brown perfection.

SEASONAL SUNDAY SUPPER

The perfect autumn meal brings
a lot to the table: the fresh vegetables of the harvest;
warm, fragrant spices; and the comfort-food
pleasures of rich braised dishes.

MENU FOR 4 TO 6

MUSTARD AND PANCETTA ROAST CHICKEN p.202

GARLIC POMEGRANATE SPINACH p.202

**GREEN BEANS
WITH FETA CRUMBLES** p.203

BRAISED CABBAGE AND BACON p.203

DOUBLE CHOCOLATE PEANUT BUTTER PIE p.205

MUSTARD AND PANCETTA ROAST CHICKEN

p.200

HANDS-ON TIME	**TOTAL TIME**	**MAKES**
20 MINUTES	1½ HOURS	6 SERVINGS

10	thin slices pancetta, (about 85 g total), finely chopped
1 tbsp	grainy mustard
1	whole chicken (1.8 to 2.25 kg)
10	fresh thyme sprigs
8	cloves garlic
pinch	each salt and pepper

In small skillet, cook pancetta over medium heat, stirring often, until golden and crisp, about 7 minutes. Using slotted spoon, transfer to paper towel–lined plate to drain. In small bowl, mix pancetta with mustard; set aside.

Remove giblets and neck (if any) from chicken; place thyme and garlic in cavity. Loosen skin from breast meat, being careful not to tear skin. Spread pancetta mixture under skin, covering breast evenly. Sprinkle chicken with salt and pepper; tuck wings behind back. Using butcher's twine, tie legs. Place chicken on rack in roasting pan. Roast in 400°F (200°C) oven until beginning to brown, about 30 minutes. Reduce heat to 375°F (190°C); roast until instant-read thermometer inserted in thickest part of thigh reads 185°F (85°C), about 40 minutes.

Discard contents of cavity. Using tongs, tip chicken, pouring juices into roasting pan. Transfer chicken to platter; cover loosely with foil. Let stand for 15 minutes before carving. Skim fat from juices; serve juices with chicken.

NUTRITIONAL INFORMATION, PER SERVING: about 296 cal, 32 g pro, 18 g total fat (5 g sat. fat), trace carb (trace dietary fibre, 0 g sugar), 122 mg chol, 320 mg sodium, 298 mg potassium. % RDI: 2% calcium, 11% iron, 5% vit A, 3% vit C, 2% folate.

GARLIC POMEGRANATE SPINACH

HANDS-ON TIME	**TOTAL TIME**	**MAKES**
15 MINUTES	15 MINUTES	4 TO 6 SERVINGS

2 tbsp	olive oil
5 cloves	garlic, thinly sliced
10 cups	packed baby spinach (about 300 g)
pinch	each salt, pepper and nutmeg
¼ cup	pomegranate seeds

In large nonstick skillet, heat oil over medium-low heat; cook garlic, stirring occasionally, until golden, 3 to 4 minutes. Using slotted spoon, transfer garlic to paper towel–lined plate. Increase heat to medium-high; cook spinach in 3 batches, stirring, until slightly wilted, about 2 minutes per batch. Return all spinach to skillet. Stir in salt, pepper and nutmeg; cook, stirring, for 1 minute. Sprinkle with ¼ cup pomegranate seeds and garlic.

NUTRITIONAL INFORMATION, PER EACH OF 6 SERVINGS: about 61 cal, 2 g pro, 5 g total fat (1 g sat. fat), 4 g carb (2 g dietary fibre, 1 g sugar), 0 mg chol, 34 mg sodium, 251 mg potassium. % RDI: 6% calcium, 13% iron, 50% vit A, 10% vit C, 33% folate.

GREEN BEANS
WITH FETA CRUMBLES

HANDS-ON TIME
20 MINUTES

TOTAL TIME
20 MINUTES

MAKES
6 SERVINGS

In large saucepan of boiling salted water, cook beans until bright green and slightly tender, about 3 minutes; drain.

In large skillet, heat oil over medium-high heat; sauté shallots and garlic until softened, 2 to 3 minutes. Add red pepper, salt and pepper; sauté until red pepper is softened, about 2 minutes.

Add beans; sauté until tender-crisp, about 2 minutes. Remove from heat; stir in lemon juice. Sprinkle with feta.

NUTRITIONAL INFORMATION, PER SERVING: about 67 cal, 2 g pro, 4 g total fat (1 g sat. fat), 7 g carb (2 g dietary fibre, 2 g sugar), 6 mg chol, 216 mg sodium, 135 mg potassium. % RDI: 6% calcium, 4% iron, 8% vit A, 33% vit C, 11% folate.

450 g	green beans, trimmed
1 tbsp	olive oil
2	shallots, diced
2	cloves garlic, minced
⅓ cup	finely diced sweet red pepper
pinch	each salt and pepper
2 tsp	lemon juice
¼ cup	crumbled feta cheese

203

BRAISED CABBAGE AND BACON

HANDS-ON TIME
15 MINUTES

TOTAL TIME
25 MINUTES

MAKES
4 TO 6 SERVINGS

In Dutch oven or large heavy-bottomed saucepan, cook bacon over medium-high heat, stirring often, until golden and crisp, about 2 minutes. Using slotted spoon, transfer to paper towel–lined plate to drain.

Drain all but 1 tsp fat from pan; cook garlic and light parts of green onions, stirring, until softened, about 1 minute. Add cabbage, salt and pepper; cook, stirring, for 2 minutes. Add broth; bring to boil. Reduce heat, cover and simmer until cabbage is tender, about 10 minutes.

Stir in mustard, dark green parts of green onions and half of the bacon; cook, stirring, for 1 minute. Sprinkle with remaining bacon.

NUTRITIONAL INFORMATION, PER EACH OF 6 SERVINGS: about 61 cal, 3 g pro, 3 g total fat (1 g sat. fat), 7 g carb (2 g dietary fibre, 4 g sugar), 5 mg chol, 191 mg sodium, 173 mg potassium. % RDI: 5% calcium, 4% iron, 3% vit A, 42% vit C, 13% folate.

3	strips bacon, chopped
2	cloves garlic, minced
6	green onions, sliced (light and dark green parts separated)
8 cups	chopped green cabbage
pinch	each salt and pepper
½ cup	sodium-reduced chicken broth
1 tbsp	Dijon mustard

DOUBLE-CHOCOLATE PEANUT BUTTER PIE

DOUBLE-CHOCOLATE PEANUT BUTTER PIE

opposite

HANDS-ON TIME	**TOTAL TIME**	**MAKES**
20 MINUTES	2 HOURS	12 SERVINGS

CRUST In bowl, mix wafer crumbs with butter. Press into bottom and up side of 9-inch (23 cm) pie plate. Bake in 350°F (180°C) oven until firm and dry, 12 to 14 minutes. Let cool completely.

FILLING Meanwhile, place chocolate in heatproof bowl. In small saucepan, bring ⅔ cup of the cream to boil; pour over chocolate, whisking until melted. Let cool until lukewarm, about 20 minutes.

Meanwhile, in bowl, beat cream cheese with peanut butter until smooth; beat in remaining cream and the icing sugar until fluffy. Beat in vanilla. Scrape into crust, smoothing top. Scrape chocolate mixture over top, spreading to edges. Sprinkle with peanuts, leaving 1½-inch (4 cm) border. Refrigerate until set, about 1 hour.

NUTRITIONAL INFORMATION, PER SERVING: about 383 cal, 7 g pro, 30 g total fat (14 g sat. fat), 21 g carb (2 g dietary fibre, 12 g sugar), 51 mg chol, 195 mg sodium, 221 mg potassium. % RDI: 4% calcium, 11% iron, 15% vit A, 11% folate.

CRUST

1¼ cups	chocolate wafer crumbs
⅓ cup	butter, melted

FILLING

120 g	dark chocolate (about 4¼ oz), finely chopped
1 cup	whipping cream (35%)
half	pkg (250 g pkg) cream cheese, softened
½ cup	smooth peanut butter
⅓ cup	icing sugar
1 tsp	vanilla
½ cup	unsalted peanuts, toasted

205

TIP FROM THE TEST KITCHEN

Store peanuts in the fridge or freezer. Because of their high fat content, they will quickly become rancid if left at room temperature.

WINTER

TREE TRIMMING PARTY p.208

HANUKKAH GET-TOGETHER p.216

MAKE-AHEAD CHRISTMAS DINNER p.224

CHRISTMAS BUFFET p.234

HOLIDAY BRUNCH p.244

NEW YEAR'S EVE DROP-IN p.250

APRÈS-SKI FONDUE p.260

GONG HEI FAT CHOI p.264

VALENTINE'S DAY DINNER p.272

RED CARPET EXTRAVAGANZA p.278

SEASONAL SUNDAY SUPPER p.284

TREE TRIMMING PARTY

It's the first party of the holiday season—a relaxed get-together before everyone gets booked up with more formal events. This collection of rustic, contemporary Canadian dishes is centred around ready-to-serve charcuterie and cheeses. And to make it even easier, most of the prep for this menu can be done ahead of time.

209

MENU FOR 12

CANADIAN KISS p.210

HICKORY HONEY PEPPER NUTS p.210

SMOKED TROUT CAKES
WITH LEMON MAYO AND SWISS CHARD KIMCHI p.211

WILD MUSHROOM PÂTÉ p.212

WILD CHARCUTERIE BOARD p.212

BISON MEATBALLS
WITH CIDER MUSTARD SAUCE p.215

CHEESE BOARD p.215

CANADIAN KISS

HANDS-ON TIME
5 MINUTES

TOTAL TIME
5 MINUTES

MAKES
1 SERVING

	ice cubes
2	thin slices fresh ginger
1 tsp	lemon juice
1½ oz	maple whisky, such as Sortilège Liqueur (about 3 tbsp)
¼ oz	raspberry liqueur, such as Chambord Black Raspberry Liqueur (about ½ tbsp)
2 tbsp	soda water (approx)
1	strip lemon zest

Add ice to cocktail glass; set aside. In cocktail shaker, using muddler or back of wooden spoon, mash ginger with lemon juice until ginger is broken into pieces. Add enough ice to fill shaker halfway. Add whisky and raspberry liqueur; close lid and shake about 6 times. Strain into glass. Top with soda; stir. Garnish with lemon zest.

NUTRITIONAL INFORMATION, PER SERVING: about 114 cal, trace pro, trace total fat (0 g sat. fat), 3 g carb (0 g dietary fibre, 3 g sugar), 0 mg chol, 7 mg sodium, 7 mg potassium. % RDI: 2% vit C.

p.214

HICKORY HONEY PEPPER NUTS

HANDS-ON TIME
15 MINUTES

TOTAL TIME
45 MINUTES

MAKES
ABOUT 4 CUPS

⅓ cup	packed brown sugar
3 tbsp	vegetable oil
2 tbsp	liquid honey
1 tsp	coarsely ground pepper
4 cups	unsalted mixed nuts
½ tsp	salt
½ tsp	hickory liquid smoke

In saucepan, bring brown sugar, oil, honey, pepper and 3 tbsp water to boil; cook for 2 minutes.

In large bowl, mix nuts with brown sugar mixture until coated; stir in salt and liquid smoke. Spread on parchment paper–lined rimmed baking sheet.

Bake in 375°F (190°C) oven, stirring 3 times, until deep golden, 20 to 25 minutes. Let cool completely on pan, stirring and breaking up nuts often to prevent clumps. *(Make-ahead: Store in airtight container for up to 2 days.)*

NUTRITIONAL INFORMATION, PER 1 TBSP: about 58 cal, 1 g pro, 5 g total fat (1 g sat. fat), 3 g carb (1 g dietary fibre, 2 g sugar), 0 mg chol, 19 mg sodium, 45 mg potassium. % RDI: 1% calcium, 2% iron, 1% folate.

SMOKED TROUT CAKES
WITH LEMON MAYO AND
SWISS CHARD KIMCHI

p.208

HANDS-ON TIME	TOTAL TIME	MAKES
1 HOUR	1½ HOURS	12 SERVINGS

SWISS CHARD KIMCHI In saucepan, bring salt and 5 cups water to boil; stir until dissolved, about 2 minutes. Let cool for 5 minutes.

Meanwhile, cut Swiss chard leaves and stems diagonally into about ¼-inch (5 mm) wide slices. In large heatproof bowl, combine leaves, stems and radishes. Pour salted water over top; let stand for 10 minutes, stirring once. Drain and rinse under cold water; let stand in colander for 10 minutes. Gently squeeze out excess liquid; transfer mixture to bowl.

Stir together garlic, ginger, sesame seeds, sugar, vinegar, Asian chili paste and fish sauce; add to Swiss chard mixture, tossing to coat. Cover and refrigerate for 1 hour. *(Make-ahead: Refrigerate in airtight container for up to 1 week.)*

LEMON MAYO While chard mixture is chilling, in small bowl, stir together mayonnaise, lemon zest and lemon juice; set aside. *(Make-ahead: Refrigerate in airtight container for up to 24 hours.)*

TROUT CAKES In large skillet, heat 1 tbsp of the oil over medium heat; cook celery and onion, stirring occasionally, until softened, 6 to 8 minutes. Scrape into large bowl; let cool completely.

To celery mixture, add trout, panko, eggs, mayonnaise and pepper; stir until combined. Shape by rounded 1 tbsp into balls; gently press into ½-inch (1 cm) thick patties. *(Make-ahead: Cover and refrigerate on parchment paper–lined baking sheets for up to 24 hours.)*

In same skillet, heat half of the remaining oil over medium heat; cook half of the patties, turning once, until golden and heated through, about 8 minutes. Repeat with remaining oil and patties. Top patties with mayo and kimchi.

NUTRITIONAL INFORMATION, PER SERVING: about 166 cal, 11 g pro, 10 g total fat (2 g sat. fat), 6 g carb (1 g dietary fibre, 4 g sugar), 44 mg chol, 921 mg sodium, 161 mg potassium. % RDI: 2% calcium, 7% iron, 15% vit A, 8% vit C, 5% folate.

SWISS CHARD KIMCHI

¼ cup	salt
225 g	Swiss chard (about 1 bunch), leaves and stems separated
5	radishes, trimmed and diced
3	cloves garlic, grated or pressed
1 tbsp	grated fresh ginger
1 tbsp	sesame seeds, toasted
1 tsp	granulated sugar
1 tsp	cider vinegar
¾ tsp	Asian chili paste (such as sambal oelek)
½ tsp	fish sauce

LEMON MAYO

⅓ cup	light mayonnaise
2 tsp	grated lemon zest
1 tsp	lemon juice

TROUT CAKES

2 tbsp	vegetable oil
2	ribs celery, finely diced
1	onion, finely diced
450 g	hot-smoked trout or hot-smoked salmon, flaked
½ cup	panko bread crumbs
2	eggs, lightly beaten
3 tbsp	light mayonnaise
¼ tsp	pepper

211

WILD MUSHROOM PÂTÉ

opposite

HANDS-ON TIME	**TOTAL TIME**	**MAKES**
30 MINUTES	45 MINUTES	2½ CUPS

2 tbsp	unsalted butter
675 g	mixed wild mushrooms (such as shiitake, oyster or chanterelle), chopped
4	green onions, thinly sliced (light and dark green parts separated)
5	sprigs fresh thyme
3 tbsp	brandy
2 tsp	lemon juice
¼ tsp	each salt and pepper
1	pkg (250 g) cream cheese, softened
2 tbsp	chopped fresh parsley

In large nonstick skillet, melt butter over medium heat; cook mushrooms, light parts of green onions and the thyme, stirring occasionally, until mushrooms are tender and just beginning to brown and no liquid remains, 12 to 15 minutes. Add brandy; cook, stirring, until no liquid remains, about 2 minutes. Stir in lemon juice, salt and pepper; let cool completely. Discard thyme.

In food processor, pulse cream cheese until smooth. Add mushroom mixture; pulse, scraping down side of bowl often, until combined. Scrape into bowl; stir in dark green parts of green onions and the parsley. Serve at room temperature. *(Make-ahead: Cover and refrigerate for up to 2 days. Bring to room temperature before serving.)*

NUTRITIONAL INFORMATION, PER 1 TBSP: about 32 cal, 1 g pro, 3 g total fat (2 g sat. fat), 1 g carb (trace dietary fibre, 1 g sugar), 8 mg chol, 36 mg sodium, 90 mg potassium. % RDI: 1% calcium, 1% iron, 3% vit A, 2% vit C, 2% folate.

WILD CHARCUTERIE BOARD

opposite

Set the mood of your holiday party with local charcuterie. Consider bison, wild boar, duck and elk as alternatives to traditional pork and beef. Variety is key. Lay out a mix of cured meat styles, such as salami, prosciutto and bresaola, as well as pâtés.

Plan for about 55 to 85 g of meat per person, served with olives or homemade pickled vegetables, a few condiments such as chutneys and mustards, and artisanal bread or crackers. Remember not to leave cured meats sitting out for more than two hours; it's much safer and more stylish to prepare two small boards and bring out a fresh one after a couple of hours.

WILD CHARCUTERIE BOARD AND WILD MUSHROOM PÂTÉ

CLOCKWISE, FROM TOP LEFT: CHEESE BOARD; BISON MEATBALLS WITH CIDER MUSTARD SAUCE;
AND HICKORY HONEY PEPPER NUTS

BISON MEATBALLS
WITH CIDER MUSTARD SAUCE

opposite

HANDS-ON TIME
1 HOUR

TOTAL TIME
1½ HOURS

MAKES
ABOUT 60 PIECES

CIDER MUSTARD SAUCE In saucepan, heat oil over medium-high heat; sauté onion and apple until tender and light golden, 10 to 12 minutes. Stir in cider, broth, molasses and Dijon mustard (not grainy Dijon mustard); bring to boil. Reduce heat; simmer, stirring occasionally, until mixture is reduced to 4 cups, about 35 minutes. Let cool slightly.

In blender, purée apple mixture until completely smooth, about 1 minute. Return to saucepan; bring to boil. Whisk in grainy Dijon mustard, salt and pepper. Whisk cornstarch with 3 tbsp water; whisk into sauce. Bring to boil; cook until thickened, 1 to 2 minutes. *(Make-ahead: Let cool for 30 minutes; refrigerate in airtight container for up to 24 hours.)*

BISON MEATBALLS Meanwhile, in large bowl, stir together onion, eggs, bread crumbs, garlic powder, salt and pepper until combined; stir in bison and bacon. Roll by 1 tbsp into balls.

In large nonstick skillet, heat half of the oil over medium heat; cook half of the meatballs, turning occasionally, until browned, no longer pink inside and instant-read thermometer inserted in centres reads 160°F (71°C), 8 to 10 minutes. Repeat with remaining oil and meatballs. *(Make-ahead: Let cool on paper towel–lined baking sheet for 30 minutes; refrigerate in airtight container for up to 24 hours.)* Return all meatballs and sauce to skillet; cook until coated and heated through.

NUTRITIONAL INFORMATION, PER PIECE: about 66 cal, 3 g pro, 5 g total fat (2 g sat. fat), 3 g carb (trace dietary fibre, 1 g sugar), 18 mg chol, 100 mg sodium, 79 mg potassium. % RDI: 1% calcium, 4% iron, 2% folate.

CIDER MUSTARD SAUCE

2 tbsp	vegetable oil
1	onion, sliced
1	McIntosh apple, peeled, cored and chopped
2 cups	dry hard (alcoholic) cider
2 cups	beef broth
3 tbsp	fancy molasses
1 tbsp	each Dijon mustard and grainy Dijon mustard
¼ tsp	each salt and pepper
3 tbsp	cornstarch

BISON MEATBALLS

1	onion, grated
2	eggs, lightly beaten
¼ cup	dried bread crumbs
1 tsp	garlic powder
¼ tsp	each salt and pepper
900 g	ground bison
6	strips bacon, finely chopped
2 tbsp	vegetable oil

215

CHEESE BOARD

opposite

Hit up your local cheese shop to try a few of our country's artisanal offerings. Then showcase your favourites on a cheese board, including some cow's and goat's milk cheeses, in three or four cheese types: hard, semi-firm, soft and blue. You'll need about 30 to 45 g of cheese (total) per person. Cheese tastes best at room temperature; take it out of the refrigerator about an hour before serving. Choose a few accompaniments, but don't overdo it: dried fruits (such as cranberries and apricots) work well, as do fresh figs, grapes and sliced pears, with good-quality crackers and crusty bread.

HANUKKAH GET-TOGETHER

Our tempting menu includes some traditional holiday treats—latkes and buñuelos—and some dishes inspired by the flavours of Israeli cuisine. We've made everything bite-size, because somehow it just tastes better that way. Happy Hanukkah!

MENU FOR 10 TO 12

FRIED CHICKEN BITES p.218

**MINI VEGETABLE LATKES
WITH CHUNKY APPLESAUCE p.219**

**EGGPLANT WALNUT DIP
WITH ZA'ATAR PITA CHIPS p.220**

**CRISP ARTICHOKES
WITH LEMON HERB DIP p.221**

MINI CHOCOLATE BABKAS p.222

**MINI CINNAMON
SUGAR BUÑUELOS p.223**

FRIED CHICKEN BITES

HANDS-ON TIME	**TOTAL TIME**	**MAKES**
40 MINUTES	40 MINUTES	10 TO 12 SERVINGS

2 cups	all-purpose flour
1 tsp	each dry mustard and garlic powder
½ tsp	pepper
¼ tsp	salt
¼ tsp	cayenne pepper (optional)
4	eggs
	vegetable oil for frying
1.35 kg	kosher boneless skinless chicken breasts and/or thighs

In shallow dish, mix together half of the flour, the mustard, garlic powder, pepper, salt and cayenne pepper (if using).

Pour remaining flour into separate shallow dish. In third shallow dish, beat eggs.

In large deep skillet or Dutch oven, pour enough oil to come 1 inch (2.5 cm) up side. Heat until deep-fryer thermometer reads 375°F (190°C) or 1-inch (2.5 cm) cube of white bread turns golden brown in 30 seconds.

Meanwhile, cut chicken into scant ½-inch (1 cm) thick slices. Coat chicken in flour, tapping off excess. Dip into eggs, allowing excess to drip back into dish. Coat with mustard mixture.

Working in batches, cook chicken, turning occasionally, until golden brown and juices run clear when chicken is pierced, about 5 minutes for white meat and 7 minutes for dark meat. Drain on rack set over paper towel–lined baking sheet.

NUTRITIONAL INFORMATION, PER EACH OF 12 SERVINGS: about 276 cal, 30 g pro, 9 g total fat (2 g sat. fat), 15 g carb (1 g dietary fibre, trace sugar), 127 mg chol, 227 mg sodium, 369 mg potassium. % RDI: 2% calcium, 12% iron, 4% vit A, 2% vit C, 19% folate.

TIP FROM THE TEST KITCHEN

For a Hanukkah version of chicken and waffles, try a piece of this fried chicken on a plain buñuelo (recipe, page 223), drizzled with a little maple syrup.

MINI VEGETABLE LATKES
WITH CHUNKY APPLESAUCE

p.216

HANDS-ON TIME
40 MINUTES

TOTAL TIME
40 MINUTES

MAKES
10 TO 12 SERVINGS

CHUNKY APPLESAUCE Peel, core and finely dice apples. In saucepan, bring apples, sugar, cinnamon, salt and ½ cup water to boil. Reduce heat and simmer, stirring occasionally and breaking up apples with back of spoon, until tender, about 15 minutes. Stir in lemon juice. Let cool completely. *(Make-ahead: Refrigerate in airtight container for up to 5 days.)*

MINI LATKES Peel and grate potatoes; squeeze out as much liquid as possible. In large bowl, stir together potatoes, carrot, celery root, onion and zucchini; mix in egg, flour, salt and pepper.

In large deep skillet or Dutch oven, pour enough oil to come 1 inch (2.5 cm) up side. Heat until deep-fryer thermometer reads 375°F (190°C) or 1-inch (2.5 cm) cube of white bread turns golden in 30 seconds.

Using 2 small spoons, shape potato mixture by scant 1 tbsp into small discs. Working in batches, slide into oil, leaving about 1 inch (2.5 cm) between latkes.

Cook, turning once, until golden brown and edges are crisp, 1 to 2 minutes. Drain on paper towel–lined baking sheet. *(Make-ahead: Transfer to rack and cover with paper towel; let stand at room temperature for up to 2 hours. Remove paper towel; place rack on baking sheet. Bake in 350°F/180°C oven until heated through, about 10 minutes.)* Serve with applesauce.

NUTRITIONAL INFORMATION, PER EACH OF 12 SERVINGS: about 191 cal, 2 g pro, 12 g total fat (1 g sat. fat), 19 g carb (2 g dietary fibre, 6 g sugar), 15 mg chol, 111 mg sodium, 228 mg potassium. % RDI: 1% calcium, 4% iron, 9% vit A, 8% vit C, 6% folate.

CHUNKY APPLESAUCE

2	Golden Delicious apples (about 450 g total)
2 tbsp	granulated sugar
pinch	each cinnamon and salt
2 tsp	lemon juice

MINI LATKES

675 g	russet potatoes (about 2)
½ cup	each grated carrot, grated celery root, grated onion and grated zucchini
1	egg, lightly beaten
⅓ cup	all-purpose flour or matzo meal
½ tsp	salt
¼ tsp	pepper
	vegetable oil for frying

219

EGGPLANT WALNUT DIP
WITH ZA'ATAR PITA CHIPS

p.216

HANDS-ON TIME	TOTAL TIME	MAKES
20 MINUTES	9 HOURS	10 TO 12 SERVINGS

EGGPLANT WALNUT DIP

1½ cups	walnut halves
2	large eggplants
1	head garlic
1	can (540 mL) chickpeas, drained and rinsed
¼ cup	lemon juice
3 tbsp	tahini
1 tsp	za'atar
½ tsp	each salt and pepper
¼ tsp	cayenne pepper
½ cup	chopped fresh parsley

ZA'ATAR PITA CHIPS

6	white or whole wheat pitas
1 tbsp	vegetable oil
1 tsp	za'atar

EGGPLANT WALNUT DIP In bowl, soak walnuts in water for 8 hours; drain and pat dry. Spread on baking sheet; toast in 350°F (180°C) oven, turning once, until crisp, about 15 minutes.

Using fork, prick eggplants all over; place on lightly greased baking sheet. Set aside.

Remove 1 clove garlic from head; peel, mince and set aside. Slice off top third of garlic head to expose cloves. Place garlic head on small square of foil; fold foil over to seal and add to baking sheet. Bake in 375°F (190°C) oven, turning eggplants once, until softened, 40 to 45 minutes. Let stand until eggplants are cool enough to handle.

Cut eggplants in half lengthwise; using spoon, scoop flesh into food processor. Discard skins. Squeeze out cloves of roasted garlic into food processor. Add chickpeas; pulse until combined.

Add walnuts, lemon juice, tahini, za'atar, salt, pepper, cayenne pepper and reserved minced garlic; pulse until walnuts are finely chopped. Stir in parsley. Cover and refrigerate for 1 hour. *(Make-ahead: Cover and refrigerate for up to 2 days.)* Serve with pita chips.

ZA'ATAR PITA CHIPS Brush 1 side of each pita with some of the oil; sprinkle with some of the za'atar. Cut each pita into 8 wedges; arrange on baking sheet. Bake in 350°F (180°C) oven until crisp, about 8 minutes. *(Make-ahead: Let cool; store in airtight container for up to 2 days.)*

NUTRITIONAL INFORMATION, PER EACH OF 12 SERVINGS: about 278 cal, 8 g pro, 12 g total fat (1 g sat. fat), 37 g carb (6 g dietary fibre, 5 g sugar), 0 mg chol, 357 mg sodium, 305 mg potassium. % RDI: 8% calcium, 18% iron, 3% vit A, 13% vit C, 34% folate.

CRISP ARTICHOKES
WITH LEMON HERB DIP

p.216

HANDS-ON TIME
40 MINUTES

TOTAL TIME
1 HOUR

MAKES
10 TO 12 SERVINGS

LEMON HERB DIP In small bowl, stir together mayonnaise, sour cream, parsley, basil, lemon zest, lemon juice and garlic. *(Make-ahead: Cover and refrigerate for up to 24 hours.)*

CRISP ARTICHOKES Squeeze juice from lemon into large bowl filled with water. Tear off tough outer leaves of each artichoke and discard. Cut off top third of 1 artichoke. Trim stem to 1-inch (2.5 cm) length, cutting away outer green part of stem. Cut artichoke and stem in half lengthwise. Using melon baller or teaspoon, remove fuzzy centre. Slice each half lengthwise. Place in bowl with lemon water. Repeat with remaining artichokes. Drain.

In large saucepan of boiling salted water, cook artichokes just until tender, about 3 minutes. Drain and let cool completely on paper towel–lined baking sheet, about 20 minutes. Cut quarters in half lengthwise. *(Make-ahead: Cover and refrigerate for up to 24 hours.)*

Meanwhile, in shallow bowl, stir together panko, garlic powder, salt, pepper and cayenne pepper. Add flour to separate shallow dish. In third shallow dish, beat eggs.

Dip artichokes in flour, tapping off excess. Dip into eggs, allowing excess to drip back into dish. Toss with panko mixture to coat.

In large deep skillet or Dutch oven, pour enough oil to come 1 inch (2.5 cm) up side. Heat until deep-fryer thermometer reads 375°F (190°C) or 1-inch (2.5 cm) cube of white bread turns golden in 30 seconds.

Working in batches, cook artichokes, turning once, until golden brown, about 1 minute. Drain on paper towel–lined baking sheet. *(Make-ahead: Let stand, uncovered, for up to 1 hour.)* Serve with dip.

NUTRITIONAL INFORMATION, PER EACH OF 12 SERVINGS: about 195 cal, 5 g pro, 10 g total fat (3 g sat. fat), 23 g carb (2 g dietary fibre, 17 g sugar), 47 mg chol, 352 mg sodium, 316 mg potassium. % RDI: 2% calcium, 19% iron, 4% vit A, 8% vit C, 8% folate.

LEMON HERB DIP

½ cup	light mayonnaise
½ cup	nondairy pareve sour cream
¼ cup	chopped fresh parsley
2 tbsp	chopped fresh basil
2 tsp	grated lemon zest
1 tbsp	lemon juice
1	small clove garlic, grated or pressed

CRISP ARTICHOKES

half	lemon
7	large artichokes (about 3.2 kg total)
2 cups	kosher panko bread crumbs
1½ tsp	garlic powder
½ tsp	each salt and pepper
¼ tsp	cayenne pepper
1 cup	all-purpose flour
4	eggs
	vegetable oil for frying

221

MINI CHOCOLATE BABKAS

HANDS-ON TIME	**TOTAL TIME**	**MAKES**
40 MINUTES	3½ HOURS	12 PIECES

BABKA DOUGH

¾ cup	kosher soy milk
1	pkg (8 g) active dry yeast
⅓ cup	granulated sugar
¼ cup	vegetable oil
½ tsp	salt
2	eggs
3¼ cups	all-purpose flour (approx)

CHOCOLATE FILLING

¼ cup	nondairy pareve margarine
⅓ cup	granulated sugar
½ tsp	cinnamon
115 g	pareve bittersweet chocolate (about 4 oz), finely chopped

TOPPING

1	egg
⅓ cup	all-purpose flour
¼ cup	granulated sugar
pinch	cinnamon
3 tbsp	nondairy pareve margarine

BABKA DOUGH In saucepan, heat soy milk over medium-low heat just until warm (100°F/38°C); pour into bowl of stand mixer. Sprinkle in yeast; let stand until frothy, about 10 minutes.

Add sugar, oil, salt and eggs; using whisk attachment, whisk to combine. Add 3 cups of the flour; using hook attachment, mix until dough is smooth, elastic and comes away from bowl, adding spoonfuls of remaining flour if necessary, about 10 minutes. Transfer to lightly floured work surface; knead into ball.

Place dough in greased bowl, turning to grease all over. Cover with plastic wrap; let rise (in warm draft-free place) until doubled in bulk, about 1½ hours.

Punch down dough; divide in half. On lightly floured work surface, roll out each half into 18- × 12-inch (45 × 30 cm) rectangle.

CHOCOLATE FILLING Spread margarine over each rectangle, leaving ½-inch (1 cm) border at long sides. Mix sugar with cinnamon; sprinkle all over margarine. Sprinkle with chocolate. Using pizza cutter or knife, cut crosswise into six 3-inch (8 cm) wide strips.

Working with 1 strip at a time and starting at 1 long side, fold in half; starting at 1 short end, simultaneously twist and roll strip into ball, pinching seam to seal. Fit into greased muffin cup. Repeat with remaining dough. Cover with greased plastic wrap; let rise (in warm draft-free place) for 1 hour.

TOPPING Whisk egg with 2 tsp water. Brush over babkas.

Stir together flour, sugar and cinnamon; using pastry blender or 2 knives, cut in margarine until crumbly. Sprinkle over babkas.

Bake in 350°F (180°C) oven until browned and bottoms sound hollow when tapped, about 18 minutes. Let stand in pan on rack for 10 minutes. Remove from pans; let cool on racks *(Make-ahead: Set aside for up to 6 hours.)*

NUTRITIONAL INFORMATION, PER PIECE: about 333 cal, 8 g pro, 12 g total fat (3 g sat. fat), 48 g carb (2 g dietary fibre, 19 g sugar), 46 mg chol, 185 mg sodium, 140 mg potassium. % RDI: 3% calcium, 21% iron, 11% vit A, 36% folate.

222

MINI CINNAMON SUGAR BUÑUELOS

HANDS-ON TIME	TOTAL TIME	MAKES
35 MINUTES	40 MINUTES	10 TO 12 SERVINGS

BUÑUELO DOUGH In large bowl, whisk together flour, sugar, baking powder and salt. Using pastry blender or 2 knives, cut in shortening until mixture resembles coarse crumbs. Whisk egg with ½ cup water; stir into flour mixture. Turn out onto lightly floured work surface; knead until smooth. *(Make-ahead: Wrap and refrigerate for up to 24 hours. Let stand at room temperature for 15 minutes before continuing with recipe.)*

On lightly floured work surface, flatten dough to scant 1-inch (2.5 cm) thickness; cut into 24 pieces. Shape each into ¼-inch (5 mm) thick disc. Cover and let rest for 5 minutes.

Meanwhile, in large deep skillet or Dutch oven, pour enough oil to come 1 inch (2.5 cm) up side. Heat until deep-fryer thermometer reads 375°F (190°C) or 1-inch (2.5 cm) cube of white bread turns golden in 30 seconds. Working in batches, cook discs, turning once, until puffed and golden, about 2 minutes. Transfer to paper towel–lined plate to drain.

CINNAMON SUGAR In bowl, whisk sugar with cinnamon; working in batches, add buñuelos and toss to coat. *(Make-ahead: Set aside for up to 1 hour.)*

NUTRITIONAL INFORMATION, PER PIECE: about 110 cal, 2 g pro, 7 g total fat (1 g sat. fat), 11 g carb (trace dietary fibre, 4 g sugar), 8 mg chol, 76 mg sodium, 14 mg potassium. % RDI: 1% calcium, 4% iron, 7% folate.

BUÑUELO DOUGH

2 cups	all-purpose flour
3 tbsp	granulated sugar
2 tsp	baking powder
½ tsp	salt
⅓ cup	shortening
1	egg
	vegetable oil for frying

CINNAMON SUGAR

½ cup	granulated sugar
1 tsp	cinnamon

223

MAKE-AHEAD CHRISTMAS DINNER

Move over, turkey: We've made a beautiful beef tenderloin the centrepiece of this festive meal. It roasts to perfection in under an hour, and the other dishes here have time-saving make-ahead options. For Christmas this year, we're giving cooks everywhere a little less to worry about.

MENU FOR 10

ROASTED CARROT AND PARSNIP SOUP
WITH WHIPPED GOAT CHEESE AND KALE CHIPS p.226

PORCINI-DUSTED BEEF TENDERLOIN
WITH SHERRY GRAVY p.229

APRICOT WILD RICE PILAF p.230

ROOT VEGETABLE CRUMBLE p.231

HARICOTS VERTS
WITH MISO BUTTER AND PEPITAS p.232

BLACK FOREST PIE p.233

ROASTED CARROT AND PARSNIP SOUP
WITH WHIPPED GOAT CHEESE AND KALE CHIPS

opposite

HANDS-ON TIME	**TOTAL TIME**	**MAKES**
30 MINUTES	1½ HOURS	10 SERVINGS

CARROT AND PARSNIP SOUP

8	carrots, chopped
4	parsnips, peeled and chopped
4	shallots, halved
3	cloves garlic
1 tbsp	olive oil
½ tsp	salt
1	pkg (900 mL) sodium-reduced chicken broth

KALE CHIPS

6 cups	torn stemmed kale
2 tsp	olive oil
¼ tsp	sweet paprika
pinch	salt

WHIPPED GOAT CHEESE

130 g	soft goat cheese
quarter	pkg (250 g pkg) cream cheese, softened
½ cup	whipping cream (35%)
1 tbsp	lemon juice
pinch	pepper

CARROT AND PARSNIP SOUP In roasting pan, toss together carrots, parsnips, shallots, garlic, oil and salt. Roast in 450°F (230°C) oven, stirring once, until softened and browned, about 1 hour.

Scrape into Dutch oven or large heavy-bottomed saucepan. Stir in broth and 1 cup water; bring to boil. Reduce heat to simmer; cook for 5 minutes. In blender or food processor, working in batches, purée mixture until smooth. *(Make-ahead: Refrigerate in airtight container for up to 3 days.)* Ladle into serving bowls.

KALE CHIPS While soup is simmering, toss together kale, oil, paprika and salt; arrange in single layer on parchment paper–lined rimmed baking sheet. Bake in 350°F (180°C) oven until crisp and darkened, 12 to 15 minutes. *(Make-ahead: Store in airtight container for up to 8 hours.)*

WHIPPED GOAT CHEESE While kale is baking, in blender or food processor, purée together goat cheese, cream cheese, cream, lemon juice and pepper until smooth and light. *(Make-ahead: Refrigerate in airtight container for up to 2 days.)* Dollop over soup. Sprinkle kale chips over top.

NUTRITIONAL INFORMATION, PER SERVING: about 292 cal, 8 g pro, 12 g total fat (6 g sat. fat), 42 g carb (9 g dietary fibre, 13 g sugar), 29 mg chol, 493 mg sodium, 969 mg potassium.
% RDI: 13% calcium, 14% iron, 195% vit A, 58% vit C, 55% folate.

ROASTED CARROT AND PARSNIP SOUP WITH WHIPPED GOAT CHEESE AND KALE CHIPS

PORCINI-DUSTED BEEF TENDERLOIN WITH SHERRY GRAVY

PORCINI-DUSTED BEEF TENDERLOIN
WITH SHERRY GRAVY

opposite

HANDS-ON TIME
30 MINUTES

TOTAL TIME
1½ HOURS

MAKES
10 SERVINGS

BEEF TENDERLOIN In spice grinder, or using mortar and pestle, grind mushrooms into fine powder. Set aside. *(Make-ahead: Store in airtight container for up to 2 days.)*

Rub beef all over with salt and pepper, pressing to adhere. In large skillet, heat butter with oil over medium-high heat; cook beef, turning occasionally, until browned all over, about 7 minutes.

Rub beef all over with half of the mushroom powder; reserve remaining mushroom powder for Sherry Gravy. Place beef on greased rack in roasting pan; roast in 400°F (200°C) oven until instant-read thermometer inserted in centre reaches 135°F (58°C) for rare, about 50 minutes.

Remove beef to cutting board; let stand for 10 minutes. Remove butcher's twine before slicing across the grain.

SHERRY GRAVY While beef is resting, in clean skillet, cook shallots over medium heat, stirring occasionally, until softened, about 5 minutes. Stir in vinegar; cook, scraping up any browned bits, until vinegar is reduced to coat shallots, about 2 minutes. Scrape into bowl. Set aside.

Remove rack from roasting pan. Heat pan over medium heat; stir in sherry, scraping up any browned bits. Bring to boil; cook until reduced to ¾ cup, about 5 minutes. Whisk in broth and reserved mushroom powder; bring to boil.

Stir butter with flour; whisk into sherry mixture. Bring to boil; cook, whisking constantly, until thickened, about 4 minutes. Strain through fine-mesh sieve into heatproof bowl; stir in shallot mixture and salt. Serve with beef.

NUTRITIONAL INFORMATION, PER SERVING: about 396 cal, 38 g pro, 20 g total fat (9 g sat. fat), 9 g carb (trace dietary fibre, 1 g sugar), 108 mg chol, 358 mg sodium, 617 mg potassium. % RDI: 2% calcium, 36% iron, 5% vit A, 7% folate.

BEEF TENDERLOIN

2	pkg (each 14 g) dried porcini mushrooms
1.7 kg	trimmed beef tenderloin premium oven roast, tied at ½-inch (1 cm) intervals
¾ tsp	salt
½ tsp	pepper
2 tbsp	butter
1 tbsp	olive oil

SHERRY GRAVY

3	shallots, thinly sliced
2 tbsp	sherry vinegar
1½ cups	dry sherry
2½ cups	sodium-reduced beef broth
3 tbsp	butter, softened
3 tbsp	all-purpose flour
pinch	salt

229

APRICOT WILD RICE PILAF

p.224

HANDS-ON TIME	**TOTAL TIME**	**MAKES**
10 MINUTES	1¾ HOURS	10 SERVINGS

2 tbsp	butter
1	onion, finely chopped
1	carrot, finely chopped
1	rib celery, finely chopped
1	clove garlic, minced
2 cups	wild rice, rinsed
3½ cups	sodium-reduced chicken broth or vegetable broth
¼ tsp	each salt and pepper
½ cup	dried apricots, finely chopped
¼ cup	chopped fresh parsley
1 tbsp	chopped fresh tarragon
1 tbsp	grated lemon zest
2 tsp	lemon juice

In saucepan, melt butter over medium heat; cook onion, carrot and celery, stirring occasionally, until softened, about 5 minutes. Add garlic; cook, stirring, until fragrant, about 1 minute. Add rice; cook, stirring, for 1 minute.

Stir in broth, salt and pepper; bring to boil. Reduce heat to low; cover and simmer until about 2 tbsp liquid remains and most of the rice is split open, about 80 minutes.

Remove from heat. Stir in apricots; cover and let stand for 10 minutes.

Stir in parsley, tarragon, lemon zest and lemon juice.

NUTRITIONAL INFORMATION, PER SERVING: about 165 cal, 6 g pro, 3 g total fat (2 g sat. fat), 31 g carb (3 g dietary fibre, 6 g sugar), 6 mg chol, 294 mg sodium, 252 mg potassium. % RDI: 2% calcium, 8% iron, 19% vit A, 7% vit C, 16% folate.

ROOT VEGETABLE CRUMBLE

p.224

HANDS-ON TIME
30 MINUTES

TOTAL TIME
1¾ HOURS

MAKES
10 SERVINGS

CREAMY ROOT VEGETABLES In 12-cup (3 L) casserole dish, combine squash, onions, sweet potato, yellow-fleshed potatoes and garlic. Set aside.

In saucepan, melt butter over medium heat. Whisk in flour; cook, whisking constantly, for 1 minute. Whisk in broth and cream; bring to boil. Reduce heat and simmer, whisking constantly, until thick enough to coat back of spoon, about 3 minutes.

Whisk in mustard, salt and pepper; pour over vegetables. Bake in 400°F (200°C) oven until tender, about 1 hour.

TOPPING In bowl, mix together bread crumbs, walnuts, sage and parsley; stir in butter. *(Make-ahead: Refrigerate in airtight container for up to 2 days.)* Sprinkle over vegetables. Bake in 400°F (200°C) oven until crumble is golden, about 15 minutes. Let stand for 5 minutes before serving.

NUTRITIONAL INFORMATION, PER SERVING: about 345 cal, 6 g pro, 21 g total fat (11 g sat. fat), 36 g carb (4 g dietary fibre, 6 g sugar), 52 mg chol, 385 mg sodium, 663 mg potassium. % RDI: 9% calcium, 14% iron, 143% vit A, 35% vit C, 25% folate.

CREAMY ROOT VEGETABLES

4 cups	cubed peeled butternut squash
2	onions, chopped
1	large sweet potato, peeled and cubed
680 g	mini yellow-fleshed potatoes, halved
4	cloves garlic, sliced
¼ cup	butter
¼ cup	all-purpose flour
2 cups	sodium-reduced chicken broth
1 cup	whipping cream (35%)
2 tsp	Dijon mustard
½ tsp	each salt and pepper

TOPPING

1½ cups	fresh bread crumbs
½ cup	walnuts, chopped
2 tbsp	chopped fresh sage
1 tbsp	chopped fresh parsley
3 tbsp	butter, melted

HARICOTS VERTS
WITH MISO BUTTER AND PEPITAS

p.224

HANDS-ON TIME
20 MINUTES

TOTAL TIME
25 MINUTES

MAKES
10 SERVINGS

800 g	haricots verts or green beans, trimmed
3 tbsp	butter, softened
1 tbsp	white miso paste
1 tsp	liquid honey
½ cup	pepitas
pinch	salt
3	shallots, thinly sliced

In large saucepan of boiling salted water, cook haricots verts in 2 batches, until bright green and slightly tender, about 3 minutes. Using slotted spoon, transfer to bowl of ice water to chill; drain well and pat dry. *(Make-ahead: Refrigerate in airtight container for up to 24 hours.)*

Meanwhile, stir together butter, miso paste and honey. *(Make-ahead: Refrigerate in airtight container for up to 3 days.)*

In large nonstick skillet, melt 1 tbsp of the miso paste mixture over medium heat; cook pepitas, stirring frequently, until fragrant, about 4 minutes. Scrape into bowl. Sprinkle with salt.

In same skillet, melt remaining miso paste mixture over medium heat; cook shallots, stirring occasionally, until tender, about 4 minutes. Add haricots verts; cook, stirring occasionally, until heated through, about 4 minutes. Remove to platter. Sprinkle with pepitas.

NUTRITIONAL INFORMATION, PER SERVING: about 103 cal, 3 g pro, 7 g total fat (3 g sat. fat), 9 g carb (2 g dietary fibre, 2 g sugar), 9 mg chol, 92 mg sodium, 187 mg potassium. % RDI: 3% calcium, 11% iron, 9% vit A, 10% vit C, 13% folate.

232

BLACK FOREST PIE

HANDS-ON TIME
1¼ HOURS

TOTAL TIME
3¼ HOURS

MAKES
8 TO 10 SERVINGS

CRUST In bowl, mix wafer crumbs with butter. Press into bottom and up side of 9-inch (23 cm) pie plate. Refrigerate until chilled, about 15 minutes. Bake in 350°F (180°C) oven until firm and dry, about 14 minutes. Let cool completely.

CHOCOLATE FILLING While crust is cooling, place chocolate in heatproof bowl. In small saucepan, heat ⅔ cup of the cream over medium heat just until bubbles form around edge of pan; pour over chocolate, whisking until smooth. Whisk in vanilla. Let stand, stirring occasionally, until slightly thickened, 15 to 20 minutes. Whip remaining cream until stiff peaks form; fold one-third into chocolate mixture. Fold in remaining whipped cream. Scrape over crust, smoothing top. Refrigerate until set, about 2 hours.

CHERRY FILLING While chocolate filling is setting, in large saucepan, bring cherries, sugar and lemon juice to boil over medium heat; cook, stirring often and breaking up cherries with back of spoon, until sauce is beginning to thicken and cherries are broken down, about 15 minutes.

Whisk cornstarch with half of the kirsch; stir into cherry mixture. Cook, stirring, until thickened, about 1 minute. Remove from heat; stir in remaining kirsch. Let cool slightly. Refrigerate until chilled, about 45 minutes. Spoon over chocolate filling, leaving ½-inch (1 cm) border. *(Make-ahead: Cover loosely with plastic wrap; refrigerate for up to 24 hours.)*

TOPPING While cherry filling is cooling, in heatproof bowl set over saucepan of hot (not boiling) water, melt three-quarters of the chopped chocolate, stirring, until smooth. Scrape onto parchment paper–lined rimmed baking sheet; spread to scant ⅛-inch (3 mm) thickness. Refrigerate just until set, about 6 minutes.

Using 3¼-inch (8 cm) tall large Christmas tree cookie cutter and 1¾-inch (4.5 cm) tall small Christmas tree cookie cutter, press 3 large and 3 small tree shapes into chocolate. Refrigerate until firm, about 20 minutes. Using cookie cutters and with a gentle twisting motion, cut shapes through to paper.

Melt remaining chopped chocolate; spoon into piping bag fitted with small plain tip. Pipe squiggles onto chocolate trees. Refrigerate until set, about 10 minutes. *(Make-ahead: Cover loosely with plastic wrap; refrigerate for up to 3 days.)*

Meanwhile, in bowl, whip cream with icing sugar until stiff peaks form; fold in kirsch. Spoon over cherry filling. Nestle chocolate trees on top of whipped cream. Sprinkle with chocolate shavings.

NUTRITIONAL INFORMATION, PER EACH OF 10 SERVINGS: about 562 cal, 4 g pro, 38 g total fat (23 g sat. fat), 56 g carb (3 g dietary fibre, 44 g sugar), 90 mg chol, 150 mg sodium, 278 mg potassium. % RDI: 5% calcium, 12% iron, 28% vit A, 5% vit C, 7% folate.

CRUST

1¼ cups	chocolate wafer crumbs
⅓ cup	butter, melted

CHOCOLATE FILLING

225 g	semisweet chocolate (8 oz), finely chopped
1⅔ cups	whipping cream (35%)
2 tsp	vanilla

CHERRY FILLING

3 cups	frozen sweet cherries
⅔ cup	granulated sugar
2 tsp	lemon juice
2 tbsp	cornstarch
3 tbsp	kirsch

TOPPING

115 g	semisweet chocolate (4 oz), chopped
¾ cup	whipping cream (35%)
4 tsp	icing sugar
2 tsp	kirsch
15 g	semisweet chocolate (½ oz), shaved

233

CHRISTMAS BUFFET

The family keeps getting bigger, louder and more boisterous every year. You started at the dining table, then annexed a second table; now there's a kids' table, too. Our menu of Christmas dinner favourites, served buffet-style, will help simplify this year's celebration. Will it make Christmas quieter? Not so much.

MENU FOR 8 TO 12

MARINATED KALE SALAD **p.236**

SWEET-AND-SOUR ONION CHUTNEY **p.236**

HERBED ROAST TURKEY **p.237**

WHITE AND WILD RICE PILAF
WITH SPINACH AND WALNUTS **p.238**

ROASTED CARROTS
WITH MUSTARD VINAIGRETTE **p.238**

WINTER VEGETABLE STEW **p.240**

CORN BREAD **p.241**

SOUR CHERRY TRIFLE **p.243**

MARINATED KALE SALAD

HANDS-ON TIME	**TOTAL TIME**	**MAKES**
10 MINUTES	1¼ HOURS	6 TO 8 SERVINGS

3 tbsp	olive oil
2 tbsp	orange juice
1 tbsp	liquid honey
1	bunch kale, stemmed and chopped
⅓ cup	dried cherries, chopped
⅓ cup	chopped hazelnuts, toasted

In large bowl, whisk together oil, orange juice and honey; add kale and cherries. Toss to coat. Let stand for 1 hour.

Serve sprinkled with hazelnuts.

NUTRITIONAL INFORMATION, PER SERVING: about 126 cal, 2 g pro, 8 g total fat (1 g sat. fat), 13 g carb (2 g dietary fibre, 8 g sugar), 0 mg chol, 20 mg sodium, 251 mg potassium. % RDI: 7% calcium, 8% iron, 39% vit A, 88% vit C, 9% folate.

SWEET-AND-SOUR ONION CHUTNEY

HANDS-ON TIME	**TOTAL TIME**	**MAKES**
15 MINUTES	45 MINUTES	3 CUPS

3 tbsp	vegetable oil
2	sweet onions (about 750 g total), finely chopped
¼ tsp	each hot pepper flakes, salt and pepper
1 cup	pure cranberry juice
⅓ cup	each dried cranberries, golden raisins and chopped dried apricots
2 tbsp	cider vinegar

In saucepan, heat oil over medium heat; cook onions, hot pepper flakes, salt and pepper, stirring occasionally, until onions are softened and just beginning to turn golden, about 15 minutes.

Stir in cranberry juice, cranberries, raisins, apricot, vinegar and ½ cup water; bring to boil. Reduce heat; simmer, stirring occasionally, until thickened and almost no liquid remains, 25 to 30 minutes. *(Make-ahead: Let cool. Refrigerate in airtight container for up to 3 days. Let come to room temperature before serving.)*

NUTRITIONAL INFORMATION, PER 1 TBSP: about 23 cal, trace pro, 1 g total fat (trace sat. fat), 4 g carb (trace dietary fibre), 0 mg chol, 14 mg sodium, 36 mg potassium. % RDI: 1% iron, 3% vit C, 1% folate.

HERBED ROAST TURKEY

p.234

HANDS-ON TIME
1 HOUR

TOTAL TIME
4½ HOURS

MAKES
16 TO 18 SERVINGS

HERBED OIL In bowl, combine tarragon, parsley, thyme and oil. Using muddler or back of wooden spoon, mash leaves until bruised and fragrant, about 1 minute. Let stand for 10 minutes. Remove herbs, squeezing out as much oil as possible; set herbs aside. Whisk butter, garlic, lemon zest, lemon juice, salt and pepper into oil.

ROAST TURKEY Remove giblets and neck from turkey; place turkey neck in roasting pan. Twist wings under back. Fill cavity with parsley, thyme, tarragon, lemon and reserved muddled herbs. Place turkey, breast side up, on rack in roasting pan. Rub all over with herbed oil.

Roast in 325°F (160°C) oven, basting every 45 minutes, until instant-read thermometer inserted in thickest part of breast reads 170°F (77°C), about 3½ hours. Wearing oven mitts and using tongs, gently tip turkey to pour liquid from cavity into roasting pan. Transfer turkey to platter; cover loosely with foil and let stand for 30 minutes before carving.

Meanwhile, discard turkey neck; pour liquid from roasting pan into heatproof bowl. Skim off fat; set aside.

Stir wine into roasting pan; bring to boil over medium-high heat. Cook for 1 minute, scraping up any browned bits.

Whisk broth with flour until smooth; stir into roasting pan along with reserved liquid and 1 cup water. Bring to boil; reduce heat and simmer, whisking often, until thickened, 5 to 8 minutes. Strain into gravy dish; serve with turkey.

NUTRITIONAL INFORMATION, PER EACH OF 18 SERVINGS: about 290 cal, 56 g pro, 12 g total fat (3 g sat. fat), 2 g carb (trace dietary fibre, trace sugar), 184 mg chol, 271 mg sodium, 760 mg potassium. % RDI: 2% calcium, 9% iron, 1% vit A, 3% vit C, 10% folate.

HERBED OIL

¼ cup	each fresh tarragon leaves and fresh parsley leaves
5	sprigs fresh thyme
3 tbsp	olive oil
1 tbsp	butter, melted
2	cloves garlic, grated
1 tbsp	grated lemon zest
1 tbsp	lemon juice
½ tsp	each salt and pepper

ROAST TURKEY

1	turkey (7 to 9 kg)
10	parsley stems
5	sprigs fresh thyme
3	sprigs fresh tarragon
1	lemon, quartered
¾ cup	dry white wine
1½ cups	sodium-reduced chicken broth
⅓ cup	all-purpose flour

237

WHITE AND WILD RICE PILAF
WITH SPINACH AND WALNUTS

opposite

HANDS-ON TIME	**TOTAL TIME**
15 MINUTES	55 MINUTES

MAKES
12 SERVINGS

⅔ cup	wild rice, rinsed
3 tbsp	vegetable oil
1	onion, finely diced
1	green onion, thinly sliced
1	bay leaf
½ tsp	salt
¼ tsp	pepper
3 cups	basmati rice
2 cups	spinach leaves, finely chopped
1 cup	toasted walnuts, coarsely chopped
¼ cup	chopped fresh parsley

In saucepan of boiling salted water, cook wild rice until tender, about 40 minutes. Drain and set aside.

Meanwhile, in separate saucepan, heat oil over medium-high heat; cook onion, half of the green onion, the bay leaf, salt and pepper until onion is softened and just beginning to turn golden, about 5 minutes. Stir in basmati rice; cook, stirring, for 1 minute.

Stir in 3½ cups water; bring to boil. Reduce heat, cover and simmer until no liquid remains and rice is tender, about 15 minutes. Turn off heat.

Stir in spinach, walnuts, parsley, remaining green onion and the wild rice; cover and let stand for 5 minutes. Discard bay leaf.

NUTRITIONAL INFORMATION, PER SERVING: about 300 cal, 7 g pro, 10 g total fat (1 g sat. fat), 46 g carb (2 g dietary fibre), 0 mg chol, 223 mg sodium, 167 mg potassium. % RDI: 3% calcium, 7% iron, 6% vit A, 3% vit C, 15% folate.

ROASTED CARROTS
WITH MUSTARD VINAIGRETTE

opposite

HANDS-ON TIME	**TOTAL TIME**
10 MINUTES	50 MINUTES

MAKES
12 SERVINGS

1.8 kg	carrots, peeled
⅓ cup	olive oil
¼ cup	lemon juice
1½ tsp	chopped fresh thyme
1 tsp	Dijon mustard
½ tsp	dried oregano
½ tsp	each salt and pepper

Halve carrots crosswise on the diagonal. Cut each piece lengthwise in half or quarters; set aside.

In large bowl, whisk together oil, lemon juice, thyme, mustard, oregano, salt and pepper; add carrots and toss to combine. Roast on foil-lined baking sheets in 375°F (190°C) oven until edges are crisp and golden and carrots are tender, 40 to 45 minutes. *(Make-ahead: Let cool; refrigerate for up to 8 hours.)*

NUTRITIONAL INFORMATION, PER SERVING: about 120 cal, 2 g pro, 6 g total fat (1 g sat. fat), 16 g carb (5 g dietary fibre), 0 mg chol, 210 mg sodium, 445 mg potassium. % RDI: 5% calcium, 6% iron, 320% vit A, 13% vit C, 12% folate.

WHITE AND WILD RICE PILAF WITH SPINACH AND WALNUTS AND ROASTED CARROTS WITH MUSTARD VINAIGRETTE

WINTER VEGETABLE STEW

HANDS-ON TIME		**TOTAL TIME**		**MAKES**	
25 MINUTES		1½ HOURS		8 SERVINGS	

1	head garlic
3 tbsp	olive oil
1	pkg (284 g) pearl onions, peeled
1.35 kg	yellow-fleshed potatoes, peeled and cut into chunks
5	sprigs fresh parsley
3	sprigs fresh thyme
2	bay leaves
1 tsp	salt
¼ tsp	pepper
pinch	saffron (optional)
¼ cup	all-purpose flour
2 cups	vegetable broth
half	head cauliflower, cut into florets
2 cups	cooked chestnuts
1	small butternut squash (about 750 g), peeled and cut into chunks

Slice off top third of garlic head to expose cloves. Place garlic head on small square of foil; drizzle cut side with 1 tsp of the oil and fold foil over to seal. Roast in 375°F (190°C) oven until tender, about 45 minutes. Let cool slightly; squeeze out cloves into bowl. Set aside.

Meanwhile, in Dutch oven or large heavy-bottomed saucepan, heat remaining oil over medium heat; cook onions, stirring occasionally, until golden, about 6 minutes.

Stir in potatoes, parsley, thyme, bay leaves, salt, pepper, saffron (if using) and roasted garlic; cook, stirring, for 2 minutes.

Stir in flour; cook, stirring, for 2 minutes. Gradually stir in broth, scraping up any browned bits. Stir in 3 cups water and bring to boil; reduce heat, cover and simmer for 10 minutes.

Stir in cauliflower and chestnuts; simmer for 5 minutes.

Stir in squash; simmer until tender, about 10 minutes. Discard parsley, thyme and bay leaves. *(Make-ahead: Let cool for 30 minutes; refrigerate for up to 24 hours. Reheat before serving, stirring gently to keep squash in chunks.)*

NUTRITIONAL INFORMATION, PER SERVING: about 263 cal, 5 g pro, 6 g total fat (1 g sat. fat), 50 g carb (8 g dietary fibre), 1 mg chol, 492 mg sodium, 751 mg potassium. % RDI: 6% calcium, 11% iron, 79% vit A, 72% vit C, 33% folate.

TIP FROM THE TEST KITCHEN

Fresh chestnuts have the best flavour and are widely available in late autumn and early winter. To prepare, cut an X in the flat side of each. Working in small batches, boil until the points of the cut curl up, about 2 minutes. Remove chestnuts using slotted spoon, peel off skin, then simmer in fresh water until tender, about 5 minutes.

Vacuum-packed and canned chestnuts are available in some grocery and specialty food shops. Of the two, vacuum-packed taste better. Both types are precooked; just drain and rinse canned chestnuts before using.

CORN BREAD

HANDS-ON TIME
10 MINUTES

TOTAL TIME
1 HOUR

MAKES
8 SERVINGS

In large bowl, whisk together flour, cornmeal, sugar, baking powder, baking soda and salt. In separate bowl, whisk together buttermilk, egg and butter; pour over flour mixture and stir to make thick batter.

Spread in greased or parchment paper–lined 8-inch (2 L) square metal cake pan. Bake in 375°F (190°C) oven until cake tester inserted in centre comes out clean, 25 to 30 minutes.

Let cool in pan on rack for 5 minutes; invert onto rack. Remove paper and let cool. *(Make-ahead: Store in airtight container for up to 24 hours.)*

NUTRITIONAL INFORMATION, PER SERVING: about 139 cal, 4 g pro, 5 g total fat (3 g sat. fat), 19 g carb (1 g dietary fibre), 28 mg chol, 154 mg sodium, 83 mg potassium. % RDI: 5% calcium, 5% iron, 5% vit A, 21% folate.

1 cup	each all-purpose flour and cornmeal
1 tbsp	granulated sugar
1 tsp	baking powder
½ tsp	baking soda
¼ tsp	salt
1¼ cups	buttermilk
1	egg
¼ cup	unsalted butter, melted

241

SOUR CHERRY TRIFLE

SOUR CHERRY TRIFLE

opposite

HANDS-ON TIME
45 MINUTES

TOTAL TIME
3 HOURS

MAKES
10 TO 12 SERVINGS

CUSTARD In bowl, whisk together egg yolks, sugar and cornstarch. In saucepan, heat milk over medium heat just until bubbles form around edge; gradually whisk one-third of the milk into egg mixture. Whisk back into pan and cook over medium heat, whisking constantly, until mixture comes to a boil. Continue to cook, whisking, until bubbling and thickened, 3 to 4 minutes. Remove from heat. Whisk in butter and vanilla. Place plastic wrap directly on surface; let cool slightly.

CAKE While custard is cooling, cut cake in half horizontally. Spread cut side of bottom with jam; replace top half, pressing to adhere. Cut into about 1-inch (2.5 cm) cubes.

Line 12-cup (3 L) trifle bowl with half of the cake pieces; brush with half of the sherry. Repeat with remaining cake pieces and sherry. Scrape warm custard over top; place plastic wrap directly on surface. Refrigerate until chilled, about 2 hours.

TOPPING While cake mixture is chilling, in saucepan, bring cherries with syrup and sugar to boil over medium-high heat; boil until syrupy and reduced by half, about 25 minutes. Scrape into bowl; let cool. Refrigerate until cold, about 1 hour.

Transfer cherry mixture to strainer set over bowl; let stand for 10 minutes to drain. Reserve liquid.

Sprinkle amaretti over custard. Spoon cherry mixture over top; drizzle with 2 tbsp of the reserved cherry liquid.

In bowl, whip cream until peaks form; spread over trifle. Sprinkle with almonds.

NUTRITIONAL INFORMATION, PER EACH OF 12 SERVINGS: about 456 cal, 7 g pro, 20 g total fat (11 g sat. fat), 61 g carb (2 g dietary fibre), 175 mg chol, 176 mg sodium, 211 mg potassium. % RDI: 11% calcium, 14% iron, 23% vit A, 3% vit C, 16% folate.

CUSTARD

5	egg yolks
⅓ cup	granulated sugar
3 tbsp	cornstarch
2 cups	whole milk
3 tbsp	butter
½ tsp	vanilla

CAKE

1	sponge cake (9 inch/23 cm)
¼ cup	raspberry jam or strawberry jam
⅔ cup	sweet sherry or Madeira

TOPPING

1	jar (796 mL) red sour cherries in light syrup
⅓ cup	granulated sugar
1¼ cups	crumbled amaretti cookies
1½ cups	whipping cream (35%)
¼ cup	sliced almonds, toasted

243

HOLIDAY BRUNCH

During this peak season for social events, how can you
bring the gang together for a good laugh over a meal?
Easy. Invite them over during the off-peak hours
for a holiday brunch. For even more fun, tell everyone
to wear a favourite Ugly Holiday Sweater.
They'll be itching to show theirs off.

245

MENU FOR 4 TO 6

CRANBERRY MIMOSAS **p.246**

ORANGE BEET SALAD **p.246**

ROASTED PEARS WITH YOGURT AND GRANOLA **p.247**

CHERRY PISTACHIO PANCAKES **p.247**

CARAMELIZED ONION AND APPLE PIZZA **p.249**

ULTRA-CRISPY ROASTED POTATOES **p.249**

CRANBERRY MIMOSAS

HANDS-ON TIME	**TOTAL TIME**	**MAKES**
10 MINUTES	10 MINUTES	12 SERVINGS

3 cups	cranberry juice
¼ cup	triple sec or orange juice
2 tbsp	grenadine
12	maraschino cherries
1	bottle (750 mL) dry sparkling white wine, chilled

In pitcher, stir together cranberry juice, triple sec and grenadine. In champagne glass, add 1 cherry; top with ¼ cup each of cranberry mixture and sparkling wine. Repeat with remaining cranberry mixture, cherries and wine.

NUTRITIONAL INFORMATION, PER SERVING: about 105 cal, trace pro, 0 g total fat (0 g sat. fat), 14 g carb (trace dietary fibre), 0 mg chol, 3 mg sodium.

ORANGE BEET SALAD

HANDS-ON TIME	**TOTAL TIME**	**MAKES**
25 MINUTES	1½ HOURS	6 SERVINGS

4	oranges
1 cup	thinly sliced celery (about 3 ribs)
2 tbsp	each liquid honey and lemon juice
1 tsp	grated fresh ginger
¼ tsp	each salt and pepper
2	cooked beets, thinly sliced
1	shallot, halved and thinly sliced
1	pkg (142 g) baby arugula
¼ cup	fresh mint leaves, chopped
2 tbsp	extra-virgin olive oil

Cut off zest and pith from oranges. Working over bowl, cut between membrane and pulp to release segments; squeeze juice from membranes into bowl. Transfer 3 tbsp juice to separate bowl. Set aside.

Toss celery with orange segments; cover and refrigerate for 1 hour.

Whisk together honey, lemon juice, ginger, salt, pepper and reserved orange juice. Stir in beets and shallot. Cover and chill in refrigerator for at least 1 hour or up to 2 days.

Just before serving, toss together orange mixture, beet mixture, arugula, mint and oil.

NUTRITIONAL INFORMATION, PER SERVING: about 130 cal, 3 g pro, 5 g total fat (1 g sat. fat), 22 g carb (3 g dietary fibre, 17 g sugar), 30 mg chol, 160 mg sodium, 461 mg potassium. % RDI: 8% calcium, 11% iron, 10% vit A, 72% vit C, 44% folate.

ROASTED PEARS
WITH YOGURT AND GRANOLA

p.244

HANDS-ON TIME	TOTAL TIME	MAKES
15 MINUTES	2¾ HOURS	8 SERVINGS

Using melon baller or teaspoon, remove cores from pears. Arrange pears, cut side up, in buttered 13- x 9-inch (3 L) baking dish. Brush lemon juice over cut side of pears; sprinkle brown sugar and salt over top. Stir together orange juice and vanilla; pour over top.

Bake in 350°F (180°C) oven, basting occasionally and turning pears halfway, until soft, 25 to 35 minutes. Let cool for 30 minutes. Refrigerate until chilled, about 2 hours. *(Make-ahead: Refrigerate for up to 24 hours.)*

Meanwhile, in small bowl, combine yogurt and maple syrup; spoon onto pears. Sprinkle with granola, almonds and orange zest.

NUTRITIONAL INFORMATION, PER SERVING: about 308 cal, 9 g pro, 8 g total fat (3 g sat. fat), 55 g carb (8 g dietary fibre), 11 mg chol, 199 mg sodium.

4	large firm ripe Bosc pears, halved lengthwise
1 tbsp	lemon
2 tbsp	packed brown sugar
¼ tsp	salt
¼ cup	orange juice
1 tsp	vanilla
1 cup	plain Greek yogurt
2 tbsp	maple syrup
¼ cup	granola
2 tbsp	toasted slivered almonds
2 tsp	grated orange zest (or triple sec)

247

CHERRY PISTACHIO PANCAKES

p.244

HANDS-ON TIME	TOTAL TIME	MAKES
10 MINUTES	10 MINUTES	12 SERVINGS

In large bowl, mix together flour, sugar, baking powder and salt. In separate bowl, whisk together egg, buttermilk and oil. Pour over flour mixture; stir until just combined but still slightly lumpy. Stir in pistachios, cherries and lemon zest.

Lightly brush skillet with some of the butter over medium heat. Working in batches and brushing on more butter as needed, pour in scant ¼ cup batter per pancake; spread slightly. Cook until bubbles appear on top, about 2 minutes. Flip and cook until bottom is golden brown, about 2 minutes. Transfer to rimmed baking sheet; cover and keep warm in 250°F (120°C) oven. Serve pancakes with maple syrup, sprinkling with more dried pistachios and cherries, if desired.

NUTRITIONAL INFORMATION, PER PANCAKE: about 165 cal, 4 g pro, 7 g total fat (2 g sat. fat), 22 g carb (1 g dietary fibre), 0 mg chol, 210 mg sodium.

1¾ cups	all-purpose flour
2 tbsp	granulated sugar
1 tbsp	baking powder
¼ tsp	salt
1	egg, lightly beaten
1½ cups	buttermilk
3 tbsp	vegetable oil
⅓ cup	chopped pistachios
⅓ cup	dried cherries
1 tsp	grated lemon zest
1 tbsp	butter (approx), melted maple syrup

CAMARELIZED ONION AND APPLE PIZZA

CARAMELIZED ONION AND APPLE PIZZA

opposite

HANDS-ON TIME
20 MINUTES

TOTAL TIME
1 HOUR

MAKES
6 SERVINGS

In large skillet, melt butter over medium heat. Cook onion, stirring occasionally, until light golden, about 15 minutes. Stir in mustard, thyme, lemon juice, maple syrup and half each of the salt and the pepper. Cook, stirring and adding water, 1 tbsp at a time, as necessary to prevent onions from sticking, until onion is golden, about 10 minutes. Set aside.

On lightly floured work surface, roll out dough into a 13- x 9-inch (33 x 23 cm) rectangle. Transfer to greased baking sheet; top with onion mixture, ham, apple, Gruyère and remaining salt and pepper. Bake on bottom rack of 450°F (230°C) oven until crust is golden, about 20 minutes.

NUTRITIONAL INFORMATION, PER SERVING: about 309 cal, 15 g pro, 10 g total fat (5 g sat. fat), 47 g carb (4 g dietary fibre, 7 g sugar), 31 mg chol, 715 mg sodium, 165 mg potassium. % RDI: 13% calcium, 19% iron, 7% vit A, 3% vit C, 40% folate.

2 tbsp	butter
1	large red onion, thinly sliced
1 tbsp	grainy mustard
2 tsp	chopped fresh thyme
1 tsp	lemon juice
½ tsp	maple syrup
¼ tsp	each salt and pepper
1	pkg (450 g) pizza dough
100 g	sliced Black Forest ham, cut into thin strips
1	small Empire or Gala apple, quartered, cored and thinly sliced
⅔ cup	shredded Gruyère cheese

ULTRA-CRISPY ROASTED POTATOES

HANDS-ON TIME
20 MINUTES

TOTAL TIME
1½ HOURS

MAKES
4 SERVINGS

In large saucepan of boiling salted water, cook potatoes just until fork-tender, about 6 minutes. Drain well.

In roasting pan, heat duck fat in 450°F (230°C) oven just until beginning to smoke, about 4 minutes. Remove from oven; standing back and averting face, add potatoes. Sprinkle with salt and pepper; stir to coat. Roast, turning potatoes every 20 minutes, until golden, 50 to 60 minutes.

NUTRITIONAL INFORMATION, PER SERVING: about 277 cal, 4 g pro, 13 g total fat (4 g sat. fat), 37 g carb (3 g dietary fibre), 13 mg chol, 780 mg sodium, 766 mg potassium. % RDI: 2% calcium, 12% iron, 50% vit C, 12% folate.

1 kg	russet potatoes, peeled and cut in 1½-inch (4 cm) pieces
¼ cup	duck, goose, beef or chicken fat (or 2 tbsp each olive oil and melted unsalted butter)
½ tsp	salt
pinch	pepper

NEW YEAR'S EVE DROP-IN

This New Year's Eve, bring back retro elegance with a classic menu of 1960s hors d'oeuvres and cocktails, updated for today's tastes. We've simplified the prep, too, so you can concentrate on what's important: having a great time hosting the last, best party of the year.

MENU FOR 12

DARK AND SNOWY **p.252**

MERRY MANHATTAN **p.252**

CLASSIC RUMAKI **p.253**

UPDATED DEVILS ON HORSEBACK **p.253**

BACON AND ONION CHEESE BALLS **p.255**

BEER AND CHEESE FONDUE DIP **p.256**

SWEET-AND-SOUR MEATBALLS **p.257**

SHRIMP COCKTAIL CANAPÉS **p.259**

CRAB RANGOON–STUFFED
MUSHROOM CAPS **p.259**

DARK AND SNOWY

HANDS-ON TIME 10 MINUTES
TOTAL TIME 25 MINUTES
MAKES 2 SERVINGS

¼	cup Ginger Syrup (approx) (recipe below)
	Allspice Rimmer (recipe below)
1 cup	ice cubes
4 oz	dark or amber rum (about ½ cup)
2 tbsp	10% cream

Moisten rims of 2 martini glasses with Ginger Syrup; dip in Allspice Rimmer to coat. In cocktail shaker, shake together ice cubes, rum, cream and ¼ cup Ginger Syrup until cold. Strain into prepared glasses.

NUTRITIONAL INFORMATION, PER SERVING: about 217 cal, 1 g pro, 2 g total fat (1 g sat. fat), 19 g carb (0 g dietary fibre, 18 g sugar), 5 mg chol, 10 mg sodium, 24 mg potassium. % RDI: 2% calcium, 1% iron, 1% vit A.

GINGER SYRUP

In large saucepan over medium heat, bring 16 slices fresh ginger and 4 cups water to boil; reduce heat and simmer until reduced to 1⅓ cup, about 20 minutes. Add 1 cup sugar, stirring until dissolved. Strain syrup into bowl; let cool. *(Make-ahead: Refrigerate in airtight container for up to 3 months.)*

ALLSPICE RIMMER

Stir together 6 tbsp each brown sugar and granulated sugar and ¾ tsp allspice, rubbing with fingers to combine. Spread in large shallow dish.

MERRY MANHATTAN

HANDS-ON TIME 10 MINUTES
TOTAL TIME 25 MINUTES
MAKES 2 SERVINGS

6	frozen cranberries
1 cup	ice cubes
4 oz	rye whisky (about ½ cup)
2 oz	dry vermouth (about ¼ cup)
2	drops Angostura bitters
2 tbsp	Spiced Syrup (recipe below)

Divide cranberries between 2 old-fashioned glasses. In cocktail shaker or glass measure, stir together ice, whisky, vermouth, bitters and Spiced Syrup until cold. Strain into prepared glasses.

NUTRITIONAL INFORMATION, PER SERVING: about 249 cal, trace pro, 0 g total fat (0 g sat. fat), 23 g carb (trace dietary fibre, 19 g sugar), 0 mg chol, 8 mg sodium, 34 mg potassium. % RDI: 1% calcium, 1% iron, 2% vit C.

SPICED SYRUP

Using bottom of small saucepan, lightly crush 2 whole star anise, 2 cinnamon sticks, 2 cardamom pods, 2 allspice berries and 2 whole cloves. In saucepan over medium heat, bring crushed spices, 3 slices fresh ginger and 2 cups water to boil. Reduce heat and simmer until reduced to ⅔ cup, about 20 minutes. Add ½ cup sugar, stirring until dissolved. Strain syrup into bowl; let cool. *(Make-ahead: Refrigerate in airtight container for up to 3 months.)*

CLASSIC RUMAKI

p.250

HANDS-ON TIME
30 MINUTES

TOTAL TIME
1½ HOURS

MAKES
36 PIECES

Trim and cut chicken livers into thirty-six ½-inch (1 cm) pieces. In bowl, stir together soy sauce, ginger, garlic and 2 tbsp of the brown sugar. Add chicken livers, tossing to coat. Cover and refrigerate for 1 hour.

For each serving, wrap 1 piece each of water chestnut and chicken liver together in 1 piece of bacon; secure with toothpick. Place on rimmed baking sheet. Sprinkle with 1 tbsp of the remaining brown sugar. Bake in 425°F (220°C) oven, turning once and sprinkling with remaining brown sugar, until bacon is browned, about 15 minutes.

NUTRITIONAL INFORMATION, PER PIECE: about 24 cal, 2 g pro, 1 g total fat (trace sat. fat), 2 g carb (trace dietary fibre, 2 g sugar), 27 mg chol, 75 mg sodium, 45 mg potassium. % RDI: 3% iron, 18% vit A, 2% vit C, 13% folate.

250 g	chicken livers
3 tbsp	sodium-reduced soy sauce
2 tsp	grated fresh ginger
2	cloves garlic, grated
¼ cup	packed brown sugar
9	water chestnuts, quartered
12	strips sodium-reduced bacon, cut crosswise in thirds

253

UPDATED DEVILS ON HORSEBACK

p.250

HANDS-ON TIME
20 MINUTES

TOTAL TIME
30 MINUTES

MAKES
48 PIECES

Stuff each fig quarter with ½ tsp of the blue cheese. Wrap each with bacon; secure with toothpick. *(Make-ahead: Cover and refrigerate for up to 6 hours.)*

Bake on rimmed baking sheet in 425°F (220°C) oven, turning once, until bacon is browned, about 13 minutes.

NUTRITIONAL INFORMATION, PER PIECE: about 26 cal, 2 g pro, 1 g total fat (1 g sat. fat), 2 g carb (trace dietary fibre, 2 g sugar), 6 mg chol, 58 mg sodium, 57 mg potassium. % RDI: 2% calcium, 1% iron, 1% vit A.

12	dried figs, quartered
120 g	blue cheese
16	strips sodium-reduced bacon, cut in thirds

FROM TOP: CRANBERRY AND PISTACHIO CHEESE BALLS; BACON AND ONION CHEESE BALLS; AND BASIL AND LEMON CHEESE BALLS

BACON AND ONION CHEESE BALLS

opposite

HANDS-ON TIME	**TOTAL TIME**	**MAKES**
20 MINUTES	20 MINUTES	ABOUT 24 PIECES

In skillet, cook bacon over medium heat until crisp, about 5 minutes. Drain on paper towel–lined plate. Chop into ¼-inch (5 mm) pieces.

Meanwhile, in food processor, pulse almonds until coarsely ground; set aside in small bowl.

In separate bowl, stir together bacon, goat cheese, green onions, garlic and pepper. Roll by scant 1 tbsp into balls. Roll in almonds, pressing to adhere. *(Make-ahead: Cover and refrigerate for up to 24 hours.)*

NUTRITIONAL INFORMATION, PER PIECE: about 61 cal, 4 g pro, 5 g total fat (2 g sat. fat), 1 g carb (trace dietary fibre, trace sugar), 9 mg chol, 60 mg sodium, 50 mg potassium. % RDI: 3% calcium, 3% iron, 4% vit A, 1% folate.

5	strips sodium-reduced bacon
½ cup	unsalted roasted natural (skin-on) whole almonds
1	pkg (300 g) soft goat cheese
2	green onions, finely chopped
1	clove garlic, finely minced
½ tsp	pepper

255

VARIATION

BASIL AND LEMON CHEESE BALLS
Omit bacon and garlic. Add 1½ tsp grated lemon zest and ¼ cup chopped fresh basil.

CRANBERRY AND PISTACHIO CHEESE BALLS
Substitute shelled unsalted pistachios for almonds. Omit bacon, green onions and garlic. Add ⅓ cup dried cranberries, finely chopped.

BEER AND CHEESE FONDUE DIP

HANDS-ON TIME	25 MINUTES
TOTAL TIME	25 MINUTES
MAKES	ABOUT 3 CUPS

1	clove garlic, halved
1⅓ cups	Weissbier
225 g	medium Cheddar cheese, shredded
170 g	Gruyère cheese, shredded
2 tbsp	cornstarch
pinch	cayenne pepper
115 g	cream cheese, cubed
1 tbsp	lemon juice
1 tbsp	Calvados or brandy

Rub cut sides of garlic all over inside of fondue pot or heavy-bottomed saucepan. Pour in Weissbier; bring to simmer over medium heat.

In bowl, toss together Cheddar, Gruyère, cornstarch and cayenne pepper. Add to beer in 3 additions, stirring constantly using wooden spoon.

Whisk in cream cheese and lemon juice until smooth. Stir in Calvados. Place over medium-low heat of fondue burner, adjusting heat as necessary to maintain low simmer and stirring often.

NUTRITIONAL INFORMATION, PER 1 TBSP: about 46 cal, 2 g pro, 4 g total fat (2 g sat. fat), 1 g carb (0 g dietary fibre, trace sugar), 11 mg chol, 49 mg sodium, 13 mg potassium. % RDI: 7% calcium, 1% iron, 3% vit A, 1% folate.

VARIATION
CHEESE FONDUE DIP
Substitute no-salt-added chicken broth for beer.

TIP FROM THE TEST KITCHEN

Weissbier is German-style wheat beer. It's a pale, crisp, light style that's often bottled unfiltered; the yeast in the bottle gives it a slightly cloudy appearance and a rich, creamy flavour. It's mild and not bitter—perfect with melted cheese.

SWEET-AND-SOUR MEATBALLS

p.250

HANDS-ON TIME	**TOTAL TIME**	**MAKES**
30 MINUTES	30 MINUTES	ABOUT 60 PIECES

MEATBALLS In bowl, stir together bread crumbs, eggs, green onions, garlic, ginger, Worcestershire sauce, pepper and salt; mix in beef. Roll by 1 tbsp into balls. *(Make-ahead: Cover and refrigerate for up to 12 hours.)*

In large nonstick skillet, heat oil over medium-high heat; working in batches, cook meatballs until browned and instant-read thermometer inserted into several reads 160°F (71°C), about 10 minutes.

SWEET-AND-SOUR SAUCE Meanwhile, in small saucepan, whisk together pineapple juice, ketchup, brown sugar, grenadine, vinegar and ¾ cup water. Bring to boil over medium-high heat; reduce heat and simmer for 5 minutes.

Stir cornstarch with 3 tbsp water; whisk into sauce and simmer until thickened, about 30 seconds. Toss three-quarters of the sauce with meatballs. Arrange in serving dish; top with remaining sauce.

NUTRITIONAL INFORMATION, PER PIECE: about 45 cal, 3 g pro, 2 g total fat (1 g sat. fat), 4 g carb (trace dietary fibre, 3 g sugar), 14 mg chol, 49 mg sodium, 57 mg potassium. % RDI: 1% calcium, 3% iron, 1% vit A, 2% vit C, 1% folate.

MEATBALLS

¼ cup	dried bread crumbs
2	eggs, lightly beaten
2	green onions, finely chopped
3	cloves garlic, minced
1 tbsp	minced fresh ginger
1 tbsp	Worcestershire sauce
½ tsp	pepper
¼ tsp	salt
900 g	lean ground beef
2 tsp	vegetable oil

SWEET-AND-SOUR SAUCE

⅔ cup	pineapple juice
½ cup	ketchup
⅓ cup	packed brown sugar
⅓ cup	grenadine
⅓ cup	white vinegar
3 tbsp	cornstarch

SHRIMP COCKTAIL CANAPÉS

SHRIMP COCKTAIL CANAPÉS

opposite

HANDS-ON TIME
25 MINUTES

TOTAL TIME
25 MINUTES

MAKES
28 PIECES

In bowl, stir together mayonnaise, cilantro, horseradish, chili sauce and Worcestershire sauce. *(Make-ahead: Cover and refrigerate for up to 24 hours.)*

Using rolling pin, flatten each slice of bread to ⅛-inch (3 mm) thickness; cut each into 4 squares. Brush cups of mini muffin pan with half of the butter. Press square into each well; brush with remaining butter. Bake in 400°F (200°C) oven until golden, about 6 minutes. Let cool on rack. *(Make-ahead: Let stand at room temperature for up to 3 hours.)*

Remove tails from shrimp; rinse and pat dry. Fill each cup with about ½ tsp of the sauce; top with shrimp. Garnish with cilantro.

NUTRITIONAL INFORMATION, PER PIECE: about 39 cal, 3 g pro, 2 g total fat (trace sat. fat), 4 g carb (trace dietary fibre, 1 g sugar), 23 mg chol, 84 mg sodium, 32 mg potassium. % RDI: 1% calcium, 4% iron, 1% vit A, 4% folate.

¼ cup	light mayonnaise
2 tbsp	chopped fresh cilantro
1 tbsp	prepared horseradish
2 tsp	tomato-based chili sauce
½ tsp	Worcestershire sauce
7	slices white sandwich bread, crusts removed
1 tbsp	butter, melted
28	cooked peeled medium shrimp (about 300 g total), tails removed
	Fresh cilantro leaves

259

CRAB RANGOON–STUFFED MUSHROOM CAPS

HANDS-ON TIME
25 MINUTES

TOTAL TIME
40 MINUTES

MAKES
30 PIECES

In bowl, stir together crabmeat, cream cheese, bread crumbs, green onions, lemon juice, garlic, Worcestershire sauce and pepper.

Spoon 1 tbsp filling into each mushroom cap, pressing to flatten slightly. *(Make-ahead: Cover and refrigerate for up to 3 hours.)* Place on foil-lined rimmed baking sheet. Stir panko with butter; press ½ tsp onto each filling.

Bake in 400°F (200°C) oven until golden and mushrooms are tender, about 18 minutes. Let cool for 5 minutes before serving.

NUTRITIONAL INFORMATION, PER PIECE: about 34 cal, 2 g pro, 2 g total fat (1 g sat. fat), 2 g carb (1 g dietary fibre, 1 g sugar), 12 mg chol, 44 mg sodium, 117 mg potassium. % RDI: 2% calcium, 1% iron, 2% vit A, 3% folate.

1	tub (212 g) pasteurized crabmeat, drained
115 g	cream cheese, softened
3 tbsp	dried bread crumbs
2	green onions, finely chopped
1 tbsp	lemon juice
1	clove garlic, minced
1 tsp	Worcestershire sauce
¼ tsp	pepper
30	cremini mushrooms (about 675 g), stemmed
⅓ cup	panko
1 tbsp	butter, melted

APRÈS-SKI FONDUE

After a day of outdoor winter activities,
cheese fondue is a fun, interactive way to spend
Saturday night at the chalet. Get your ski or toboggan
buddies involved from start to finish—choosing
ingredients, shredding cheese, chopping vegetables and,
of course, pouring you a mug of spicy mulled wine.

261

MENU FOR 4

CHEDDAR AND OKA FONDUE p.262

LIME-GLAZED COCONUT BUTTER COOKIES p.263

MULLED RED WINE AND MADEIRA p.263

CHEDDAR AND OKA FONDUE

p.260

HANDS-ON TIME	**TOTAL TIME**
20 MINUTES	20 MINUTES

MAKES
ABOUT 4 CUPS

1	clove garlic, halved
1 cup	unsweetened apple cider
1 tbsp	lemon juice
340 g	5-year-old Cheddar cheese, shredded
225 g	Oka cheese, shredded
1 tsp	Dijon mustard
pinch	each cayenne pepper and ground nutmeg
1 tbsp	cornstarch

Rub cut sides of garlic all over inside of fondue pot or heavy-bottomed saucepan. Pour in all but 2 tbsp of the cider, the lemon juice and ¼ cup water; bring to simmer over medium heat.

Add Cheddar and Oka; stir with wooden spoon until melted, about 7 minutes.

Stir in mustard, cayenne and nutmeg. Dissolve cornstarch in remaining cider; whisk into fondue. Bring to simmer, stirring; simmer for 1 minute.

Place over medium-low heat of fondue burner on table, adjusting heat as necessary to maintain low simmer and stirring often.

NUTRITIONAL INFORMATION, PER ¼ CUP: about 148 cal, 9 g pro, 11 g total fat (7 g sat. fat), 4 g carb (0 g dietary fibre), 34 mg chol, 134 mg sodium, 50 mg potassium. % RDI: 25% calcium, 1% iron, 9% vit A, 2% folate.

VARIATION

EMMENTAL AND CHEDDAR FONDUE
Substitute Emmental for the 5-year-old Cheddar, and 2-year-old Cheddar for the Oka.

TIP FROM THE TEST KITCHEN

Bread cubes are classic dippers for cheese fondue, but providing vegetable options (cooked beforehand) makes the fondue more balanced and nutritious. Try a mix of boiled mini potatoes; sautéed whole mushrooms; blanched sweet pepper slices; and lightly steamed broccoli, cauliflower, and green beans.

Have a heatproof spoon in the fondue pot, so you can stir the cheese mixture occasionally. Instead of dipping, you may prefer to spoon the cheese over the vegetables on your fork, although half the fun of a fondue is spearfishing the ones that got away.

LIME-GLAZED COCONUT BUTTER COOKIES

HANDS-ON TIME
25 MINUTES

TOTAL TIME
1¾ HOURS

MAKES
ABOUT 40 COOKIES

BUTTER COOKIES In large bowl, beat butter with sugar until fluffy; beat in egg and vanilla. Whisk together flour, coconut, cornstarch, lime zest, baking soda and salt; stir into butter mixture. Divide dough in half; shape into discs. Wrap each in plastic wrap and refrigerate until firm, about 30 minutes.

Between waxed paper, roll out dough to ¼-inch (5 mm) thickness. Using 2½-inch (6 cm) round cookie cutter, cut out shapes, rerolling scraps as necessary and refrigerating dough if it becomes too soft. Arrange, 1 inch (2.5 cm) apart, on parchment paper–lined rimless baking sheets; freeze just until firm, about 15 minutes.

Bake in 350°F (180°C) oven until firm and edges are golden, 10 to 12 minutes. Transfer to racks; let cool completely.

LIME GLAZE In small bowl, whisk together icing sugar, lime zest and lime juice; spread scant 1 tsp over each cookie. Let stand until set, about 10 minutes.

NUTRITIONAL INFORMATION, PER COOKIE: about 112 cal, 1 g pro, 5 g total fat (3 g sat. fat), 16 g carb (trace dietary fibre), 17 mg chol, 51 mg sodium, 17 mg potassium. % RDI: 3% iron, 4% vit A, 2% vit C, 7% folate.

BUTTER COOKIES

1 cup	unsalted butter, softened
⅔ cup	granulated sugar
1	egg
1 tsp	vanilla
2¼ cups	all-purpose flour
½ cup	sweetened desiccated coconut
2 tbsp	cornstarch
2 tsp	grated lime zest
1 tsp	baking soda
¼ tsp	salt

LIME GLAZE

2 cups	icing sugar
2 tsp	grated lime zest
¼ cup	lime juice

263

MULLED RED WINE AND MADEIRA

HANDS-ON TIME
10 MINUTES

TOTAL TIME
15 MINUTES

MAKES
8 SERVINGS

In saucepan over medium heat, bring wine, Madeira, brown sugar, liqueur, cloves, cinnamon and oranges just to simmer.

Reduce heat to low; cook, without simmering, for 10 minutes. Strain; discard cloves, cinnamon and oranges. Ladle into heatproof glasses or mugs.

NUTRITIONAL INFORMATION, PER SERVING: about 110 cal, 0 g pro, 0 g total fat (0 g sat. fat), 17 g carb (0 g dietary fibre), 0 mg chol, 11 mg sodium, 172 mg potassium. % RDI: 2% calcium, 4% iron, 8% vit C, 2% folate.

1	bottle (750 mL) red wine
1 cup	Madeira
¼ cup	packed brown sugar
2 oz	orange-flavoured liqueur (about ¼ cup)
4	whole cloves
¾	cinnamon stick
1	Seville orange or navel orange, sliced

GONG HEI FAT CHOI
CHINESE NEW YEAR

This menu might grace a northern Chinese table during the two-week Chinese New Year Festival or, for that matter, any time of the year. In the traditional manner, start the meal with a group of cold dishes together with drinks or tea, then serve one or two types of dumplings along with a simple soup. Mmm, dumplings!

265

MENU FOR 6 TO 8

GARLIC CUCUMBER STRIPS **p.266**

BEIJING-STYLE BOILED PEANUTS **p.266**

KELP WITH SZECHUAN PEPPERCORNS **p.267**

CHICKEN AND CELERY IN MUSTARD SAUCE **p.267**

ORANGE-CHILI CRISP BEEF STRIPS **p.268**

BOK CHOY, MUSHROOM AND TOFU SOUP **p.269**

CHINESE CHICKEN BROTH **p.269**

CHINESE DUMPLINGS **p.270**

GARLIC CUCUMBER STRIPS

HANDS-ON TIME	**TOTAL TIME**	**MAKES**
10 MINUTES	45 MINUTES	6–8 SERVINGS

340 g	cucumbers, halved and seeded
½ tsp	salt
1 tbsp	rice vinegar
1 tsp	granulated sugar
3	cloves garlic, grated or pressed
½ tsp	sesame oil

Cut cucumbers into 1½- × ⅓- × ⅓-inch (4 cm × 8 mm × 8 mm) sticks.

In bowl, mix cucumbers with salt; let stand for 30 minutes. Strain through sieve or colander, pressing out as much liquid as possible.

In bowl, stir vinegar with sugar until dissolved. Add cucumbers and garlic; toss. Drizzle oil over top. Let stand for 5 minutes. *(Make-ahead: Cover and refrigerate for up to 8 hours.)*

NUTRITIONAL INFORMATION, PER EACH OF 8 SERVINGS: about 13 cal, trace pro, trace total fat (0 g sat. fat), 3 g carb (trace dietary fibre), 0 mg chol, 72 mg sodium. % RDI: 1% calcium, 1% iron, 3% vit C, 1% folate.

BEIJING-STYLE BOILED PEANUTS

HANDS-ON TIME	**TOTAL TIME**	**MAKES**
15 MINUTES	2¾ HOURS	6 TO 8 SERVINGS

225 g	raw or blanched skinned peanuts
3	thin slices fresh ginger
2	whole star anise
½ cup	each finely diced daikon radish and finely diced carrot
⅓ cup	finely chopped Chinese or regular celery
½ tsp	salt
1¼ tsp	fish sauce

In saucepan, bring peanuts, ginger, star anise and 2¾ cups water to boil; reduce heat to medium. Uncover and boil, adding water if necessary to just cover peanuts, until tender-crisp, about 30 minutes. If there is more water than needed to barely cover peanuts, boil down over high heat. Scrape into bowl; let cool. Discard ginger and star anise.

Meanwhile, in separate bowl, sprinkle radish, carrot and celery with salt; mix well. Let stand for 30 minutes.

Add salted vegetables to peanuts; mix in fish sauce. Refrigerate for 2 hours. *(Make-ahead: Cover and refrigerate up to 3 days.)*

NUTRITIONAL INFORMATION, PER EACH OF 8 SERVINGS: about 177 cal, 7 g pro, 12 g total fat (2 g sat. fat), 13 g carb (3 g dietary fibre), 0 mg chol, 232 mg sodium. % RDI: 3% calcium, 4% iron, 9% vit A, 3% vit C, 21% folate.

KELP WITH SZECHUAN PEPPERCORNS

HANDS-ON TIME	TOTAL TIME	MAKES
20 MINUTES	50 MINUTES	6 TO 8 SERVINGS

Rinse kelp several times in cold water. Soak in 8 cups water until tender and not salty, 20 to 30 minutes. Drain well, squeezing out excess moisture. Place in heatproof bowl; mound garlic, hot pepper and sugar on top.

In small saucepan, heat oil and peppercorns over medium heat until bubbling, fragrant and seeds darken, 4 to 5 minutes. Strain through heatproof sieve over kelp mixture (garlic will sizzle).

Return peppercorns to skillet. Add soy sauce and vinegar; boil until reduced by half, about 1 minute. Strain through sieve over kelp; discard peppercorns. Toss kelp; let cool. Stir in green onion.

NUTRITIONAL INFORMATION, PER EACH OF 8 SERVINGS: about 73 cal, 1 g pro, 7 g total fat (1 g sat. fat), 3 g carb (trace dietary fibre), 0 mg chol, 291 mg sodium. % RDI: 3% calcium, 4% iron, 2% vit C, 1% folate.

30 g	dried shredded kelp
2	cloves garlic, minced
1	red finger chili pepper, thinly sliced
½ tsp	granulated sugar
¼ cup	sesame oil
4 tsp	Szechuan peppercorns
2 tbsp	soy sauce
1 tbsp	black rice vinegar or balsamic vinegar
1	green onion, thinly sliced

CHICKEN AND CELERY IN MUSTARD SAUCE

HANDS-ON TIME	TOTAL TIME	MAKES
30 MINUTES	40 MINUTES	6 TO 8 SERVINGS

In saucepan of boiling salted water, blanch celery until tender-crisp, about 20 seconds; using tongs, transfer to bowl of ice water. Drain and pat dry.

Add ginger to boiling water; reduce heat to low. Add chicken; cover and poach until no longer pink inside, about 15 minutes. Remove chicken and let cool. Remove and discard skin and bones. *(Make-ahead: Wrap and refrigerate celery and chicken separately for up to 6 hours.)* Shred chicken.

In bowl, mix mustard powder with 1 tbsp water to make paste; let stand for 10 minutes. Whisk in soy sauce, sesame oil, vinegar and sugar until sugar is dissolved. Stir in onions.

Place celery on serving plate; top with chicken. Spoon mustard sauce over top. Garnish with cilantro.

NUTRITIONAL INFORMATION PER EACH OF 8 SERVINGS: about 46 cal, 4 g pro, 3 g total fat (trace sat. fat), 2 g carb (trace dietary fibre), 11 mg chol, 140 mg sodium. % RDI: 1% calcium, 2% iron, 2% vit A, 3% vit C, 3% folate.

3	ribs celery, cut crosswise in 2-inch (5 cm) pieces
4	slices fresh ginger
1	bone-in, skin-on chicken breast (about 375 g)
1 tbsp	mustard powder
1 tbsp	sodium-reduced soy sauce
1 tbsp	sesame oil
2 tsp	rice vinegar
1 tsp	granulated sugar
2	green onions, minced
¼ cup	loosely packed fresh cilantro leaves

ORANGE-CHILI CRISP BEEF STRIPS

HANDS-ON TIME	25 MINUTES
TOTAL TIME	35 MINUTES
MAKES	6 SERVINGS

225 g	beef sirloin grilling steak
4 tsp	soy sauce
2 tsp	Chinese rice wine, sake or dry sherry
½ tsp	five-spice powder
3 tbsp	cornstarch
1 tbsp	all-purpose flour
1	orange
	vegetable oil for frying
3	cloves garlic, minced
1	hot red pepper, seeded and very thinly sliced
2 tsp	granulated sugar
2 tsp	rice vinegar
pinch	salt
1 tsp	toasted sesame seeds

Slice beef across the grain into very thin 2-inch (5 cm) long strips. In bowl, mix together soy sauce, rice wine, five-spice powder and beef. In separate bowl, blend cornstarch, flour and ¼ cup water to make paste; stir into beef mixture to coat. Let stand for 10 minutes.

Using paring knife or vegetable peeler, pare off half of the orange zest (without white pith) in strips. Stack and slice into fine threads. Squeeze ⅓ cup juice from orange; set aside.

In wok or large skillet, pour enough oil to come 2 inches (5 cm) up side. Heat until deep-fryer thermometer reads 350°F or wooden chopstick inserted in oil bubbles immediately around edges. Cook beef in 2 batches, breaking up with spoon, until crisp and dry, 4 to 5 minutes per batch. Using slotted spoon, transfer to sieve over heatproof bowl to drain off oil.

Pour off all but 1 tbsp of the oil in wok; stir-fry garlic over medium-high heat until fragrant but not browned, about 20 seconds. Add orange strips and hot pepper; stir-fry for 20 seconds.

Stir in orange juice, sugar, vinegar and salt; boil over high heat until reduced to thick glaze. Add beef; stir-fry to coat. Toss with sesame seeds.

NUTRITIONAL INFORMATION, PER SERVING: about 139 cal, 9 g pro, 7 g total fat (1 g sat. fat), 9 g carb (1 g dietary fibre), 20 mg chol, 224 mg sodium. % RDI: 1% calcium, 9% iron, 2% vit A, 20% vit C, 4% folate.

BOK CHOY, MUSHROOM
AND TOFU SOUP

p.264

HANDS-ON TIME
15 MINUTES

TOTAL TIME
15 MINUTES

MAKES
6 TO 8 SERVINGS

In Dutch oven or large saucepan, bring broth to boil; add tofu and mushrooms. Reduce heat and simmer until mushrooms are tender, about 3 minutes.

Add bok choy; simmer until tender-crisp, about 3 minutes. Taste and add salt if desired. Transfer to serving bowls. Sprinkle with green onion, sesame oil, pepper and cilantro (if using).

NUTRITIONAL INFORMATION, PER EACH OF 8 SERVINGS: about 59 cal, 6 g pro, 3 g total fat (trace sat. fat), 3 g carb (1 g dietary fibre), 1 mg chol, 325 mg sodium. % RDI: 8% calcium, 10% iron, 20% vit A, 22% vit C, 18% folate.

5 cups	Chinese Chicken Broth (recipe, below)
1	pkg (300 g) regular or medium tofu, cut into ¾-inch (2 cm) cubes
1 cup	thinly sliced button, cremini or shiitake mushrooms
4 cups	chopped bok choy, spinach or napa cabbage (about 375 g)
½ tsp	salt (approx) (optional)
1	green onion, thinly sliced
½ tsp	sesame oil
pinch	white pepper
	fresh cilantro leaves (optional)

269

CHINESE CHICKEN BROTH

In Dutch oven or large saucepan, bring 900 g chicken backs, legs or other pieces and 10 cups water to boil; reduce heat to simmer and skim off scum. Add 3 slices fresh ginger, 2 green onions, 1 sprig fresh cilantro, 2 tbsp Chinese rice wine, 1 tsp peppercorns and ½ tsp salt; cook until flavourful, about 2 hours. Strain through fine sieve. Skim off any fat. (*Make-ahead: Let cool; cover and refrigerate for up to 2 days.*)

MAKES ABOUT 8 CUPS

NUTRITIONAL INFORMATION, PER 1 CUP: about 26 cal, 3 g pro, 1 g total fat (0 g sat. fat), 1 g carb (0 g dietary fibre), 1 mg chol, 163 mg sodium. % RDI: 1% iron, 1% folate.

CHINESE DUMPLINGS

Who doesn't love Chinese dumplings? Hundreds of types are made throughout China, but northern-style dumplings, using white wheat-flour wrappers, are wildly popular throughout China and abroad. Chinese dumpling (*jiaozi*) wrappers are available at most large grocery stores.

HOW TO WRAP DUMPLINGS

Using finger, wet edge of wrapper with water. Place about 2½ tsp filling in centre; fold wrapper over and pinch edge together. Pleat edge, pinching to secure. Stand on cornstarch-dusted tray and cover with tea towel. *(Make-ahead: Cover towel with plastic wrap; refrigerate for up to 8 hours. Or freeze, uncovered, on tray; transfer to airtight container and freeze for up to 3 months. Cook from frozen.)*

HOW TO COOK DUMPLINGS

• Boiled fresh dumplings: Drop dumplings into large saucepan of vigorously boiling water; return to boil. Continue to cook until dumplings float to surface and filling is firm. Remove dumplings with Chinese wire strainer or slotted spoon.

• Boiled frozen dumplings: Proceed as for boiled fresh dumplings, above.

• Fried dumplings: Add 2 tbsp peanut oil or vegetable oil to unheated cast-iron or nonstick skillet; add enough dumplings to fit snugly without touching. Heat over medium-high heat until oil sizzles; pour in enough water to come up side of pan by scant ½ inch (1 cm). Cover and cook until dry and spattering ceases; uncover and cook, if necessary, until bottoms are golden.

• Leftover dumplings: Cooked dumplings can be reheated and crisped by cooking in a little oil.

SPINACH AND MUSHROOM VEGETARIAN FILLING

HANDS-ON TIME 20 MINUTES

TOTAL TIME 40 MINUTES

MAKES ABOUT 3 CUPS (ENOUGH FOR ABOUT 60 DUMPLINGS)

1	pkg (50 g) bean threads (mung bean vermicelli)
2	bunches spinach (about 750 g total), blanched and drained
170 g	shiitake mushrooms, stemmed and chopped
1 tbsp	peanut oil or vegetable oil
1 tbsp	soy sauce
2 tsp	Chinese rice wine, dry sherry or sake
½ tsp	granulated sugar
2	eggs
1 tbsp	sesame oil
¾ tsp	salt
¼ tsp	white pepper

In heatproof bowl, cover bean threads with about 2 cups boiling water; soak for 10 minutes. Drain. Using scissors, cut into 1-inch (2.5 cm) lengths and place in large bowl.

Squeeze moisture out of spinach; chop finely. Add to bean threads.

In small skillet, heat peanut oil over medium-high heat; sauté mushrooms until lightly browned. Add soy sauce, rice wine and sugar; sauté until no liquid remains. Scrape into separate bowl; let cool.

Beat together eggs, sesame oil, ¼ tsp of the salt and the pepper. Heat 8-inch (20 cm) nonstick or cast-iron skillet over medium heat; cook half of the egg mixture until egg is set. Slide onto plate. Repeat with remaining egg mixture. Roll up egg sheets; cut into shreds and chop.

Add egg shreds, mushroom mixture and remaining salt to spinach mixture; mix well.

NUTRITIONAL INFORMATION, PER 2½ TSP: about 13 cal, 1 g pro, 1 g total fat (trace sat. fat), 1 g carb (trace dietary fibre), 6 mg chol, 54 mg sodium. % RDI: 1% calcium, 4% iron, 12% vit A, 2% vit C, 8% folate.

PORK FILLING

HANDS-ON TIME 15 MINUTES

TOTAL TIME 55 MINUTES

MAKES ABOUT 3 CUPS (ENOUGH FOR ABOUT 60 DUMPLINGS)

2 tbsp	dried shrimp (optional)
3 cups	finely chopped napa cabbage (225 g)
1 tsp	salt
450 g	lean ground pork
½ cup	minced green onion
1	egg, lightly beaten
1 tbsp	soy sauce
1 tsp	grated fresh ginger
1 tsp	sesame oil
¼ tsp	white or black pepper
pinch	cayenne pepper (optional)

Soak shrimp (if using) in cold water for 20 minutes; drain. In small skillet, cook shrimp over medium-low heat until fragrant and lightly toasted, 2 to 3 minutes; let cool. Mince and set aside.

Toss cabbage with salt; let stand for 20 minutes. Squeeze out moisture. Transfer to large bowl.

Add pork, green onion, egg, soy sauce, ginger, sesame oil, white pepper, cayenne pepper (if using) and shrimp (if using); mix well.

NUTRITIONAL INFORMATION, PER 2½ TSP: about 19 cal, 2 g pro, 1 g total fat (trace sat. fat), trace carb (0 g dietary fibre), 8 mg chol, 39 mg sodium. % RDI: 1% iron, 1% folate.

BEEF AND DILL FILLING

HANDS-ON TIME 15 MINUTES

TOTAL TIME 35 MINUTES

MAKES ABOUT 3 CUPS (ENOUGH FOR ABOUT 60 DUMPLINGS)

2 cups	finely chopped napa cabbage (150 g)
¾ tsp	salt
450 g	medium or lean ground beef
1½ cups	finely chopped fresh dill
⅔ cup	minced green onion
1	egg, lightly beaten
1	hot pepper, seeded and minced (optional)
1 tbsp	soy sauce
2 tsp	sesame oil
1 tsp	grated fresh ginger
¼ tsp	black pepper

Toss cabbage with ½ tsp of the salt; let stand for 20 minutes. Squeeze out moisture. Transfer to large bowl.

Add beef, dill, green onion, egg, hot pepper (if using), soy sauce, sesame oil, ginger, pepper and remaining salt; mix well.

NUTRITIONAL INFORMATION, PER 2½ TSP: about 21 cal, 2 g pro, 1 g total fat (trace sat. fat), trace carb (0 g dietary fibre), 8 mg chol, 36 mg sodium. % RDI: 1% iron, 1% vit A, 1% folate.

SHRIMP AND LEEK FILLING

HANDS-ON TIME 15 MINUTES

TOTAL TIME 45 MINUTES

MAKES ABOUT 2½ CUPS (ENOUGH FOR ABOUT 45 DUMPLINGS)

2 cups	minced leeks (white and light green parts only)
1 tsp	salt
450 g	shrimp, peeled and deveined
90 g	ground pork
1	egg yolk
¼ cup	finely chopped fresh cilantro
2 tsp	light or sodium-reduced soy sauce
2 tsp	Chinese rice wine, dry sherry or sake
1 tsp	grated fresh ginger
1 tsp	fish sauce or sodium-reduced soy sauce
1 tsp	sesame oil
pinch	white or black pepper

Toss leeks with salt; let stand for 30 minutes. Squeeze out moisture. Transfer to large bowl.

In food processor, pulse shrimp until finely chopped. Add shrimp, pork, egg yolk, cilantro, soy sauce, rice wine, ginger, fish sauce, sesame oil and pepper to leeks; stir to combine.

NUTRITIONAL INFORMATION, PER 2½ TSP: about 17 cal, 2 g pro, 1 g total fat (trace sat. fat), 1 g carb (0 g dietary fibre), 17 mg chol, 56 mg sodium. % RDI: 1% calcium, 2% iron, 1% vit A, 1% folate.

VALENTINE'S DAY DINNER

This year, we suggest you skip the noisy restaurant packed with dozens of other couples. Instead, stay home and enjoy your own special meal with the one you love. No reservation required.

MENU FOR 2

SPARKLING RASPBERRY COCKTAIL **p.274**

LEMON HERB SCALLOPS **p.274**

SPICY BUCATINI WITH ROASTED TOMATOES **p.277**

MINI CHOCOLATE PUDDING CAKES **p.277**

SPARKLING RASPBERRY COCKTAIL

opposite

HANDS-ON TIME	**TOTAL TIME**	**MAKES**
5 MINUTES	5 MINUTES	2 SERVINGS

2	raspberries
3 oz	vodka (about 6 tbsp)
2 tbsp	raspberry coulis or cranberry cocktail
1	small bottle (375 mL) sparkling white wine

Place 1 raspberry in each of 2 ice cube–tray moulds. Fill with water and freeze.

In 2 chilled champagne flutes, divide vodka and raspberry coulis. Top with sparkling wine. Garnish with a raspberry ice cube.

NUTRITIONAL INFORMATION, PER SERVING: about 183 cal, trace pro, trace total fat (0 g sat. fat), 3 g carb (0 g dietary fibre, 3 g sugar), 0 mg chol, 6 mg sodium, 74 mg potassium. % RDI: 1% calcium, 2% iron, 10% vit C.

LEMON HERB SCALLOPS

p.272

HANDS-ON TIME	**TOTAL TIME**	**MAKES**
25 MINUTES	25 MINUTES	2 SERVINGS

LEMON CILANTRO OIL

1 cup	packed fresh cilantro leaves
⅓ cup	olive oil
1 tbsp	grated lemon zest
2 tbsp	lemon juice
½ tsp	each salt and pepper
¼ tsp	crumbled saffron threads

SCALLOPS

1 tbsp	butter
2 tsp	olive oil
1	small leek (white and light green parts only), thinly sliced
½ cup	frozen shelled edamame, thawed
¼ tsp	each salt and pepper
4 large	sea scallops (about 225 g total), patted dry

LEMON CILANTRO OIL In blender, blend cilantro, oil, lemon zest, lemon juice, salt and pepper until smooth, about 2 minutes. Stir in saffron. Set aside. *(Make-ahead: Refrigerate in airtight container for up to 5 days; bring to room temperature to use.)*

SCALLOPS In nonstick skillet, heat half each of the butter and oil over medium-high heat; sauté leek until softened, 5 to 6 minutes. Stir in edamame and half each of the salt and pepper. Remove from pan and keep warm; wipe skillet clean.

In same skillet, heat remaining butter and oil over medium-high heat until foaming. Sprinkle scallops with remaining salt and pepper; sear all over until browned and centres are opaque, 4 to 6 minutes.

Divide leek mixture between 2 small plates. Top each with 2 scallops; drizzle each with 2 tsp of the lemon cilantro oil. Serve immediately.

NUTRITIONAL INFORMATION, PER SERVING: about 317 cal, 23 g pro, 22 g total fat (6 g sat. fat), 7 g carb (2 g dietary fibre, 1 g sugar), 59 mg chol, 696 mg sodium, 589 mg potassium. % RDI: 12% calcium, 28% iron, 9% vit A, 12% vit C, 55% folate.

SPARKLING RASPBERRY COCKTAIL

SPICY BUCATINI WITH ROASTED TOMATOES

SPICY BUCATINI
WITH ROASTED TOMATOES

opposite

HANDS-ON TIME	TOTAL TIME	MAKES
25 MINUTES	40 MINUTES	2 SERVINGS

In small bowl, toss together tomatoes, 1 tsp of the oil and the pepper. Arrange, cut side up, on foil-lined baking sheet; roast in 325°F (160°C) oven until shrivelled and starting to brown, about 25 minutes.

Meanwhile, in nonstick skillet, cook pancetta over medium-high heat until crisp, about 6 minutes. Using slotted spoon, remove to paper towel–lined plate to drain. Add remaining oil, the garlic and hot pepper flakes to skillet; cook over medium heat until fragrant, about 1 minute. Add olives and tomatoes.

Meanwhile, in large saucepan of boiling salted water, cook pasta according to package directions until al dente, 8 to 10 minutes. Drain and return to pan. Toss with tomato mixture, basil and salt. Serve topped with pancetta and Parmesan.

NUTRITIONAL INFORMATION, PER SERVING: about 566 cal, 18 g pro, 23 g total fat (5 g sat. fat), 72 g carb (6 g dietary fibre, 5 g sugar), 23 mg chol, 746 mg sodium, 460 mg potassium. % RDI: 7% calcium, 28% iron, 15% vit A, 32% vit C, 86% folate.

2 cups	cherry tomatoes, halved
2 tbsp	olive oil
pinch	pepper
¼ cup	chopped pancetta
2	cloves garlic, minced
½ tsp	hot pepper flakes
4	Kalamata olives, pitted and coarsely chopped
170 g	bucatini
2 tbsp	coarsely chopped fresh basil
pinch	salt
1 tbsp	grated Parmesan cheese

277

MINI CHOCOLATE PUDDING CAKES

HANDS-ON TIME	TOTAL TIME	MAKES
10 MINUTES	35 MINUTES	2 SERVINGS

In bowl, whisk together flour, 2 tsp of the cocoa powder, the granulated sugar and baking powder. In separate bowl, whisk together egg yolk, milk, butter and vanilla; stir into flour mixture. Fold in chocolate chips. Divide batter among 2 lightly greased 6-oz (175 mL) ramekins.

In bowl, whisk together hot water, brown sugar and remaining cocoa powder. Pour over batter.

Bake on rimmed baking sheet in 350°F (180°C) oven until firm to the touch, about 18 minutes. Let stand for 10 minutes before serving.

NUTRITIONAL INFORMATION, PER SERVING: about 324 cal, 5 g pro, 11 g total fat (6 g sat. fat), 56 g carb (242 g sugar), 107 mg chol, 84 mg sodium, 228 mg potassium. % RDI: 7% calcium, 17% iron, 9% vit A, 19% folate.

¼ cup	all-purpose flour
5 tsp	cocoa powder, sifted
4 tsp	granulated sugar
¼ tsp	baking powder
1	egg yolk, lightly beaten
4 tsp	milk
2 tsp	butter, melted
½ tsp	vanilla
2 tbsp	semisweet chocolate chips
⅓ cup	hot water
¼ cup	packed brown sugar

RED CARPET EXTRAVAGANZA

279

Fill out your ballots, fans. It's awards season,
and the party everyone wants to attend is at your place!
Whether your friends are serious aficionados or just want
to review the outfits, everyone will enjoy this evening.
So, without further ado, it's our great honour to present
the nominees for Best Finger Food in a Feature Role.

MENU FOR 12

HOT SWISS CHARD
AND ARTICHOKE DIP **p.280**

SPANISH SALT COD FRITTERS **p.281**

EDAMAME AND
ROASTED TOMATO CANAPÉS **p.282**

BACON, ONION AND
GOAT CHEESE PIZZA BITES **p.283**

HOT SWISS CHARD AND ARTICHOKE DIP

HANDS-ON TIME	**TOTAL TIME**	**MAKES**
10 MINUTES	40 MINUTES	4 CUPS

1	bunch Swiss chard, stems removed
2	cans (each 400 mL) artichoke hearts, drained, rinsed and coarsely chopped
¾ cup	rinsed drained canned cannellini beans
¾ cup	grated Parmesan cheese
½ cup	ricotta cheese
⅓ cup	sour cream
1 tbsp	olive oil
2 tsp	lemon juice
1	clove garlic, minced
pinch	each salt and pepper

In large saucepan of boiling water, blanch Swiss chard, stirring, until wilted, about 1 minute. Strain through sieve over bowl, squeezing out and reserving liquid.

In food processor, purée together Swiss chard, ¼ cup reserved liquid, all but 1 cup of the artichoke hearts, the beans, all but ¼ cup of the Parmesan, the ricotta, sour cream, olive oil, lemon juice, garlic, salt and pepper until almost smooth. Stir in remaining artichokes.

Scrape into 4-cup (1 L) ovenproof dish; sprinkle with remaining Parmesan. Bake in 350°F (180°C) oven until browned and bubbly, about 35 minutes.

NUTRITIONAL INFORMATION, PER 1 TBSP: about 19 cal, 1 g pro, 1 g total fat (1 g sat. fat), 2 g carb (1 g dietary fibre), 2 mg chol, 61 mg sodium, 63 mg potassium. % RDI: 2% calcium, 1% iron, 2% vit A, 3% vit C, 3% folate.

TIP FROM THE TEST KITCHEN

We lightened up this classic dip and gave it a modern twist with ricotta, Swiss cheese and cannellini beans (white kidney beans). Serve with an array of vegetables.

SPANISH SALT COD FRITTERS

p.278

HANDS-ON TIME
35 MINUTES

TOTAL TIME
37 HOURS

MAKES
ABOUT 46 PIECES

Cut fish into 4 pieces; rinse well with cold water. In large deep bowl, soak in cold water in refrigerator for 36 hours, changing water 4 times. Taste fish; if still too salty, continue changing water and soaking for up to 8 hours longer. Drain and rinse.

In saucepan, cover fish with cold water and bring to simmer over medium-high heat. Turn off heat; let stand until fish flakes easily when tested, about 20 minutes. Drain well, reserving water; let cool. Remove skin and bones; flake. Set aside.

In saucepan of reserved water, boil potatoes until tender, about 15 minutes; drain well. Return to pan over medium-low heat to dry for 30 seconds; mash. Scrape into bowl.

In clean saucepan, bring olive oil and ¾ cup water to boil over medium heat; vigorously whisk in flour until smooth, about 2 minutes. Remove from heat. Whisk for 1 minute. Whisk in eggs, 1 at a time.

Stir in potatoes, green onions, parsley, garlic and pepper. Stir in fish just until combined; let cool.

In Dutch oven or large saucepan, pour enough vegetable oil to come 2 inches (5 cm) up side. Heat until deep-fryer thermometer registers 375°F (190°C) or 1-inch (2.5 cm) cube of white bread turns golden in 30 seconds. Working in batches, drop fish mixture by heaping 1 tbsp into hot oil; cook, turning once, until golden brown, 3 to 5 minutes. Drain on rack.

1	pkg (400 g) bone-in salt cod
750 g	russet potatoes, peeled and quartered
3 tbsp	extra-virgin olive oil
¼ cup	all-purpose flour
3	eggs
⅓ cup	finely chopped green onions
⅓ cup	chopped fresh parsley
1	clove garlic, minced
¼ tsp	pepper
	vegetable oil for frying

281

NUTRITIONAL INFORMATION, PER PIECE: about 114 cal, 6 g pro, 9 g total fat (1 g sat. fat), 3 g carb (trace dietary fibre), 25 mg chol, 583 mg sodium, 159 mg potassium. % RDI: 2% calcium, 3% iron, 1% vit A, 3% vit C, 3% folate.

TIP FROM THE TEST KITCHEN

Since the amount of salt left in the fish after soaking can vary slightly, cook 1 test fritter and taste it. If necessary, add up to ½ tsp salt to potato mixture.

EDAMAME AND
ROASTED TOMATO CANAPÉS

📷
p.278

HANDS-ON TIME	**TOTAL TIME**	**MAKES**
20 MINUTES	1¾ HOURS	36 PIECES

ROASTED TOMATOES

2 cups	cherry tomatoes, halved
2 tbsp	olive oil
pinch	each salt, pepper and granulated sugar

CANAPÉS

1¼ cups	frozen shelled edamame
½ cup	chopped fresh mint
¼ cup	extra-virgin olive oil
1	clove garlic, minced
¾ tsp	grated lemon zest
2 tbsp	lemon juice
¾ tsp	salt
36	whole grain crackers or gluten-free crackers
½ cup	crumbled feta cheese (optional)

ROASTED TOMATOES Toss together tomatoes, oil, salt, pepper and sugar. Arrange, cut side up, on parchment paper–lined baking sheet; roast in 300°F (150°C) oven until shrivelled and dry in centre, about 1½ hours.

CANAPÉS While tomatoes are roasting, in small saucepan of boiling water, cook edamame until tender, about 5 minutes. Drain, reserving ¼ cup of the cooking liquid; let cool.

Rinse edamame under cold water. In food processor, purée together edamame, half of the mint, the oil, garlic, lemon zest, lemon juice and salt, adding reserved cooking liquid, 1 tbsp at a time, as needed until smooth.

Spoon generous 1 tsp edamame mixture onto each cracker; top with tomatoes, remaining mint and the feta (if using).

NUTRITIONAL INFORMATION, PER PIECE: about 36 cal, 1 g pro, 3 g total fat (trace sat. fat), 2 g carb (1 g dietary fibre), 0 mg chol, 57 mg sodium, 46 mg potassium. % RDI: 1% calcium, 2% iron, 1% vit A, 3% vit C, 7% folate.

TIP FROM THE TEST KITCHEN

Colourful and healthy, this hors d'oeuvre appeals to everyone, including friends who prefer gluten-free food. For a stylish presentation, break the crackers into pieces or shards.

BACON, ONION AND
GOAT CHEESE PIZZA BITES

p.278

HANDS-ON TIME
25 MINUTES

TOTAL TIME
3¾ HOURS

MAKES
72 PIECES

PIZZA DOUGH In bowl, stir together 1 cup of the flour, the oil, honey, yeast and 2 cups warm water. Cover with plastic wrap and let rise (in warm, draft-free place) until bubbly and almost doubled in bulk, about 1 hour.

Using wooden spoon, stir in all but ½ cup of the remaining flour, the sesame seeds and salt to form ragged dough. Turn out onto floured work surface; knead until smooth and elastic, about 6 minutes, adding as much of the remaining flour as necessary.

Place dough in greased bowl, turning to grease all over. Cover with plastic wrap and let rise (in warm, draft-free place) until doubled in bulk, about 1½ hours.

Divide dough in half. Place each half on greased 16- × 12-inch (40 × 30 cm) rimmed baking sheet. Pressing with fingertips and gently pulling at edges, stretch to fit sheets.

TOPPINGS Sprinkle bacon, red onions, green onions and pepper evenly over dough; top with Romano.

Bake, 1 sheet at a time, on bottom rack of 450°F (230°C) oven until bottom of crust is golden, about 18 minutes. Sprinkle goat cheese over top; bake until cheese is slightly melted, about 4 minutes. Let cool for 5 minutes. Cut each pizza into 36 squares.

NUTRITIONAL INFORMATION, PER PIECE: about 61 cal, 2 g pro, 3 g total fat (1 g sat. fat), 8 g carb (trace dietary fibre), 4 mg chol, 83 mg sodium, 27 mg potassium. % RDI: 2% calcium, 4% iron, 1% vit A, 10% folate.

PIZZA DOUGH

5 cups	all-purpose flour (approx)
2 tbsp	olive oil
1 tbsp	liquid honey
1	pkg (8 g) active dry yeast
3 tbsp	sesame seeds
1½ tsp	salt

TOPPINGS

175 g	thick-sliced bacon, diced (about 1⅓ cups)
2 cups	thinly sliced red onion
1	bunch green onions, cut in 1-inch (2.5 cm) pieces
½ tsp	pepper
⅔ cup	grated Romano cheese
175 g	goat cheese, crumbled (about 1¼ cups)

TIP FROM THE TEST KITCHEN

For traditional, thicker-crust, round pizzas, use two 14-inch (35 cm) round pizza pans instead of rectangular baking sheets.

SEASONAL SUNDAY SUPPER

Every cook's recipe file needs a show-stopping roast for a special Sunday meal. Our foolproof, no-fuss method leaves you lots of time to prepare all the traditional sides. To keep your family happy, you may have to make this menu next week, too. And the week following. After all, there's a reason it's called a Sunday roast.

285

MENU FOR 10

THE ULTIMATE STANDING RIB ROAST
WITH GREEN PEPPERCORN HORSERADISH SAUCE **p.286**

IRISH MASHED POTATOES **p.287**

GLAZED CARROTS **p.287**

SAUTÉED BRUSSELS SPROUTS
AND GREEN BEANS WITH PARMESAN **p.288**

APPLE CINNAMON CRUMBLE **p.291**

THE ULTIMATE STANDING RIB ROAST
WITH GREEN PEPPERCORN HORSERADISH SAUCE

p.284

HANDS-ON TIME	TOTAL TIME	MAKES
20 MINUTES	4 HOURS	8 TO 10 SERVINGS

STANDING RIB ROAST

3 kg	beef standing rib premium oven roast
2	cloves garlic, minced
2 tsp	chopped fresh rosemary
½ tsp	pepper
¼ tsp	salt
4 tsp	Dijon mustard

GREEN PEPPERCORN SAUCE

1 tbsp	butter
3	shallots, finely chopped
¼ cup	brandy
2¼ cups	sodium-reduced beef broth
2 tbsp	green peppercorns in brine, drained
½ cup	whipping cream (35%)
3 tbsp	prepared horseradish
1 tsp	Worcestershire sauce
¼ tsp	pepper
3 tbsp	cornstarch

STANDING RIB ROAST Place roast, bone side down, on rack in roasting pan. Mash together garlic, rosemary, pepper and salt. Brush mustard over top and sides of roast; spread garlic mixture over mustard, pressing to adhere. Let stand at room temperature for 45 minutes.

Roast in 500°F (260°C) oven for 11 minutes per kilogram, or 33 minutes for a 3 kg roast. Turn off oven; do not open door. Let stand in oven for 2 hours.

GREEN PEPPERCORN SAUCE Meanwhile, in saucepan, melt butter over medium heat; cook shallots, stirring often and reducing heat if browning too quickly, until golden and softened, about 5 minutes. Add brandy; cook, stirring, until almost no liquid remains, about 1 minute. Stir in broth and peppercorns; simmer over medium-low heat for 5 minutes. Stir in cream, horseradish, Worcestershire sauce and pepper. Blend cornstarch with 3 tbsp water; whisk into broth mixture. Cook, whisking, until thickened, about 1 minute. Serve with roast.

NUTRITIONAL INFORMATION, PER EACH OF 10 SERVINGS: about 501 cal, 44 g pro, 31 g total fat (15 g sat. fat), 5 g carb (1 g dietary fibre, 1 g sugar), 123 mg chol, 399 mg sodium, 526 mg potassium. % RDI: 4% calcium, 28% iron, 5% vit A, 3% vit C, 6% folate.

TIP FROM THE TEST KITCHEN

This method requires exact timing to achieve the perfect medium-rare roast, so keep an eye on the clock to guarantee the best results. It also depends on the oven's residual heat, so be sure to fully preheat the oven and resist opening it while the roast cooks. The bonus: The meat doesn't require the usual resting time because it finishes cooking—and cools a bit—as the oven slowly cools. There's no need to let it stand before carving.

286

IRISH MASHED POTATOES

HANDS-ON TIME
15 MINUTES

TOTAL TIME
30 MINUTES

MAKES
10 SERVINGS

In large saucepan of boiling salted water, cook potatoes, onion, garlic and bay leaf until potatoes are tender, about 18 minutes. Drain and return to pan; shake over low heat to dry, about 1 minute. Discard onion and bay leaf. Remove from heat; mash until smooth or press through food mill or ricer.

Meanwhile, in small saucepan, heat cream with butter over medium-low heat until hot. Stir into potatoes along with ½ cup of the green onions, the salt, nutmeg and pepper. *(Make-ahead: Refrigerate in covered ovenproof dish for up to 24 hours; reheat, covered, in 350°F/180°C oven until hot, about 25 minutes.)* Serve sprinkled with remaining green onions.

NUTRITIONAL INFORMATION, PER SERVING: about 176 cal, 3 g pro, 9 g total fat (5 g sat. fat), 23 g carb (2 g dietary fibre), 24 mg chol, 418 mg sodium, 448 mg potassium. % RDI: 4% calcium, 4% iron, 8% vit A, 25% vit C, 6% folate.

1.35 kg	potatoes, peeled and quartered
1	onion, halved
3	cloves garlic
1	bay leaf
1 cup	10% cream or milk
⅓ cup	butter
⅔ cup	finely chopped green onions
½ tsp	salt
pinch	each ground nutmeg and pepper

GLAZED CARROTS

HANDS-ON TIME
5 MINUTES

TOTAL TIME
13 MINUTES

MAKES
10 SERVINGS

Cut carrots in half crosswise on diagonal. Halve top ends lengthwise.

In large skillet, cover and bring carrots, butter, honey, sugar, salt and ⅓ cup water to boil over high heat; cook until carrots are slightly tender, about 4 minutes. Reduce heat to medium-high; uncover and cook, stirring occasionally, until tender and liquid has evaporated, 3 to 4 minutes. Sprinkle with pistachios.

NUTRITIONAL INFORMATION, PER SERVING: about 88 cal, 2 g pro, 5 g total fat (2 g sat. fat), 10 g carb (3 g dietary fibre), 6 mg chol, 60 mg sodium, 239 mg potassium. % RDI: 3% calcium, 4% iron, 130% vit A, 5% vit C, 6% folate.

900 g	small thin carrots, peeled
2 tbsp	butter
1 tbsp	liquid honey
½ tsp	granulated sugar
pinch	salt
½ cup	unsalted pistachios, chopped

SAUTÉED BRUSSELS SPROUTS AND GREEN BEANS
WITH PARMESAN

HANDS-ON TIME	**TOTAL TIME**	**MAKES**
20 MINUTES	20 MINUTES	10 SERVINGS

450 g	brussels sprouts, halved
450 g	green beans, trimmed
3 tbsp	olive oil
1 cup	thinly sliced shallots
1½ tsp	fennel seeds, crushed
¼ cup	pine nuts
¼ tsp	each salt and pepper
4 tsp	lemon juice
⅓ cup	shaved Parmesan cheese or Romano cheese

In large saucepan of boiling salted water, blanch brussels sprouts until slightly tender, about 1 minute. Using slotted spoon, transfer to large bowl of ice water to chill; drain and set aside. Repeat with green beans. *(Make-ahead: Refrigerate in separate airtight containers for up to 24 hours.)*

In large skillet or wok, heat oil over medium-high heat; sauté shallots with fennel seeds until golden and crisp, about 2 minutes.

Add brussels sprouts, beans, pine nuts, salt and pepper. Sauté until vegetables are slightly browned, about 3 minutes. Toss with lemon juice; sprinkle with Parmesan.

NUTRITIONAL INFORMATION, PER SERVING: about 113 cal, 4 g pro, 8 g total fat (1 g sat. fat), 10 g carb (3 g dietary fibre), 3 mg chol, 301 mg sodium, 279 mg potassium. % RDI: 7% calcium, 9% iron, 8% vit A, 53% vit C, 20% folate.

SAUTÉED BRUSSELS SPROUTS AND GREEN BEANS WITH PARMESAN

APPLE CINNAMON CRUMBLE

APPLE CINNAMON CRUMBLE

HANDS-ON TIME	**TOTAL TIME**	**MAKES**
15 MINUTES	55 MINUTES	10 TO 12 SERVINGS

APPLE FILLING In large bowl, toss together apples, sugar, flour and cinnamon. Set aside.

CRUMBLE TOPPING In separate large bowl, whisk together oats, flour, brown sugar, cinnamon and salt. Using fork, mash in butter, pressing together with fingers, until crumbly.

ASSEMBLY Spread filling evenly in 2 greased 8-inch (2 L) square baking dishes; sprinkle oat mixture over filling.

Bake in top and bottom thirds of 350°F (180°C) oven, switching and rotating dishes halfway through, until filling is bubbling, fruit is tender and topping is crisp and golden, 40 to 60 minutes. Serve with whipping cream (if using).

NUTRITIONAL INFORMATION, PER EACH OF 12 SERVINGS: about 347 cal, 4 g pro, 12 g total fat (7 g sat. fat), 60 g carb (4 g dietary fibre), 27 mg chol, 79 mg sodium. % RDI: 3% calcium, 13% iron, 9% vit A, 7% vit C, 14% folate.

APPLE FILLING

16 cups	sliced peeled Golden Delicious or Empire apples
½ cup	granulated sugar
4 tbsp	all-purpose flour
1 tsp	cinnamon

CRUMBLE TOPPING

2 cups	large-flake rolled oats
1 cup	all-purpose flour
⅔ cup	packed brown sugar
½ tsp	cinnamon
¼ tsp	salt
⅔ cup	butter, softened
	whipping cream (35%) (optional)

You love to cook, and we want you to feel great about every meal that comes out of your kitchen—so creating delicious, trustworthy recipes is the top priority for us in the Canadian Living Test Kitchen. We are chefs, recipe developers and food writers, all from different backgrounds but equally dedicated to the art and science of creating delicious recipes you can make right at home.

What Does Tested Till Perfect Mean?

Every year, the food specialists in the Canadian Living Test Kitchen work together to produce approximately 500 Tested-Till-Perfect recipes. So what does Tested Till Perfect mean? It means we follow a rigorous process to ensure you'll get the same results in your kitchen as we do in ours.

Here's What We Do:

- In the Test Kitchen, we use the same everyday ingredients and equipment that you use in your own kitchen.
- We start by researching ideas and brainstorming as a team.
- We write up the recipe and go straight into the kitchen to try it out.
- We taste, evaluate and tweak the recipe until we really love it.
- Each recipe then gets handed off to different food editors for another test and another tasting session.
- We meticulously test and retest each recipe as many times as it takes to make sure it turns out as perfectly in your kitchen as it does in ours.
- We carefully weigh and measure all ingredients, record the data and send the recipe out for nutritional analysis.
- The recipe is then edited and rechecked to ensure all the information is correct and it's ready for you to cook.

INDEX

A

A Day at the Cottage, *117-123*
Afternoon Tea, *49-55*
Allspice Rimmer, *252*
almonds
Bacon and Onion Cheese Balls, *255*
Basil and Lemon Cheese Balls, *255*
Green Beans Amandine, *67*
Lemon Amaretto Tiramisu, *23*
Pumpkin Cheesecake With White Chocolate Almond Bark, *185*
Spinach Salad With Apples and Goat Cheese Croutons, *194*
Wild Rice and Lentil Salad, *137*
amaretto liqueur
Lemon Amaretto Tiramisu, *23*
anchovy fillets
Boston Lettuce Salad With Green Goddess Dressing, *44*
Angostura bitters
Merry Manhattan, *252*
apple cider. See also cider (alcoholic).
Cheddar Oka Fondue, *262*
Emmental and Cheddar Fondue, *262*
Roast Pork With Cider Cream Sauce, *13*
apples
Apple Cheddar Drop Biscuits, *46*
Apple Cinnamon Crumble, *291*
Apple Mint Iced Tea, *123*
Apple Walnut Chutney, *27*
Barbecued Pork Loin Stuffed With Bacon and Apples, *180*
Bison Meatballs With Cider Mustard Sauce, *215*
Caramelized Onion and Apple Pizza, *249*
Chard and Apple Salad With Maple Bacon Vinaigrette, *37*
Chunky Applesauce, *219*
Jicama and Apple Spinach Salad With Honey-Dijon Dressing, *178*
Oven-Roasted Pork Loin Stuffed With Bacon and Apples, *180*
Roast Pork With Cider Cream Sauce, *13*
Roasted Onions and Apples With Thyme, *197*
Sausage, Apple and Sage Stuffing, *168*
Spinach Salad With Apples and Goat Cheese Croutons, *194*
Après-Ski Fondue, *261-263*
apricots (dried)
Apple Walnut Chutney, *27*
Apricot Wild Rice Pilaf, *230*
Sweet-and-Sour Onion Chutney, *236*
aquavit
Garden Martinis, *115*
artichokes
Crisp Artichokes With Lemon Herb Dip, *221*
Hot Swiss Chard and Artichoke Dip, *280*
Mediterranean Kale Salad, *138*
asparagus
Asparagus and Ricotta Crostini, *85*
Asparagus With Herbed Dipping Sauce, *87*
Lemony Red Pepper and Asparagus Pasta Salad, *97*
Pinwheel Sandwiches, *50*
Roasted Asparagus Salad With Parmesan Croutons, *19*
Sautéed Spring Asparagus and Mushrooms, *32*

avocados
Avocado Coco Lime Pops, *107*
Grilled Corn and Avocado Salad, *150*
Tomatillo Salsa, *134*

B

Babkas, *222*
Baby Shower, *57-63*
Baby Sleeper Cake, *63*
bacon. See also pancetta.
Bacon and Onion Cheese Balls, *255*
Bacon and Onion Grilled Cheese, *119*
Bacon, Onion and Goat Cheese Pizza Bites, *283*
Barbecued Pork Loin Stuffed With Bacon and Apples, *180*
Bison Meatballs With Cider Mustard Sauce, *215*
Braised Cabbage and Bacon, *203*
Chard and Apple Salad With Maple Bacon Vinaigrette, *37*
Classic Rumaki, *253*
Grilled Bacon and Feta Mini Pizzas, *114*
Jalapeño Baked Beans, *78*
Oven-Roasted Pork Loin Stuffed With Bacon and Apples, *180*
Slow Cooker Scalloped Potatoes, *20*
Surf and Turf Caesar, *158*
Updated Devils on Horseback, *253*
Wine and Bacon Steamed Mussels, *162*
Baked Beans, *78*
Baked Pita Chips, *191*
Barbecued Breakfast Packets, *118*
Barbecued Pork Loin Stuffed With Bacon and Apples, *180*

Basil and Lemon Cheese Balls, *255*
bean threads
Spinach and Mushroom Dumplings, *270*
beans. See cannellini beans; green beans; pinto beans.
beef
Beef and Dill Dumplings, *271*
Orange Chili Crisp Beef Strips, *268*
Porcini-Dusted Beef Tenderloin With Sherry Gravy, *229*
Slow Cooker Balsamic-Braised Pot Roast, *196*
Steakhouse Sliders, *94*
Sweet-and-Sour Meatballs, *257*
Texas Barbecue Brisket, *76*
Ultimate Standing Rib Roast With Green Peppercorn Horseradish Sauce, *286*
beer
Beer and Cheese Fondue Dip, *256*
Ginger Beer Shandy, *131*
Jalapeño Baked Beans, *78*
Texas Barbecue Brisket, *76*
beets
Orange Beet Salad, *246*
Beijing-Style Boiled Peanuts, *266*
beverages. See also cocktails.
Apple Mint Iced Tea, *123*
Chai Mango Lemonade, *138*
Hazelnut Irish Coffee, *15*
Mulled Red Wine and Madeira, *263*
Nonalcoholic Cosmopolitans, *61*
Peach Tea, *89*
Perfect Cup of Tea, *54*
Pitcher Lime Squash, *131*
Tea Sangria, *115*

biscuits. See also scones.
  Apple Cheddar Drop
  Biscuits, *46*
  Cheddar Chive
  Biscuits, *161*
**Bison Meatballs With Cider
  Mustard Sauce,** *215*
Black Forest ham
  Caramelized Onion and
  Apple Pizza, *249*
  Ham Pickle Spread
  Sandwiches, *51*
Black Forest Pie, *233*
blue cheese
  Irish Root Soup With
  Cashel Blue Cheese, *12*
  Lightened-Up Blue Cheese
  Dip, *191*
  Updated Devils on
  Horseback, *253*
bocconcini cheese
  Grilled Panzanella
  Bites, *92*
**Boiled Fresh Lobsters With
  Seasoned
  Butters,** *163*
**Bok Choy, Mushroom and
  Tofu Soup,** *269*
**Boston Lettuce Salad
  With Green Goddess
  Dressing,** *44*
Boursin cheese
  Crisp Cheese-Stuffed
  Jalapeños, *188*
Boxty Potato Cakes, *14*
**Braised Cabbage and
  Bacon,** *203*
brandy
  Beer and Cheese Fondue
  Dip, *256*
  Cheese Fondue Dip, *256*
  Ultimate Standing
  Rib Roast With Green
  Peppercorn Horseradish
  Sauce, *286*
  Wild Mushroom Pâté, *212*
breads
  Corn Bread, *241*
  Irish Brown Bread, *10*

Breakfast Packets, *118*
**Brined Maple Mustard Pork
  Chops,** *102*
brisket
  Texas Barbecue Brisket, *76*
broth
  Chinese Chicken
  Broth, *269*
brunches
  Holiday Brunch, *245-249*
  Mother's Day Brunch, *43-47*
brussels sprouts
  Lemon Brussels Sprouts, *14*
  Sautéed Brussels Sprouts
  and Green Beans With
  Parmesan, *288*
  Sautéed Brussels Sprouts
  With Shaved Parmesan,
  182
**Bucatini With Roasted
  Tomatoes,** *277*
Buñuelos, *223*
Butter Cookies, *263*
Butter Tart Ice Cream, *81*
butternut squash
  Roasted Butternut Squash
  and Cheddar Gratin, *172*
  Root Vegetable
  Crumble, *231*
  Winter Vegetable Stew, *240*
butters
  Curried Ginger
  Butter, *163*
  Lemony Dill Butter, *163*
  Miso Butter, *232*
  Roasted Garlic Butter, *20*
  Spicy Garlic Butter, *163*
button mushrooms
  Creamy Mushroom and
  Gruyère Gratin, *181*

C
**Cabane à Sucre (Sugar
  Shack),** *35-41*
cabbage
  Beef and Dill
  Dumplings, *271*
  Bok Choy, Mushroom and
  Tofu Soup, *269*

  Braised Cabbage and
  Bacon, *203*
  Kale and Cabbage
  Slaw, *103*
  Pork Dumplings, *271*
  Tangy Summer
  Coleslaw, *96*
  Tropical Coleslaw, *96*
Caesars, *158*
cakes. See also
  cheesecakes.
  Baby Sleeper Cake, *63*
  Dairy-Free Gluten-Free
  Molten Chocolate Lava
  Cakes, *33*
  Flourless Chocolate Lava
  Cakes, *33*
  Mini Carrot Cake Trifles, *71*
  Mini Chocolate
  Babkas, *222*
  Mini Chocolate Pudding
  Cakes, *277*
  Raspberry Lemon Cream
  Cake, *99*
Calvados
  Beer and Cheese Fondue
  Dip, *256*
  Cheese Fondue Dip, *256*
Camembert cheese
  Chard and Apple Salad
  With Maple Bacon
  Vinaigrette, *37*
Campari
  Negroni Spritzer, *79*
Canada Day Barbecue,
  101-107
**Canada Day Make-Ahead
  Menu,** *91-99*
Canadian Kiss, *210*
canapés
  Edamame and Roasted
  Tomato Canapés, *282*
  Shrimp Cocktail Canapés,
  259
cannellini beans
  Hot Swiss Chard and
  Artichoke Dip, *280*
  Pesto White Bean
  Crostini, *85*

**Caramelized Onion and
  Apple Pizza,** *249*
carrots
  Glazed Carrots, *287*
  Honey-Glazed Carrots, *32*
  Honey-Lime Carrots With
  Cipollini Onions, *22*
  Kimchi Slaw, *134*
  Mini Carrot Cake
  Trifles, *71*
  Roasted Carrot and Parsnip
  Soup With Whipped Goat
  Cheese and Kale Chips, *226*
  Roasted Carrots With
  Mustard Vinaigrette, *238*
cauliflower
  Winter Vegetable Stew, *240*
celery
  Chicken and Celery in
  Mustard Sauce, *267*
celery root
  Celery Root Garlic
  Mash, *198*
  Mini Vegetable Latkes With
  Chunky Applesauce, *219*
**Chai Mango
  Lemonade,** *138*
chanterelle mushrooms
  Wild Mushroom Pâté, *212*
Char Siu-Style Ribs, *103*
charcuterie, *88, 212*
**Chard and Apple Salad
  With Maple Bacon
  Vinaigrette,** *37*
Cheddar cheese
  Apple Cheddar Drop
  Biscuits, *46*
  Bacon and Onion Grilled
  Cheese, *119*
  Beer and Cheese Fondue
  Dip, *256*
  Cheddar Oka Fondue, *262*
  Cheddar Chive
  Biscuits, *161*
  Cheese and Maple
  Soufflés, *38*
  Cheese Fondue Dip, *256*
  Cheesy Barbecued
  Breakfast Packets, *118*

Crisp Cheese-Stuffed
Jalapeños, *188*
Emmental and Cheddar
Fondue, *262*
Mini Cheddar and Onion
Galette Bites, *59*
Pimiento Cheese Spread
Sandwiches, *51*
Roasted Butternut Squash
and Cheddar Gratin, *172*
**Cheese and Charcuterie
Platters,** *88, 212, 215*
**Cheese and Maple
Soufflés,** *38*
Cheese Board, *215*
Cheese Balls, *255*
Cheese Fondue Dip, *256*
cheesecakes
Pumpkin Cheesecake
With White Chocolate
Almond Bark, *185*
White Chocolate
Cheesecake Dip, *61*
**Cheesy Barbecued
Breakfast Packets,** *118*
cherries
Black Forest Pie, *233*
Cherry Pistachio Mini
Pancakes, *247*
Cranberry Mimosas, *246*
Marinated Kale Salad, *236*
Sour Cherry Trifle, *243*
Tea Sangria, *115*
chestnuts
Creamy Mushroom and
Gruyère Gratin, *181*
Winter Vegetable Stew, *240*
chicken
Chicken and Celery in
Mustard Sauce, *267*
Chicken With Morel
Sauce, *68*
Chinese Chicken Broth, *269*
Fried Chicken Bites, *218*
Grilled Caribbean
Chicken, *126*
Grilled Honey-Garlic
Chicken Wings, *104*
Grilled Jerk Chicken
Wings, *112*
Maple Buttermilk Grilled
Chicken, *93*
Moroccan Chicken With
Grilled Vegetables, *120*
Mustard and Pancetta
Roast Chicken, *202*
Spicy Honey-Garlic
Boneless Wings, *191*
chicken livers
Chopped Liver Pâté, *26*
Classic Rumaki, *253*

chickpeas
Eggplant Walnut Dip With
Za'atar Pita Chips, *220*
Marinated Chickpea
Salad, *119*
Roasted Vegetable
Hummus, *58*
chimichurri
Grilled Vegetables With
Cilantro Chimichurri, *145*
**Chinese Chicken
Broth,** *269*
Chinese Dumplings,
270-271
Chinese New Year, *265-271*
**chocolate. See also white
chocolate.**
Black Forest Pie, *233*
Dairy-Free Gluten-Free
Molten Chocolate Lava
Cakes, *33*
Double-Chocolate Peanut
Butter Pie, *205*
Flourless Chocolate Lava
Cakes, *33*
Mini Chocolate
Babkas, *222*
Mini Chocolate Pudding
Cakes, *277*
Mini Chocolate Scones, *54*
Chopped Liver Pâté, *26*
Christmas Buffet, *235-243*
Chunky Applesauce, *219*
chutneys
Apple Walnut Chutney, *27*
Sweet-and-Sour Onion
Chutney, *236*
**cider (alcoholic). See also
apple cider.**
Bison Meatballs With
Cider Mustard Sauce, *215*
Roast Pork With Cider
Cream Sauce, *13*
Cilantro Chimichurri, *145*
Classic Rumaki, *253*
**cocktails. See also
beverages.**
Canadian Kiss, *210*
Cranberry Mimosas, *246*
Dark and Snowy, *252*
Garden Martinis, *115*
Gin Chiller, *89*
Ginger Beer Shandy, *131*
Merry Manhattan, *252*
Negroni Spritzer, *79*
Orange Fizz, *89*
Pineapple Mimosas, *44*
Pitcher Cosmopolitans, *61*
Portuguese Summer Daisy
Cocktail, *142*
Rum Punch, *131*

Sparkling Raspberry
Cocktail, *274*
Surf and Turf Caesar, *158*
coconut
Lime-Glazed Coconut
Butter Cookies, *263*
Maple French Toast
Sticks, *38*
coconut milk
Avocado Coco Lime
Pops, *107*
Cookup Rice, *127*
cod. See salt cod.
coffee
Hazelnut Irish Coffee, *15*
coleslaws. See slaws.
cookies
Lemon Cream Sandwich
Cookies, *53*
Lime-Glazed Coconut
Butter Cookies, *263*
Rosehip Cream Sandwich
Cookies, *53*
Cookup Rice, *127*
corn
Corn and Zucchini
Sauté, *144*
Creamed Corn
Potatoes, *161*
Grilled Corn and Avocado
Salad, *150*
Grilled Garam Masala
Corn, *136*
Za'atar Lamb Flatbread
With Pea Shoots, *143*
Corn Bread, *241*
Cosmopolitans, *61*
**Crab Rangoon–Stuffed
Mushroom Caps,** *259*
cranberries
Cranberry and Pistachio
Cheese Balls, *255*
Merry Manhattan, *252*
Nonalcoholic
Cosmopolitans, *61*
Pitcher Cosmopolitans, *61*
Red Wine Cranberry Jelly,
173
Sweet-and-Sour Onion
Chutney, *236*
Cranberry Mimosas, *246*
cream cheese
Beer and Cheese Fondue
Dip, *256*
Cheese Fondue Dip, *256*
Crab Rangoon–Stuffed
Mushroom Caps, *259*
Creamy Herbes de
Provence Dip, *58*
Double-Chocolate Peanut
Butter Pie, *205*

Mini Carrot Cake Trifles, *71*
Pimiento Cheese Spread
Sandwiches, *51*
Pumpkin Cheesecake
With White Chocolate
Almond Bark, *185*
Roasted Carrot and Parsnip
Soup With Whipped Goat
Cheese and Kale Chips, *226*
White Chocolate
Cheesecake Dip, *61*
Wild Mushroom Pâté, *212*
**Creamed Corn
Potatoes,** *161*
Creamy Cilantro Dip, *111*
**Creamy Herbes de
Provence Dip,** *58*
**Creamy Lemon Meringue
Pie,** *47*
**Creamy Mushroom and
Gruyère Gratin,** *181*
cremini mushrooms
Crab Rangoon–Stuffed
Mushroom Caps, *259*
Creamy Mushroom and
Gruyère Gratin, *181*
Ham Hock Hash and
Poached Eggs, *45*
Sautéed Spring Asparagus
and Mushrooms, *32*
Steakhouse Sliders, *94*
**Crisp Artichokes With
Lemon Herb Dip,** *221*
**Crisp Cheese-Stuffed
Jalapeños,** *188*
Crostini Bar, *85*
Crudités With Herb Dip, *51*
crumbles
Apple Cinnamon
Crumble, *291*
Root Vegetable
Crumble, *231*
cucumbers
Garlic Cucumber
Strips, *266*
Kimchi Slaw, *134*
Marinated Chickpea
Salad, *119*
Quinoa Tabbouleh, *151*
Spicy Cucumber Salad, *126*
Tzatziki, *135*
**Curried Egg Salad
Sandwiches,** *50*
**Curried Ginger
Butter,** *163*
Curried Potato Salad, *105*

D
daikon radishes
Beijing-Style Boiled
Peanuts, *266*

Dairy-Free Gluten-Free Molten Chocolate Lava Cakes, 33
Dark and Snowy, 252
dates
    Sticky Date Pudding With Irish Whiskey Toffee Sauce, 15
Devilled Eggs, 136
dips. See also sauces.
    Beer and Cheese Fondue Dip, 256
    Creamy Herbes de Provence Dip, 58
    Crisp Artichokes With Lemon Herb Dip, 221
    Crudités With Herb Dip, 51
    Eggplant Walnut Dip With Za'atar Pita Chips, 220
    Grilled Radishes With Creamy Cilantro Dip, 111
    Hot Swiss Chard and Artichoke Dip, 280
    Lightened-Up Blue Cheese Dip, 191
    Roasted Eggplant Dip, 29
    Roasted Vegetable Hummus, 58
    Tamarind Dip, 130
    White Chocolate Cheesecake Dip, 61
Double-Chocolate Peanut Butter Pie, 205
doughnuts
    Mini Cinnamon Sugar Buñuelos, 223
Dumplings, 270-271

E
Easter Dinner, 17-23
edamame
    Edamame and Roasted Tomato Canapés, 282
    Grilled Sesame Edamame, 111
    Lemon Herb Scallops, 274
eggplants
    Eggplant Walnut Dip With Za'atar Pita Chips, 220
    Roasted Eggplant Dip, 29
eggs
    Barbecued Breakfast Packets, 118
    Cheese and Maple Soufflés, 38
    Cheesy Barbecued Breakfast Packets, 118
    Curried Egg Salad Sandwiches, 50
    Ham Hock Hash and Poached Eggs, 45

Mini Smoked Salmon and Goat Cheese Quiches, 60
Mini Smoked Salmon Quiches, 60
Smashed Potato Salad, 77
Thai Devilled Eggs, 136
elderflower liqueur
    Garden Martinis, 115
Emmental and Cheddar Fondue, 262
endives
    Spinach Salad With Apples and Goat Cheese Croutons, 194

F
Family Reunion Picnic, 133-139
Fan Potatoes, 67
Father's Day Cookout, 75-81
fennel
    Fennel Apple Spinach Salad With Honey-Dijon Dressing, 178
    Grilled Vegetables With Cilantro Chimichurri, 145
    Mixed Greens With Orange Chive Dressing, 66
    Slow Cooker Scalloped Potatoes, 20
feta cheese
    Edamame and Roasted Tomato Canapés, 282
    Green Beans With Feta Crumbles, 203
    Grilled Bacon and Feta Mini Pizzas, 114
    Swiss Chard, Strawberry and Feta Salad With Honey Vinaigrette, 142
    Tzatziki, 135
    Village Salad Bites, 92
figs
    Devils on Horseback, 253
fish
    Mini Smoked Salmon and Goat Cheese Quiches, 60
    Mini Smoked Salmon Quiches, 60
    Pistachio-Crusted Salmon, 151
    Salt Fish Cakes, 128
    Smoked Mackerel Pâté, 10
    Smoked Trout Cakes With Lemon Mayo and Swiss Chard Kimchi, 211
    Spanish Salt Cod Fritters, 281
    Tuna Olive Salad Sandwiches, 50

flatbread
    Za'atar Lamb Flatbread With Pea Shoots, 143
Flourless Chocolate Lava Cakes, 33
fondue
    Beer and Cheese Fondue Dip, 256
    Cheddar Oka Fondue, 262
    Cheese Fondue Dip, 256
    Emmental Cheddar Fondue, 262
fool
    Rhubarb Ginger Fool, 153
Frangelico
    Hazelnut Irish Coffee, 15
French Toast Sticks, 38
Fresh Shucked Oysters, 12
Fried Chicken Bites, 218
Fried Okra, 79
fritters
    Spanish Salt Cod Fritters, 281
    Split Pea Fritters, 129
fudge
    Maple Fudge, 41

G
Game Night, 187-191
Garden Martinis, 115
Garden Party Grill, 109-115
Garlic Cucumber Strips, 266
gin
    Garden Martinis, 115
    Gin Chiller, 89
    Negroni Spritzer, 79
Ginger Beer Shandy, 131
Ginger Syrup, 252
Glazed Carrots, 287
goat cheese
    Bacon and Onion Cheese Balls, 255
    Bacon, Onion and Goat Cheese Pizza Bites, 283
    Basil and Lemon Cheese Balls, 255
    Cranberry and Pistachio Cheese Balls, 255
    Mini Smoked Salmon and Goat Cheese Quiches, 60
    Peas and Prosciutto Crostini, 85
    Roasted Carrot and Parsnip Soup With Whipped Goat Cheese and Kale Chips, 226
    Spinach Salad With Apples and Goat Cheese Croutons, 194
Gong Hei Fat Choi (Chinese New Year), 265-271

green beans
    Green Beans Amandine, 67
    Green Beans With Feta Crumbles, 203
    Haricots Verts With Miso Butter and Pepitas, 232
    Sautéed Brussels Sprouts and Green Beans With Parmesan, 288
Green Peppercorn Horseradish Sauce, 286
Grilled Bacon and Feta Mini Pizzas, 114
Grilled Balsamic Vegetables, 95
Grilled Caribbean Chicken, 126
Grilled Cheese, 77
Grilled Corn and Avocado Salad, 150
Grilled Fruit With Honeyed Crème Fraîche, 123
Grilled Garam Masala Corn, 136
Grilled Honey-Garlic Chicken Wings, 104
Grilled Jerk Chicken Wings, 112
Grilled Panzanella Bites, 92
Grilled Radicchio, 104
Grilled Radishes With Creamy Cilantro Dip, 111
Grilled Sausage Bar, 134-135
Grilled Sesame Edamame, 111
Grilled Shrimp With Sriracha-Lime Cocktail Sauce, 114
Grilled Vegetables With Cilantro Chimichurri, 145
Gruyère cheese
    Beer and Cheese Fondue Dip, 256
    Caramelized Onion and Apple Pizza, 249
    Cheese Fondue Dip, 256
    Creamy Mushroom and Gruyère Gratin, 181
    Slow Cooker Scalloped Potatoes, 20

H
ham. See also prosciutto.
    Barbecued Breakfast Packets, 118
    Caramelized Onion and Apple Pizza, 249
    Cheesy Barbecued Breakfast Packets, 118

Ham Hock Hash and Poached Eggs, *45*
Ham Pickle Spread Sandwiches, *51*
Pineapple and Maple Ham, *36*
Pineapple-Glazed Ham, *18*
Hanukkah Get-Together, *217-223*
Haricots Verts With Miso Butter and Pepitas, *232*
Harvest Table, *193-199*
Hazelnut Irish Coffee, *15*
hazelnuts
Marinated Kale Salad, *236*
Herb-Rubbed Roast Turkey With Fresh Sage Gravy, *166*
Herbed Mini Potato Skewers, *96*
Herbed Roast Turkey, *237*
Hickory Honey Pepper Nuts, *210*
Holiday Brunch, *245-249*
Honey-Glazed Carrots, *32*
Honey-Lime Carrots With Cipollini Onions, *22*
Hot Swiss Chard and Artichoke Dip, *280*
hummus
Roasted Vegetable Hummus, *58*

I
ice cream
Butter Tart Ice Cream, *81*
Maple Taffy on Vanilla Ice Cream, *41*
iced teas
Apple Mint Iced Tea, *123*
Chai Mango Lemonade, *138*
Peach Tea, *89*
Tea Sangria, *115*
Irish Brown Bread, *10*
Irish cream liqueur
Hazelnut Irish Coffee, *15*
Irish Mashed Potatoes, *287*
Irish Root Soup With Cashel Blue Cheese, *12*
Irish whiskey
Sticky Date Pudding With Irish Whiskey Toffee Sauce, *15*
It's a Parade, *83-89*

J
jalapeño peppers
Crisp Cheese-Stuffed Jalapeños, *188*
Grilled Jerk Chicken Wings, *112*

Jalapeño Baked Beans, *78*
Tomatillo Salsa, *134*
Jicama and Apple Spinach Salad With Honey-Dijon Dressing, *178*

K
kale
Kale and Cabbage Slaw, *103*
Marinated Kale Salad, *236*
Mediterranean Kale Salad, *138*
Roasted Carrot and Parsnip Soup With Whipped Goat Cheese and Kale Chips, *226*
Kelp With Szechuan Peppercorns, *267*
kimchi
Kimchi Slaw, *134*
Smoked Trout Cakes With Lemon Mayo and Swiss Chard Kimchi, *211*

L
lamb
Roast Leg of Lamb With Caramelized Onion Gravy, *30*
Za'atar Lamb Flatbread With Pea Shoots, *143*
latkes
Mini Vegetable Latkes With Chunky Applesauce, *219*
Layered "Knish" Bake, *31*
lemons
Basil and Lemon Cheese Balls, *255*
Creamy Lemon Meringue Pie, *47*
Crisp Artichokes With Lemon Herb Dip, *221*
Lemon Amaretto Tiramisu, *23*
Lemon Brussels Sprouts, *14*
Lemon Cream Sandwich Cookies, *53*
Lemon Herb Scallops, *274*
Lemon Mayo, *211*
Lemony Dill Butter, *163*
Lemony Red Pepper and Asparagus Pasta Salad, *97*
Mini Lemon Scones, *54*
Raspberry Lemon Cream Cake, *99*
lemonade
Chai Mango Lemonade, *138*
lentils
Wild Rice and Lentil Salad, *137*

Lightened-Up Blue Cheese Dip, *191*
limes
Avocado Coco Lime Pops, *107*
Grilled Shrimp With Sriracha-Lime Cocktail Sauce, *114*
Honey-Lime Carrots With Cipollini Onions, *22*
Lime-Glazed Coconut Butter Cookies, *263*
Pitcher Lime Squash, *131*
lobster
Boiled Fresh Lobsters With Seasoned Butters, *163*
lychees
Gin Chiller, *89*

M
mackerel
Smoked Mackerel Pâté, *10*
Madeira
Mulled Red Wine and Madeira, *263*
Sour Cherry Trifle, *243*
Make-Ahead Christmas Dinner, *225-233*
Make-Ahead Easter Dinner, *17-23*
Make-Ahead Thanksgiving, *165-174*
mango nectar
Chai Mango Lemonade, *138*
mangoes
Grilled Fruit With Honeyed Crème Fraîche, *123*
Mango Sauce, *130*
Tropical Coleslaw, *96*
maple syrup
Avocado Coco Lime Pops, *107*
Brined Maple Mustard Pork Chops, *102*
Chard and Apple Salad With Maple Bacon Vinaigrette, *37*
Cheese and Maple Soufflés, *38*
Maple Buttermilk Grilled Chicken, *93*
Maple French Toast Sticks, *38*
Maple Fudge, *41*
Maple Mayo, *39*
Maple Pots de Crème With Warm Pears, *174*
Maple Taffy on Vanilla Ice Cream, *41*

Pineapple and Maple Ham, *36*
Roasted Pears With Yogurt and Granola, *247*
maple whisky
Canadian Kiss, *210*
Marinated Chickpea Salad, *119*
Marinated Kale Salad, *236*
Marinated Mozzarella, *84*
Market Day, *141-147*
martinis
Garden Martinis, *115*
mascarpone cheese
Lemon Amaretto Tiramisu, *23*
mayos
Lemon Mayo, *211*
Maple Mayo, *39*
meatballs
Bison Meatballs With Cider Mustard Sauce, *215*
Sweet-and-Sour Meatballs, *257*
Mediterranean Kale Salad, *138*
Merry Manhattan, *252*
mimosas
Cranberry Mimosas, *246*
Pineapple Mimosas, *44*
Mini Carrot Cake Trifles, *71*
Mini Cheddar and Onion Galette Bites, *59*
Mini Chocolate Babkas, *222*
Mini Chocolate Pudding Cakes, *277*
Mini Chocolate Scones, *54*
Mini Cinnamon Sugar Buñuelos, *223*
Mini Lemon Scones With Strawberries and Cream, *54*
Mini Smoked Salmon and Goat Cheese Quiches, *60*
Mini Smoked Salmon Quiches, *60*
Mini Vegetable Latkes With Chunky Applesauce, *219*
miso paste
Haricots Verts With Miso Butter and Pepitas, *232*
Mixed Greens With Orange Chive Dressing, *66*
morel mushrooms
Chicken With Morel Sauce, *68*
Moroccan Chicken With Grilled Vegetables, *120*
Mother's Day Brunch, *43-47*
mozzarella balls
Marinated Mozzarella, *84*

Mulled Red Wine and
Madeira, *263*
mung bean vermicelli
Spinach and Mushroom
Dumplings, *270*
mushrooms
Bok Choy, Mushroom and
Tofu Soup, *269*
Chicken With Morel
Sauce, *68*
Crab Rangoon–Stuffed
Mushroom Caps, *259*
Creamy Mushroom and
Gruyère Gratin, *181*
Grilled Balsamic
Vegetables, *95*
Ham Hock Hash and
Poached Eggs, *45*
Moroccan Chicken With
Grilled Vegetables, *120*
Porcini-Dusted Beef
Tenderloin, *229*
Sautéed Spring Asparagus
and Mushrooms, *32*
Spinach and Mushroom
Dumplings, *270*
Steakhouse Sliders, *94*
Wild Mushroom Pâté, *212*
mussels
Wine and Bacon Steamed
Mussels, *162*
**Mustard and Pancetta
Roast Chicken,** *202*

N
nachos
Turkey Chili Nachos, *189*
Negroni Spritzer, *79*
New Year's Eve Drop-In,
251-259
**Nonalcoholic
Cosmopolitans,** *61*
**Non-Kosher Roast Leg of
Lamb With Caramelized
Onion Gravy,** *30*
nuts
Beijing-Style Boiled
Peanuts, *266*
Hickory Honey Pepper
Nuts, *210*

O
Oat Demerara Shortbread,
52
Oka cheese
Cheddar Oka Fondue, *262*
Okonomiyaki Topping, *135*
okra
Fried Okra, *79*
olives
Orange-Spiced Olives, *84*

Spicy Bucatini With
Roasted Tomatoes, *277*
Tuna Olive Salad
Sandwiches, *50*
Village Salad Bites, *92*
oranges
Mixed Greens With
Orange Chive Dressing, *66*
Mulled Red Wine and
Madeira, *263*
Negroni Spritzer, *79*
Orange Beet Salad, *246*
Orange Chili Crisp Beef
Strips, *268*
Orange Fizz, *89*
Orange-Spiced Olives, *84*
Tea Sangria, *115*
**Oven-Roasted Pork Loin
Stuffed With Bacon and
Apples,** *180*
oyster mushrooms
Creamy Mushroom and
Gruyère Gratin, *181*
Sautéed Spring Asparagus
and Mushrooms, *32*
Wild Mushroom Pâté, *212*
oysters
Fresh Shucked Oysters, *12*
Oysters on the Half
Shell, *158*

P
pancakes
Cherry Pistachio Mini
Pancakes, *247*
pancetta
Fennel Apple Spinach
Salad With Honey-Dijon
Dressing, *178*
Jicama and Apple Spinach
Salad With Honey-Dijon
Dressing, *178*
Mustard and Pancetta
Roast Chicken, *202*
Shrimp and Pancetta
Skewers, *87*
Spicy Bucatini With
Roasted Tomatoes, *277*
parsnips
Roasted Carrot and Parsnip
Soup With Whipped Goat
Cheese and Kale Chips, *226*
Party on the Block, *125-131*
Passover Dinner, *25-33*
pastas
Lemony Red Pepper and
Asparagus Pasta Salad, *97*
Spicy Bucatini With
Roasted Tomatoes, *277*
pâtés
Chopped Liver Pâté, *26*

Smoked Mackerel Pâté, *10*
Wild Mushroom Pâté, *212*
pea shoots
Za'atar Lamb Flatbread
With Pea Shoots, *143*
peaches
Grilled Fruit With Honeyed
Crème Fraîche, *123*
Peach Tea, *89*
Ultimate Peach Pie, *147*
peanut butter
Double-Chocolate Peanut
Butter Pie, *205*
peanuts
Beijing-Style Boiled
Peanuts, *266*
Double-Chocolate Peanut
Butter Pie, *205*
pears
Apple Walnut Chutney, *27*
Maple Pots de Crème With
Warm Pears, *174*
Roasted Pears With Yogurt
and Granola, *247*
**peas. See also chickpeas;
pigeon peas; split peas.**
Curried Potato Salad, *105*
Peas and Prosciutto
Crostini, *85*
Twin Peas With Roasted
Garlic Butter, *20*
pecans
Ultimate Pecan Pie, *199*
pepitas
Haricots Verts With Miso
Butter and Pepitas, *232*
Swiss Chard, Strawberry
and Feta Salad With
Honey Vinaigrette, *142*
Perfect Cup of Tea, *54*
Perfect Poached Eggs, *45*
**Pesto White Bean
Crostini,** *85*
pies
Black Forest Pie, *233*
Creamy Lemon Meringue
Pie, *47*
Double-Chocolate Peanut
Butter Pie, *205*
Ultimate Peach Pie, *147*
Ultimate Pecan Pie, *199*
pigeon peas
Cookup Rice, *127*
pilafs
Apricot Wild Rice
Pilaf, *230*
White and Wild Rice
Pilaf With Spinach and
Walnuts, *238*
**Pimiento Cheese Spread
Sandwiches,** *51*

pine nuts
Sautéed Brussels Sprouts
and Green Beans With
Parmesan, *288*
pineapple
Grilled Fruit With Honeyed
Crème Fraîche, *123*
Mini Carrot Cake Trifles, *71*
Pineapple and Maple
Ham, *36*
Tropical Coleslaw, *96*
pineapple juice
Pineapple-Glazed Ham, *18*
Pineapple Mimosas, *44*
Sweet-and-Sour
Meatballs, *257*
pinto beans
Jalapeño Baked Beans, *78*
pistachios
Cherry Pistachio Mini
Pancakes, *247*
Cranberry and Pistachio
Cheese Balls, *255*
Glazed Carrots, *287*
Pistachio-Crusted Salmon
With Garlic Rapini, *151*
pita bread
Baked Pita Chips, *191*
Za'atar Pita Chips, *220*
Grilled Bacon and Feta
Mini Pizzas, *114*
Pitcher Cosmopolitans, *61*
Pitcher Lime Squash, *131*
pizzas. See also flatbread.
Bacon, Onion and Goat
Cheese Pizza Bites, *283*
Caramelized Onion and
Apple Pizza, *249*
Grilled Bacon and Feta
Mini Pizzas, *114*
poached eggs
Ham Hock Hash and
Poached Eggs, *45*
pomegranate seeds
Garlic Pomegranate
Spinach, *202*
Spinach Salad With
Apples and Goat Cheese
Croutons, *194*
pops
Avocado Coco Lime
Pops, *107*
**Porcini-Dusted Beef
Tenderloin With Sherry
Gravy,** *229*
pork. See also bacon; ham.
Barbecued Pork Loin
Stuffed With Bacon and
Apples, *180*
Brined Maple Mustard
Pork Chops, *102*

Char Siu–Style Ribs, *103*
Cookup Rice, *127*
Oven-Roasted Pork Loin Stuffed With Bacon and Apples, *180*
Pork Dumplings, *271*
Roast Pork With Cider Cream Sauce, *13*
Sausage, Apple and Sage Stuffing, *168*
portobello mushrooms
Grilled Balsamic Vegetables, *95*
Moroccan Chicken With Grilled Vegetables, *120*
Portuguese Summer Daisy Cocktail, *142*
pot roast
Slow Cooker Balsamic-Braised Pot Roast, *196*
potatoes. See also sweet potatoes.
Boxty Potato Cakes, *14*
Celery Root Garlic Mash, *198*
Creamed Corn Potatoes, *161*
Curried Potato Salad, *105*
Fan Potatoes, *67*
Grilled Vegetables With Cilantro Chimichurri, *145*
Ham Hock Hash and Poached Eggs, *45*
Herbed Mini Potato Skewers, *96*
Irish Mashed Potatoes, *287*
Layered "Knish" Bake, *31*
Mini Vegetable Latkes With Chunky Applesauce, *219*
Potato and Turnip Mash With Roasted Garlic, *182*
Root Vegetable Crumble, *231*
Slow Cooker Scalloped Potatoes, *20*
Smashed Potato Salad, *77*
Smooth and Creamy Mashed Potatoes, *167*
Spanish Salt Cod Fritters, *281*
Spicy Roasted Potato Skins, *188*
Spinach, Onion and Potato Bake, *31*
Ultra-Crispy Roasted Potatoes, *249*
Winter Vegetable Stew, *240*
pots de crème
Maple Pots de Crème With Warm Pears, *174*

prosciutto
Peas and Prosciutto Crostini, *85*
puddings
Mini Chocolate Pudding Cakes, *277*
Sticky Date Pudding With Irish Whiskey Toffee Sauce, *15*
Pumpkin Cheesecake With White Chocolate Almond Bark, *185*
punch. See also beverages; cocktails.
Rum Punch, *131*

Q

quiches
Mini Smoked Salmon and Goat Cheese Quiches, *60*
Mini Smoked Salmon Quiches, *60*
Quinoa Tabbouleh, *151*

R

radicchio
Chard and Apple Salad With Maple Bacon Vinaigrette, *37*
Grilled Radicchio, *104*
radishes. See also daikon radishes.
Asparagus and Ricotta Crostini, *85*
Boston Lettuce Salad With Green Goddess Dressing, *44*
Grilled Radishes With Creamy Cilantro Dip, *111*
Smoked Trout Cakes With Lemon Mayo and Swiss Chard Kimchi, *211*
Tangy Summer Coleslaw, *96*
Tropical Coleslaw, *96*
rapini
Pistachio-Crusted Salmon With Garlic Rapini, *151*
raspberries
Orange Fizz, *89*
Raspberry Lemon Cream Cake, *99*
Sparkling Raspberry Cocktail, *274*
Red Carpet Extravaganza, *279*
red wine
Mulled Red Wine and Madeira, *263*
Red Wine Cranberry Jelly, *173*

Rhubarb Ginger Fool, *153*
ribs
Char Siu–Style Ribs, *103*
rice
Apricot Wild Rice Pilaf, *230*
Cookup Rice, *127*
White and Wild Rice Pilaf With Spinach and Walnuts, *238*
Wild Rice and Lentil Salad, *137*
ricotta cheese
Asparagus and Ricotta Crostini, *85*
Hot Swiss Chard and Artichoke Dip, *280*
Za'atar Lamb Flatbread, *143*
Roast Leg of Lamb With Caramelized Onion Gravy, *30*
Roast Pork With Cider Cream Sauce, *13*
Roasted Asparagus Salad With Parmesan Croutons, *19*
Roasted Butternut Squash and Cheddar Gratin, *172*
Roasted Carrot and Parsnip Soup With Whipped Goat Cheese and Kale Chips, *226*
Roasted Carrots With Mustard Vinaigrette, *238*
Roasted Eggplant Dip, *29*
Roasted Onions and Apples With Thyme, *197*
Roasted Pears With Yogurt and Granola, *247*
roasted red peppers
Lemony Red Pepper and Asparagus Pasta Salad, *97*
Roasted Vegetable Hummus, *58*
Root Vegetable Crumble, *231*
Rosehip Cream Sandwich Cookies, *53*
rum
Dark and Snowy, *252*
Rum Punch, *131*
Rumaki, *253*
rutabaga
Irish Root Soup With Cashel Blue Cheese, *12*
rye whisky
Merry Manhattan, *252*

S

salads. See also slaws.
Boston Lettuce Salad With Green Goddess Dressing, *44*

Chard and Apple Salad With Maple Bacon Vinaigrette, *37*
Curried Potato Salad, *105*
Fennel Apple Spinach Salad With Honey-Dijon Dressing, *178*
Grilled Corn and Avocado Salad, *150*
Jicama and Apple Spinach Salad With Honey-Dijon Dressing, *178*
Lemony Red Pepper and Asparagus Pasta Salad, *97*
Marinated Chickpea Salad, *119*
Marinated Kale Salad, *236*
Mediterranean Kale Salad, *138*
Mixed Greens With Orange Chive Dressing, *66*
Orange Beet Salad, *246*
Quinoa Tabbouleh, *151*
Roasted Asparagus Salad With Parmesan Croutons, *19*
Smashed Potato Salad, *77*
Spicy Cucumber Salad, *126*
Spinach Salad With Apples and Goat Cheese Croutons, *194*
Swiss Chard, Strawberry and Feta Salad With Honey Vinaigrette, *142*
Wild Rice and Lentil Salad, *137*
salmon
Mini Smoked Salmon and Goat Cheese Quiches, *60*
Mini Smoked Salmon Quiches, *60*
Pistachio-Crusted Salmon With Garlic Rapini, *151*
salsa
Tomatillo Salsa, *134*
salt cod
Salt Fish Cakes, *128*
Spanish Salt Cod Fritters, *281*
salt pork
Cookup Rice, *127*
sandwiches
Bacon and Onion Grilled Cheese, *119*
Curried Egg Salad Sandwiches, *50*
Ham Pickle Spread Sandwiches, *51*
Pimiento Cheese Spread Sandwiches, *51*

300

Tea Sandwiches, *50-51*
Tuna Olive Salad
Sandwiches, *50*
sangria
Tea Sangria, *115*
sauces. See also dips.
Chunky Applesauce, *219*
Cider Cream Sauce, *13*
Cider Mustard Sauce, *215*
Green Peppercorn
Horseradish Sauce, *286*
Herbed Dipping Sauce, *87*
Horseradish Sauce, *94*
Irish Whiskey Toffee
Sauce, *15*
Mango Sauce, *130*
Sriracha-Lime Cocktail
Sauce, *114*
Sweet-and-Sour Sauce, *257*
sausages
Grilled Sausage Bar,
134-135
Sausage, Apple and Sage
Stuffing, *168*
**Sautéed Brussels Sprouts
and Green Beans With
Parmesan, *288***
**Sautéed Brussels Sprouts
With Shaved Parmesan,
*182***
**Sautéed Garlic Swiss
Chard, *46***
**Sautéed Spring Asparagus
and Mushrooms, *32***
Scalloped Potatoes, *20*
scallops. See sea scallops.
scones
Mini Chocolate Scones, *54*
Mini Lemon Scones
With Strawberries and
Cream, *54*
sea scallops
Lemon Herb Scallops, *274*
Surf and Turf Caesar, *158*
Seafood Supper, *157-163*
**Seasonal Sunday Suppers,
*65-71, 149-153, 201-205,
285-291***
shiitake mushrooms
Sautéed Spring Asparagus
and Mushrooms, *32*
Spinach and Mushroom
Dumplings, *270*
Wild Mushroom Pâté, *212*
shortbread
Oat Demerara Shortbread,
52
shrimp
Grilled Shrimp With
Sriracha-Lime Cocktail
Sauce, *114*

Pork Dumplings, *271*
Shrimp and Leek
Dumplings, *271*
Shrimp and Pancetta
Skewers, *87*
Shrimp Cocktail Canapés
259
Simple Syrup, *89*
skewers
Herbed Mini Potato
Skewers, *96*
Shrimp and Pancetta
Skewers, *87*
slaws
Kale and Cabbage
Slaw, *103*
Kimchi Slaw, *134*
Tangy Summer
Coleslaw, *96*
Tropical Coleslaw, *96*
sliders
Steakhouse Sliders, *94*
**Slow Cooker Balsamic-
Braised Pot Roast, *196***
**Slow Cooker Scalloped
Potatoes, *20***
Smashed Potato Salad, *77*
Smoked Mackerel Pâté, *10*
smoked salmon
Mini Smoked Salmon and
Goat Cheese Quiches, *60*
Mini Smoked Salmon
Quiches, *60*
smoked trout
Smoked Trout Cakes With
Lemon Mayo and Swiss
Chard Kimchi, *211*
**Smooth and Creamy
Mashed Potatoes, *167***
soufflés
Cheese and Maple
Soufflés, *38*
soups. See also broth.
Bok Choy, Mushroom and
Tofu Soup, *269*
Irish Root Soup With
Cashel Blue Cheese, *12*
Roasted Carrot and Parsnip
Soup With Whipped Goat
Cheese and Kale Chips, *226*
Sour Cherry Trifle, *243*
**Spanish Salt Cod
Fritters, *281***
**Sparkling Raspberry
Cocktail, *274***
sparkling white wine
Cranberry Mimosas, *246*
Orange Fizz, *89*
Pineapple Mimosas, *44*
Portuguese Summer Daisy
Cocktail, *142*

Sparkling Raspberry
Cocktail, *274*
Spiced Syrup, *252*
**Spicy Bucatini With
Roasted Tomatoes, *277***
**Spicy Cucumber
Salad, *126***
Spicy Garlic Butter, *163*
**Spicy Honey-Garlic
Boneless Wings, *191***
**Spicy Roasted Potato Skins,
*188***
spinach
Bok Choy, Mushroom and
Tofu Soup, *269*
Boston Lettuce Salad
With Green Goddess
Dressing, *44*
Fennel Apple Spinach
Salad With Honey-Dijon
Dressing, *178*
Garlic Pomegranate
Spinach, *202*
Jicama and Apple Spinach
Salad With Honey-Dijon
Dressing, *178*
Roasted Asparagus
Salad With Parmesan
Croutons, *19*
Spinach and Mushroom
Dumplings, *270*
Spinach, Onion and Potato
Bake, *31*
Spinach Salad With
Apples and Goat Cheese
Croutons, *194*
Tzatziki, *135*
White and Wild Rice
Pilaf With Spinach and
Walnuts, *238*
Split Pea Fritters, *129*
**Sriracha-Lime Cocktail
Sauce, *114***
St. Patrick's Day Feast, *9-15*
Steakhouse Sliders, *94*
stew
Winter Vegetable Stew, *240*
**Sticky Date Pudding
With Irish Whiskey Toffee
Sauce, *15***
strawberries
Dairy-Free Gluten-Free
Chocolate Lava Cakes, *33*
Flourless Chocolate Lava
Cakes, *33*
Mini Lemon Scones
With Strawberries and
Cream, *54*
Swiss Chard, Strawberry
and Feta Salad With
Honey Vinaigrette, *142*

stuffings
Bacon and Apple Stuffing,
180
Sausage, Apple and Sage
Stuffing, *168*
sugar snap peas
Twin Peas With Roasted
Garlic Butter, *20*
**Sunday Suppers, *65-71, 149-
153, 201-205, 285-291***
Surf and Turf Caesar, *158*
**Sweet-and-Sour
Meatballs, *257***
**Sweet-and-Sour Onion
Chutney, *236***
sweet potatoes
Barbecued Breakfast
Packets, *118*
Root Vegetable
Crumble, *231*
Sweet Potato Cakes, *39*
Swiss chard
Chard and Apple Salad
With Maple Bacon
Vinaigrette, *37*
Hot Swiss Chard and
Artichoke Dip, *280*
Sautéed Garlic Swiss
Chard, *46*
Smoked Trout Cakes With
Lemon Mayo and Swiss
Chard Kimchi, *211*
Swiss Chard, Strawberry
and Feta Salad With
Honey Vinaigrette, *142*
Swiss Chard With Frizzled
Onions, *171*
syrups
Ginger Syrup, *252*
Simple Syrup, *89*
Spiced Syrup, *252*

T
Tabbouleh, *151*
Tamarind Dip, *130*
**Tangy Summer
Coleslaw, *96***
tea
Afternoon Tea, *49-55*
Apple Mint Iced Tea, *123*
Chai Mango
Lemonade, *138*
Peach Tea, *89*
Perfect Cup of Tea, *54*
Tea Sangria, *115*
Tea Sandwiches, *50-51*
Texas Barbecue Brisket, *76*
Thai Devilled Eggs, *136*
Thanksgiving
Make-Ahead Thanksgiving,
165-174

Thanksgiving Feast,
177-185
Tiramisu, *23*
tofu
Bok Choy, Mushroom and
Tofu Soup, *269*
Tomatillo Salsa, *134*
Tomato Curry Topping, *135*
Tree Trimming Party,
209-212
trifles
Mini Carrot Cake Trifles, *71*
Sour Cherry Trifle, *243*
Tropical Coleslaw, *96*
trout
Smoked Trout Cakes With
Lemon Mayo, *211*
**Tuna Olive Salad
Sandwiches,** *50*
turkey
Herb-Rubbed Roast
Turkey With Fresh Sage
Gravy, *166*
Herbed Roast Turkey, *237*
Turkey Chili Nachos, *189*
turnips
Potato and Turnip Mash
With Roasted Garlic, *182*
**Twin Peas With Roasted
Garlic Butter,** *20*
Tzatziki, *135*

U
Ultimate Peach Pie, *147*
Ultimate Pecan Pie, *199*
**Ultimate Standing Rib Roast
With Green Peppercorn
Horseradish Sauce,** *286*
**Ultra-Crispy Roasted
Potatoes,** *249*
**Updated Devils on
Horseback,** *253*

V
Valentine's Day Dinner,
273-277
vermouth
Merry Manhattan, *252*
Negroni Spritzer, *79*
Village Salad Bites, *92*
vodka
Pitcher Cosmopolitans, *61*
Sparkling Raspberry
Cocktail, *274*
Surf and Turf Caesar, *158*

W
walnuts
Apple Walnut Chutney, *27*
Eggplant Walnut Dip With
Za'atar Pita Chips, *220*
Mini Carrot Cake Trifles, *71*

Root Vegetable
Crumble, *231*
White and Wild Rice
Pilaf With Spinach and
Walnuts, *238*
water chestnuts
Classic Rumaki, *253*
**White and Wild Rice
Pilaf With Spinach and
Walnuts,** *238*
white chocolate
Avocado Coco Lime
Pops, *107*
Pumpkin Cheesecake
With White Chocolate
Almond Bark, *185*
White Chocolate
Cheesecake Dip, *61*
**white kidney beans. See
cannellini beans.**
**white wine. See also
sparkling white wine.**
Wine and Bacon Steamed
Mussels, *162*
**Wild Charcuterie
Board,** *212*
Wild Mushroom Pâté, *212*
wild rice
Apricot Wild Rice
Pilaf, *230*
White and Wild Rice

Pilaf With Spinach and
Walnuts, *238*
Wild Rice and Lentil
Salad, *137*
**wine. See red wine;
sparkling white wine;
white wine.**
wings
Grilled Honey-Garlic
Chicken Wings, *104*
Grilled Jerk Chicken
Wings, *112*
Spicy Honey-Garlic
Boneless Wings, *191*
Winter Vegetable Stew, *240*

Z
za'atar
Eggplant Walnut Dip With
Za'atar Pita Chips, *220*
Za'atar Lamb Flatbread
With Pea Shoots, *143*
zucchini
Corn and Zucchini
Sauté, *144*
Grilled Balsamic
Vegetables, *95*
Mini Vegetable Latkes With
Chunky Applesauce, *219*

CREDITS

RECIPES

All recipes Tested Till Perfect by the Canadian Living Test Kitchen.

PHOTOGRAPHY

RYAN BROOK: pages 62 and 200

JEFF COULSON: cover, bottom left; cover, bottom right; pages 24, 28, 70, 100, 116, 121, 122, 13, 139. 146, 148, 156, 158, 159, 176, 179, 183, 184, 186, 190, 208, 213, 214, 216, 234 and 284

JOHN CULLEN: pages 250, 254 and 258

YVONNE DUIVENVOORDEN: cover, top right; pages 11, 98, 108, 113, 124, 264, 278 and 289

JOE KIM: pages 90, 272 and 276

STEVE KRUG: pages 16 and 21

HANS LAURENDEAU/SHOOT STUDIO: page 106

JEAN LONGPRÉ: page 195

JODI PUDGE: pages 6, 8, 42, 48, 55, 64, 69, 72, 74, 152, 154, 206, 239, 242, 260 and 290

DAVID SCOTT: page 56

RYAN SZULC: pages 80, 82, 86, 88

TANGO PHOTOGRAPHIE: pages 34, 40, 244, 248 and 275

RONALD TSANG: pages 204, 224, 227 and 228

JAMES TSE: cover, top left; pages 164, 169, 170 and 175

MAYA VISNEYI: page 140

FOOD STYLING

STÉPHAN BOUCHER: pages 106 and 195

AHSLEY DENTON: pages 108, 113, 272 and 276

MICHAEL ELLIOTT/JUDY INC.: pages 8, 42, 4, 55, 64, 69, 74, 140, 152, 204, 239, 242, 260 and 290

VÉRONIQUE GAGNON LALANNE: page 275

DAVID GRENIER: pages 100, 175, 234, 250, 254 and 258

ADELE HAGAN: pages 132 and 139

MIRANDA KEYES: page 200

LUCIE RICHARD: cover, top right; pages 56, 124, 264, 278 and 289

DENYSE ROUSSIN: pages 34, 40, 244 and 248

HEATHER SHAW: page 70

CHRISTOPHER ST. ONGE: cover, top left; pages 164, 169, 170, 224, 227 and 228

CLAIRE STUBBS: pages 11, 16, 2, 24, 28, 82, 86, 88, 90, 98, 216 and 284

MELANIE STUPARYK: pages 62, 116, 121, 122, 148, 186 and 190

NOAH WHITENOFF: cover, bottom left; cover, bottom right; pages 146, 176, 179, 183, 184, 208, 213 and 214

NICOLE YOUNG: pages 80, 156, 158 and 159

PROP STYLING

KARINE BLACKBURN: pages 244 and 248

LAURA BRANSON: pages 70, 116, 121, 122, 132, 139, 175, 204 and 284

AURELIE BRYCE: pages 82, 86, 88, 156, 158 and 159

ALANNA DAVEY: pages 16, 21, 224, 227 and 228

CATHERINE DOHERTY: cover, top right; pages 6, 8, 24, 28, 42, 48, 55, 64, 69, 72, 74, 152, 154, 186, 190, 206, 216, 234, 239, 242, 260, 272, 276, 289 and 290

JEN EVANS: cover, top left; pages 140, 164, 169 and 170

MARC-PHILIPPE GAGNÉ: page 98

VÉRONIQUE GAGNON LALANNE: page 275

MADELEINE JOHARI: cover, bottom left; cover, bottom right; pages 80, 90, 176, 179, 183, 184, 208, 213 and 214

MONIQUE MACOT: page 195

SABRINA LINN: pages 100 and 146

SASHA SEYMOUR: pages 106, 113, 148 and 200

CAROLINE SIMON: pages 34, 40 and 106

OKSANA SLAVUYTCH: pages 1, 5, 124 and 264

PAIGE WIER/JUDY INC.: pages 250, 254 and 258

GENEVIEVE WISEMAN: pages 62 and 278

ABOUT OUR NUTRITION INFORMATION

To meet nutrient needs each day, moderately active women 25 to 49 need about 1,900 calories, 51 g protein, 261 g carbohydrate, 25 to 35 g fibre and not more than 63 g total fat (21 g saturated fat). Men and teenagers usually need more. Canadian sodium intake of approximately 3,500 mg daily should be reduced, whereas the intake of potassium from food sources should be increased to 4,700 mg per day.

The percentage of recommended daily intake (% RDI) is based on the values used for Canadian food labels for calcium, iron, vitamins A and C, and folate.

Figures are rounded off. They are based on the first ingredient listed when there is a choice and do not include optional ingredients or those with no specified amounts.

ABBREVIATIONS

cal = calories **pro** = protein **carb** = carbohydrate **sat. fat** = saturated fat **chol** = cholesterol

Canadian Living

Complete your collection of Tested-Till-Perfect recipes!

The Ultimate Cookbook

The Special Occasions Cookbook

The Complete Chicken Book
The Complete Chocolate Book
The Complete Preserving Book

400-Calorie Dinners
Dinner in 30 Minutes or Less
Essential Salads
Fish & Seafood
Make It Ahead!
Make It Chocolate!
Pasta & Noodles
Sweet & Simple

New Slow Cooker Favourites

The Affordable Feasts Collection
The Appetizer Collection
The Barbecue Collection
The International Collection
The One Dish Collection
The Slow Cooker Collection
The Vegetarian Collection

150 Essential Beef, Pork & Lamb Recipes
150 Essential Salads
150 Essential Whole Grain Recipes

Available wherever books are sold or online at
canadianliving.com/books